MYTHS of HARMONY

PITT LATIN AMERICAN SERIES

George Reid Andrews, General Editor

Catherine M. Conaghan, Associate Editor

MYTHS *of* HARMONY

Race and Republicanism during the Age of Revolution,

Colombia 1795–1831

MARIXA LASSO

University of Pittsburgh Press

Published by the University of Pittsburgh Press, Pittsburgh PA 15260

Copyright © 2007, University of Pittsburgh Press

Manufactured in the United States of America

Printed on acid-free paper

10 9 8 7 6 5 4 3 2 1

Library of Congress Cataloging-in-Publication Data

Lasso, Marixa.
  Myths of harmony : race and republicanism during the age of revolution : Colombia 1795–1831
/ Marixa Lasso.
    p. cm. — (Pitt Latin American series)
  Includes bibliographical references and index.
  ISBN-13: 978-0-8229-4311-2 (cloth : alk. paper)
  ISBN-10: 0-8229-4311-5 (cloth : alk. paper)
  ISBN-13: 978-0-8229-5965-6 (pbk. : alk. paper)
  ISBN-10: 0-8229-5965-8 (pbk. : alk. paper)
  1. Blacks—Colombia—Politics and government—19th century. 2. Colombia—Race relations.
3. Colombia—History—War of Independence, 1810-1822—Participation, Blacks. I. Title.
  F2349.B55L37 2007
  305.896'086109034—dc22
                              2007016301

CONTENTS

ACKNOWLEDGMENTS

In the course of thinking through and developing this project, I have incurred many personal and institutional debts. In the United States, I received financial support from the Social Sciences Research Council/American Council of Learned Societies, with funding from the Andrew Mellon Foundation; the Wenner Gren Foundation for Anthropological Research; the Tinker Foundation; and the University of Florida College of Arts and Sciences. I began this project at the University of Florida where I received crucial support and intellectual stimulation from David Geggus and Mark Thurner. I remember with fondness our conversations and the kindness with which they read and commented on many versions of my manuscript. I am also thankful for the advice and encouragement of Alvaro Feliz Bolaños, Frederick Corney, and Jeffrey Needell. While writing the book, I encountered other historians who generously read and commented on my work: thanks to Jeremy Adelman, Reid Andrews, Nancy Appelbaum, Choi Chatterjee, Dan Cohen, Laurent Dubois, Chris Endy, Susan Fitzpatrick, John Garrigus, Aims McGuinness, Kym Morrison, Mary Roldan, James Sanders, Pete Sigal, and Gillian Weiss. I also would like to thank my colleagues at Case Western Reserve University for a wonderful intellectual and collegial environment. A semester-long leave granted by the university provided needed writing time.

In Colombia, I am most grateful to the staff of the Archivo Historico Nacional de Colombia, the Biblioteca Luis Angel Arango, and the Biblioteca Nacional. In particular, I would like to thank the director and staff of the Archivo Legislativo, who without institutional support or resources resolved to organize and make available their nineteenth-century documents. I thank historians Anamaría Bidegain, Meri Clark, Muriel Laurent, Raúl Roman, Antonino Vidal Ortega, and Fabio Zambrano for their friendship and advice. My special thanks go to Alfonso Múnera for his inspiring intellectual support and wonderful hospitality. I would also like to thank Tatiana, Mayttee, Antonio, Julia, William, and Anamaría for their friendship and hospitality. My stay in Colombia would not have been the same without them.

In Panama, my friends and family provided love and needed emotional stability in my nomadic academic life. I am most grateful to historian Alfredo Castillero Calvo from the University of Panama. He and his wife, Angeles Barquero, welcomed me into their home, where I first learned to love history and archival research. Finally, I thank Jim for his love and companionship and for helping me build a bridge between Ohio and Panama.

MYTHS *of* HARMONY

Introduction

The Wars of Independence

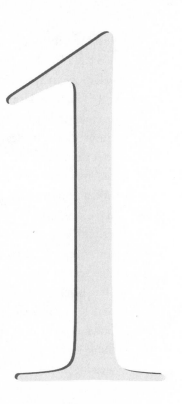

ON NOVEMBER 11, 1811, an angry mob of black and mulatto patriots stormed into the Cartagena town council hall. Armed with lances, daggers, and guns, they gave their petition for independence to the undecided members of the local revolutionary junta. After insulting and beating its members, they forced the helpless junta to sign the declaration of independence against its will.[1] The scene described above faithfully follows most contemporary eyewitness accounts of Cartagena's Independence Day and conforms to historical research that demonstrates the political influence of blacks and mulattoes in the independence movements. Yet to many it still seems incredible to narrate an independence scene in which blacks and mulattoes called the day.[2] To do so challenges two popular assumptions about the Wars of Independence: that the lower classes were mere cannon fodder and had little, if any, political influence; and that the Wars of Independence were led by elites fueled by foreign "enlightened illusions" with no relevance to Spanish American reality.[3]

The latter idea can be traced back to the first histories of the Wars of Independence, in which the lower classes were counted among the numerous obstacles that creole patriots had to overcome to create an independent, free, and modern nation.[4] José Manuel Restrepo—protagonist in the struggles for independence, minister of the interior under Simón Bolívar, and historian and author of the first history of the Colombian Wars of Independence—assessed the lower classes as primitive, in need of education, and prone to follow demagogues; if uncontrolled, they would push the nation down the road to anarchy.[5] Restrepo acknowledged the presence and decisive influence of *pardos* (free blacks and mulattoes) in Cartagena's revolution, but he immediately depoliticized their actions. Booze and cash rather than patriotism explained their participation in the independence movement.[6] *Pardo* involvement was not a positive proof of popular patriotism; instead it demonstrated the "insolence and preponderance of people of color, which became fatal for public peace."[7] Restrepo's foundational history inscribed the acts of *pardo* patriots within a discourse of danger and irrationality that set their behavior in sharp contrast to the noble and politicized conduct of the creole elite.[8]

In such nineteenth-century creole writings, modernity is the commendable aspiration of creole patriots and one of the principles justifying independence from Spain.[9] Yet early narratives of the independence wars also contain some of the first denunciations of modern democratic politics as unsuitable for Spanish American societies. These texts did not condemn democracy per se, but rather its excesses. Simón Bolívar is perhaps the most influential representative of this tradition. His attacks on lawyers, demagogues, and incendiary theoreticians for their failure to grasp that modern politics could not be transferred to Spanish America without sufficient attention to local geography and culture are well known.[10] What often goes unacknowledged is his influence on the development of an intellectual tradition that erased the contribution of the Spanish American popular classes in the history of modern democracy, making modernity seem a mere illusion of the elite. Bolívar sought to prove that fully representative politics did not suit South Americans. He created a dichotomy that distinguished between politically virtuous North Americans and South Americans, whose "character, habits and present enlightenment does not suit perfect representative institutions." An "entirely popular system," he insisted, was not appropriate for this region.[11] He also cast local demands for popular and regional representation as the political pipedreams of a handful of enlightened lawyers.[12] In his address to the Constitutional Congress of Angostura, he criticized the current constitution by reminding legislators that "not all eyes are capable of looking at the light of celestial perfection."[13] Representative democracy might belong in paradise, but not in South America. By making representative politics look like the exclusive aspiration of self-deluded lawyers, he detached the new constitutional governments from the societies that birthed them. This narrative's legacy erased from historical memory local struggles over the nature of the new political system. Yet if Bolívar lashed out against lawyers' inability to realize that liberal and perfect institutions did not fit the geography of Colombia, this was because he feared not that the popular classes would remain aloof from modern politics but that they would participate too much. As Germán Carrera-Damas has shown, he feared that democracy in Spanish America could lead to the end of elite rule.[14] He blamed lawyers for not understanding that representative institutions among "the Caribes from the Orinoco, the sailors of Maracibo, the *bogas* [river boatmen] of Magdalena, the bandits of Patia . . . and all the savage hordes of Africa and America" would lead to Colombia's ruin, perhaps to a second Haiti.[15] In his famous "Jamaica Letter," he noted that in Lima "the rich would not tolerate democracy, and the slaves and *pardos* would not tolerate aristocracy."[16] Years later, he would warn José Antonio Paez against changing Colombia's republican system, arguing that "the height and brilliance of a throne would be frightful. Equality would be broken and *los colores* [the colored classes] would see all their rights lost to a new aristocracy."[17] Future interpretations of Bolívar would tend to forget the strong linkage between *pardos* and democracy in his writings. Mostly remembered instead is his attack on lawyers' inability to comprehend local society.[18]

Paradoxically, this binary discourse of elite illusion and lower-class primitiveness reached new levels in the 1960s and 1970s, when a new generation of historians sought to denounce the elitism of traditional narratives that glorified independence and the historical role of the founding fathers. They wanted instead to understand the social effects of independence and to incorporate the popular classes into national histories. As historians compared the nature and degree of social and economic change from colonial times through the nineteenth century, they concluded that the lower classes had gained nothing by independence; if anything, they had lost.[19] The lower classes had been betrayed by an elite illusion of modernity that proclaimed the equality of all citizens but was characterized by *caciquismo* (patron-client relations) and electoral fraud—that proclaimed racial equality but continued colonial practices of racial discrimination.[20] Therefore, changes in political culture were quickly dismissed as mirages that hid cruel social inequalities.[21] The wars had secured independence from Spain, but nothing else. The work of Colombian historian Indalecio Lievano-Aguirre is typical of this perspective. Although he highlighted the participation of the popular classes in the wars, he disconnected them from the political ideology of their times. According to him, "the showing of false erudition of creole lawyers was unintelligible to slaves, Indians, the dispossessed, and the colored races." In spite of his critique of traditional narratives, Lievano-Aguirre remained trapped by the elitist characterization of the lower classes as prepolitical primitives.[22] Ironically, it is this focus on the lower classes that makes the Revolution a political chimera; it is their assumed disconnection from modern politics that makes revolutionary politics a mere illusion of the Spanish American elite. Thus, local intellectual and political debates became false erudition, implicitly contrasted with some true—perhaps European?—erudition. Spanish America's crucial, pioneering role in the history of democracy and republicanism became further erased.[23]

But in Venezuela and Caribbean Colombia, which were central war theaters and important exporters of revolutionary armies, people of African descent were a demographic majority. They not only constituted the corps of the patriot army but also participated actively in the construction of the new political systems. Even so, some historians still insisted on their irrelevance. Significantly, this blind spot was not due to historians' ignorance of lower-class participation in the wars and receptiveness to certain revolutionary ideas. One of the most complex and brilliant political analysts of the period, François-Xavier Guerra, acknowledged the involvement of people of African descent, as well as the influence of French, particularly Haitian, revolutionary ideas in slave revolts.[24] Yet he quickly dismissed such events as exceptional and inconsequential occurrences that at most tended to make the elite more conservative. Thus Guerra's grand generalization was that the lower classes' lack of participation in modern politics set the Spanish American revolutions apart from other contemporary revolutions.[25]

This persistence in denying *pardos'* contribution to republican politics speaks to the weight given to nineteenth-century political narratives, which continue to be read as documentary evidence of lower-class attitudes.[26] Anthony Pagden's analysis of Dominique De Pradt's 1829 writings about the blacks and mulattoes at the Constitutional Congress of Angostura provides a clear example of the limits of such narratives. De Pradt described the congress in the following terms:

> Sybarites of the civilization of Europe, preachers of liberty, I would wish to see your tribunals set by the banks of the Orinoco, your benches of senators mingled with a horrible mixture of Blacks, mulattos, plainsmen, Creoles, of men suddenly dragged out of the depths of slavery and barbarity to be transformed into legislators and heads of state! The same blood, the same language, the same customs, a common heritage of grandeur and of tal-

ent, an advanced civilization, all these hold together all the several parts of the societies of Europe. In America all is diversity, the principles of division, and absence of civilization. In Europe one plays, in America one must create.[27]

One of the most striking features of De Pradt's observation is its endurance. Pagden uses De Pradt to point out Bolívar's failure to understand that his lofty republican ideals would do poorly within such a social environment. Oddly, he accuses Bolívar of not following his own precept—the need to adapt laws to regional specificities—and of not being able to see the chimerical nature of his own program. According to Pagden, local people needed a nationalist ideology based on emotional historical or religious nationalism instead of abstract republican precepts with which they had no connection.[28]

In Pagden's analysis, one of the salient characteristics of De Pradt's description—the presence of black and mulatto legislators in Angostura —goes unnoticed. One wonders who these senators were; what they thought about their legislative duties; how they experienced, participated in, or followed the congressional debates. Did they influence the debates' outcome? Did Bolívar or any of the other legislators have them in mind as an important public in preparing their addresses? Addressing these questions may cause a different picture of the origins of modernity in Spanish America to emerge. However, this would require going beyond the conservative narrative of the Wars of Independence, which reiterates the unsuitability of republican ideals for Spanish American societies, the proclivity of the lower classes to follow demagogues, and the need for strong governments in societies riven by racial and social differences. This historical interpretation, as Antonio Annino has pointed out, is the result of the "Black legend" of Spanish American political history, which in its national version denounces nineteenth-century suffrage as a practice dominated by caudillos, corruption, and ignorance. This legend tends to have a checklist model of revolution, which inevitably compares Spanish American revolutions to the French and U.S. models in an effort to determine where they failed.[29]

The problem with this perspective is that it does not help us understand the revolutions and their legacy. It does not do justice to the political and intellectual richness of this period. As Pagden, Guerra, Annino, Jaime Rodriguez, Margarita Garrido, and Jeremy Adelman, among others, have shown, this period witnessed serious and vigorous debates about the nature and future of representative politics.[30] The conservative narrative should be seen not as a description of lower-class political characteristics but as only one of several political programs and commentaries that emerged during the wars. Such readings need to be confronted with others that emerged during the Revolution.[31] They should be understood as part of a larger debate over the nature of political change and the role of the lower classes in the new states, as part of a general nineteenth-century debate over how to reconcile social order and hierarchy with the politics of citizenship and representation. Further, seeing republican politics as an imported concept does not explain how the nineteenth-century Spanish American republics lasted longer than their European counterparts and why they survived in the midst of European monarchical backlash. It does not explain why these early republics enjoyed some of the most ample suffrage laws of their time or why they were replaced with more restrictive codes in the late nineteenth century.[32] Moreover, it does not help us understand the mentality of the people who lived through the wars: the protagonists surely wondered at their changing times, at witnessing unprecedented transformations. Perhaps more important, the binary discourse of elite illusion and lower-class primitiveness deprives the Latin American popular classes of their historical role in the construction and development of modern politics. At stake are the very origins of Spanish American modernity.

Building on the methodological developments in peasant studies literature, works on the Wars of Independence have begun to provide a more nuanced conception of the appropriation of elite political discourse by the lower classes and their participation in the processes of state formation in the new republics. These narratives have challenged the assumption of a strong ideological divide between the elite and the lower classes.[33] Peter Guardino, Alfonso Múnera, and Peter Blanchard have taught us that blacks and mulattoes were not mere cannon fodder in the Spanish American Wars of Independence; they participated in and influenced the political debates about citizenship in the revolutionary period, sometimes pushing the elites to acquiesce to radical measures that they had not initially contemplated.[34] The historical literature on slavery during the Age of Revolution—in particular the historiography on the French Caribbean—is further changing our understanding of blacks' politics during this crucial period. This literature has examined the multiple ways in which enslaved and free people of African descent appropriated French revolutionary discourse. It has also highlighted the importance of lower-class, geographically mobile men and women in disseminating news about the Haitian Revolution and abolitionist politics among the Caribbean slave population. In addition, it has shown the importance of colonial revolutionary events in the development of European notions of race and citizenship.[35] My work follows this literature. I am particularly indebted to the work of Alfonso Múnera, the first historian to acknowledge the crucial importance of Afro-Colombians in Cartagena's independence movement.

In spite of this new research, the revolutionary nature of the wars continues to be hotly contested. Even Eric Van Young's recent insightful and sophisticated analysis of the Mexican Wars of Independence continues to question the relevance of modern politics for the Mexican lower classes.[36] In Colombia, as in the rest of Latin America, lower-class protagonism continues to be challenged. Aline Helg builds on Múnera's account of blacks' and mulattoes' participation in Cartagena's independence but reaches the traditional conclusion that the drive for independence "was a fragmented and conflictive elite-led movement." According to her, "Afro-Colombian culture remained local and mostly festive. It seldom made claims against or directly challenged the power of the wealthy."[37] It is not yet clear how historical summaries of the independence period will incorporate the debate about popular politics and reconcile various interpretations. Still, many *pardos* embraced the rhetoric of the Age of Revolution and actively pressured for the realization of their vision of social and political equality.[38] Their political activities would have enormous consequences for Colombian politics and racial ideology. They would lead to the declaration of racial equality among all free people and the construction of a nationalist mythology of racial harmony and equality.

The Myth of Racial Democracy

During the Wars of Independence, Colombian patriots declared the end of colonial caste laws and decreed legal racial equality among all free citizens. They also constructed a powerful nationalist ideology that proclaimed the harmony and fraternity of Colombians of all colors and denounced racial hierarchies and conflicts as unpatriotic. Twentieth-century scholars called this link between nationalism and racial harmony "the myth of racial democracy." Although this was a momentous political, legal, and ideological change, studies of race relations have tended to approach the declaration of equality only to denounce its failures. They correctly point out that legal equality did not eliminate racial discrimination. Moreover, they condemn the elites' use of the republican rhetoric of equality to attract the black population to their side during the Wars of Independence and the nineteenth-century civil wars.[39] The fact that slavery remained legal in most of Spanish America until the 1850s seems to confirm the emptiness of this rhetoric. In addition, the nationalist discourse of racial harmony allowed the elite to maintain informal patterns of discrimination by impeding the formation of racially based political associations.[40]

However, the powerful association among republicanism, nationalism, and racial equality that characterized the Spanish American independence period cannot be taken for granted. To do so not only fails to address the complex processes of myth construction but also trivializes a major and fascinating historical moment. In the Western world, republican notions of citizenship have not always led to nationalist rhetorics of racial equality; on the contrary, the height of nineteenth-century liberalism coincided with increasing scientific racism.[41] Moreover, when the notion of racial equality became firmly established in patriot rhetoric during the 1810s and 1820s, contemporary American republics did not provide compelling examples of racial equality to local elites. In the United States, nonwhite inferiority was part of the mainstream political landscape; only a few radical abolitionists favored full legal equality for blacks and whites.[42] In Haiti, revolutionary France's declaration of racial equality was associated with civil war, slave rebellion, the defeat of the French planter class, and the formation of a black independent state—hardly an appealing image for Spanish American white creoles. Further, as race-war rumors show, early republican race relations were charged with deep tensions. With the emergence of a powerful black political and military class— including generals and congressmen—and the enfranchisement of a sector of the free black population, *pardos* had developed new expectations of freedom and equality. They now exerted a political pressure that the creole elite could not ignore. Clearly, the future of race relations was one of the most controversial and significant problems of the independence period and the myth of racial harmony one of the most important political legacies of the Age of Revolution.[43]

Since Gilberto Freyre, José Vasconcelos, and Fernando Ortiz popularized the notion of Latin American racial democracy in the 1920s and 1930s, historians have searched the colonial past for the origins of the relative flexibility that characterizes Latin American as opposed to U.S. race relations. Scholars have explained this flexibility as a result of the demographic and economic weight of people of mixed descent and of a history of transculturation, patent in colonial culture, law, and religion.[44] A new generation of scholars has successfully challenged this perspective, denouncing racial democracy as a myth, a hegemonic construction of Latin American elites. More than four decades of comparative analysis of slavery in the Americas have dismissed the notion of a benign and paternalist Iberian planter class, showing that these historical constructions are an intrinsic part of the myth itself. Research over the past decades has turned to an analysis of continuing patterns of racial discrimination in Latin America.[45] An unintended consequence of this intellectual shift has been the abandonment of the question of origins. Even recent works that look explicitly at the connection between nationalism and race in Latin America are more concerned with understanding how modern racial identities work once they are in place, rather than with asking how they emerged.[46] When and how the myth itself was constructed has been largely neglected.[47]

The first decades of independence are crucial for understanding the myth's origins. The historical role of Gran Colombia (contemporary Colombia, Ecuador, Panama, and Venezuela) in its development can hardly be overstated. In more than one way, the Colombian struggle for independence represents a foundational moment in the history of modern race relations in Latin America. Gran Colombia was not only one of the first Latin American regions where racial equality became government policy but one of the first to elaborate a nationalist rhetoric of racial harmony and equality. Further, the important role of Colombian blacks and mulattoes precedes the similar part played by people of African descent in the better-studied Cuban war.[48] Yet most works on the myth of racial democracy tend to ignore the Age of Revolution.[49] Even recent comparative works on postemancipation societies usually analyze the later part of the nineteenth century— Reconstruction (1866–77), the Cuban Wars of Independence (1865–98), and Brazilian manumission (1888).[50] Studies on the history of the myth of racial democracy usually begin with the Cuban liberator José Martí and his call for a republic "with all and for all" in the 1890s.[51] This focus, which reflects the weight and richness of the scholarship on Brazil, Cuba, and the United States, tends to leave out the anticolonial struggles of the early nineteenth century. Yet in Latin America, patriots linked nationalism with racial harmony and equality for the first time in the 1810s and 1820s, during the Wars of Independence.[52] When Cuban liberators made racial equality a fundamental slogan of the patriot camp, they were not inventing a novel concept but building on an entrenched Spanish American tradition that linked nationalism with racial equality.[53]

Focusing on the province of Cartagena in Caribbean Colombia, this work examines the construction of a nationalist rhetoric of racial harmony and equality by examining the relationship among race, war, and nation. It analyzes how belief in racial equality evolved during the Wars of Independence from a notion shared by only a few American and Spanish radicals to a fundamental patriot nationalist construct that neatly separated Americans from Spaniards.[54] The tactical need to attract black soldiers to the patriot side is the common explanation for how racial harmony became associated with nationalism, but this does not suffice to explain this notion's strength and longevity or its association with patriotic love of country. The myth of racial harmony, like all nationalist myths, needed something further to provoke love and alliance: it is difficult to profess love to Machiavellian military tactics. What first captured the imagination of creole patriots was the Cádiz constitutional debates of 1810–12, which linked racial harmony to insurgent nationalism, thus endowing it with emotional power.

This work also examines the emergence of the phantom of race war and its impact on racial constructs. While elite racial fears are well known to historians, in particular Bolívar's constant reference to "pardocracy," we know little about the social basis of these fears and even less about the historical and political repercussions of talk about race war. Neither is it clear when or how the concept of race war disappeared.[55] Sedition cases in which *pardos* were accused of enmity toward whites can enhance our understanding of the historical significance of constant references to race war. Specifically, these cases illuminate how the explicit expression of racial grievances became a mark of unpatriotic divisiveness. The linkage between racial equality and nationalism per se did not exclude the expression of grievances. The ideal of racial harmony and equality had the potential to either empower the disenfranchised or keep them in their place. The question was who controlled the concept of equality. Blacks' and mulattoes' demands, their active participation in patriot politics, gave this issue special urgency and concrete implications. Only through analysis of specific conflicts and negotiations among Afro-Colombians, local elites, and the state can we obtain a full appreciation of the origins of modern racial constructs in Colombia.

A Note on Region, Sources, and Terms

The region including the city of Cartagena and the Magdalena River valley up to the city of Honda is a privileged site for examining Afro-Colombian politics during the Age of Revolution. This was a crucial war theater in which people of African descent—a demographic majority—played a key political and military role. Moreover, its close links with other Caribbean regions such as Haiti, Jamaica, Venezuela, and Panama make it an excellent sphere for examining the transmission of revolutionary ideas to the Spanish mainland.

During the Wars of Independence and their immediate aftermath, Cartagena formed part of a territory larger than contemporary Colombia. In late colonial times, it was part of the viceroyalty of New Granada, which included today's Colombia, Ecuador, Panama, and Venezuela. From independence, in 1821, until 1830, Cartagena was part of the new Republic of Colombia, which then included the regions administered by the old viceroyalty of New Granada—what historians today call Gran Colombia. Thus, until 1830, mentions of Colombia or the

Colombian state refer to Gran Colombia. This distinction is important: the foundations of racial imaginaries in Colombia were linked to this wider political area. The racial policies developed by the central state in Bogotá were thought to apply to a larger political entity, the region of Cartagena but one of a series of Colombian regions where people of African descent were numerous and politically active. When state authorities confronted racial conflicts in Cartagena, they tended to also take into consideration Venezuela, Panama, and Guayaquil.[56] The connections among these regions were also apparent to Afro-Colombians, many of whom traveled throughout South America and the Caribbean following the Bolivarian army.

The term *pardo* describes free people of African descent regardless of color. Although originally this term was used to describe mulattoes, by the early nineteenth century, it was commonly used in Colombia as a generic term for free people of African descent.[57] The term *castas* refers to all free people of mixed racial descent. The word *creole* refers to members of the white elite who were born in Spanish America. Finally, *myth of racial harmony* is used to describe the nationalist racial ideology of this period: it better reflects early nineteenth-century language than does *racial democracy*, a term coined much later. As we will see, some of this myth's ideological characteristics changed from the early nineteenth century to the twentieth—highlighting the need to historicize its cultural evolution. However, the linkage between nationalism and racial harmony and equality did not change.

A variety of documentary sources can help us to understand how race was used in different public and private spaces. I use parliamentary debates, newspaper articles, judiciary sentences, military speeches, manumission ceremonies, and personal diaries to trace the cultural, intellectual, and political bases of the new nationalist myth of racial harmony. I also use a series of criminal accusations against Afro-Colombians for "enmity toward whites" to illuminate certain aspects of race relations that are not apparent in other documents. These judicial records offer rich insights into the racial politics of the early republican period. They provide a glimpse into the lives of Afro-Colombians at this time, emerging from the political activities of *pardos* whose names, professions, and words have come down to us. They give us a sense of how these people understood their changing times. They also reveal the presence of *pardos* in local politics. The 1812 Constitution of Cartagena enfranchised all men with independent means of support, either from property or from a profession or trade, regardless of income.[58] The 1821 Constitution, however, set property requirements for office holders and members of the electoral college.[59] In the Caribbean cities of Colombia, these electoral laws gave suffrage rights to a large number of *pardo* artisans who dominated the trades. Yet the available records do not reveal the percentage of *pardo* artisans (or independent peasants) who exercised this right. This obscurity derives not only from the paucity of contemporary public documents but also from republican laws that forbade the use of racial markers in these documents. Because of their very nature, however, accusations of race war are explicit about the race of the actors involved. Even though these records do not tell us how many *pardos* occupied public office, they do permit us a glimpse of political conflicts involving *pardos* who had reached positions of authority. Moreover, judicial records provide access to a variety of political expressions: voting was not the only political act.[60] Judicial cases illustrate what changes *pardos* expected the Republic to bring and how they sought to pressure the government to bring these changes about through petitions, pamphlets, and the support of political figures in the streets.

Racial Tensions in

Late Colonial Society

The Magdalena River Region

IN THE LATE eighteenth and early nineteenth centuries, the Magdalena River was Colombia's undisputed commercial artery, and its three port cities, Cartagena, Mompox, and Honda, controlled most of the legal and illegal trade between the Caribbean and the Andes.[1] Among these three cities, Cartagena reigned. With its impressive walls, rich houses, and magnificent churches and convents, it was the seat of the merchant guild (*consulado de comercio*), the Inquisition, and the office of the provincial governor. A prosperous town of 13,396 habitants, Cartagena dominated New Granada's trade and had the viceroyalty's highest concentration of merchants. Here, New Granada's gold was exchanged for European merchandise destined for as far away as

Quito.[2] Cartagena was also the hub of the viceroyalty's slave trade, which supplied the rich mining areas of western New Granada. It further benefited from its strategic role in the Spanish defense system. The *situado* (a military subsidy) injected the city's economy with hundreds of thousands of pesos annually for the construction and repair of the defense system and the support of the military garrison.[3]

According to Alfonso Múnera, by end of the eighteenth century, the composition of Cartagena's merchant and military elite had gone through a radical change. The city elite, traditionally dominated by peninsular merchants, had become increasingly creole. Americans also dominated the military, including middle-ranking officers, as a result of the Bourbon policy of relying on colonials to fill the army. The Spanish continued to dominate only the highest commands. Even though most members of the merchant guild continued to be Spanish, when the nineteenth century began, most of them had lived more than twenty years in Cartagena, where they had developed strong connections and family ties. In addition, their creole sons had grown to become Cartagena's new intellectual elite. After finishing their higher education in Bogotá, these sons returned to Cartagena with novel ideas about science and technology and new projects to develop their region.

By 1809, most members of the *cabildo* (town council) belonged to this generation of creoles. Two of the most powerful men in the city—the wealthy merchant and leading intellectual José Ignacio de Pombo and the field marshal Antonio Narvaez de la Torre, the highest-ranking soldier in the viceroyalty—were creole. The Americanization of Cartagena's elite was further consolidated by a growing awareness that peninsular and local economic interests were diverging. Bourbon free-trade reforms and the disruption of Spanish Atlantic commerce during the wars with France and England in the 1790s made Cartagena's elite acutely aware of their conflicting interests with Bogotá and Spain. While Cartagena's elite saw free trade as an appropriate means to export commercial agriculture and import European manufactures,

Spanish merchants saw it as a threat to their colonial monopoly. Cartagena's and Bogotá's economic interests were in similar opposition. Again and again, Cartagena unsuccessfully asked the viceroy for permission to import U.S. flour. Although the distance and difficult communications between Bogotá and Cartagena made Andean flour more expensive (and often scarce), the viceroy repeatedly denied Cartagena's petition under pressure from Bogotá's elite, which feared losing an important market. Thus, during the crisis of the Spanish empire in 1808, the actions of Cartagena's creoles were influenced by their increasing association of economic and political well-being with regional autonomy from Spain and Bogotá.[4]

Cartagena's economic and military activities also fostered the growth of a populous *pardo* artisan and military class. In 1780, at least one thousand artisans lived in the city, more than 80 percent of them *pardos*.[5] Their demographic weight explains *pardos'* dominance of the city's crafts. Indeed, according to the 1780 census, free people of color constituted 56.7 percent of Cartagena's population; slaves 15.7 percent; whites, including clergy, 27.0 percent; and Indians 0.5 percent. *Pardo* artisans included shoemakers, tailors, masons, and silversmiths. Some of them became relatively wealthy and could afford to live in two-story houses and own slaves.[6]

The *pardos'* demographic weight also made them crucial to the new Bourbon military organization. In the second half of the eighteenth century, the Bourbons carried out a series of sweeping military reforms with the goal of creating a disciplined and well-trained militia that could share the burden of defense. Reformers sought to achieve this goal by relying on qualified leadership and, importantly, on the development of corporate pride by granting special legal privileges, the *fuero militar*, to militia members. It soon became clear to Spanish authorities that in regions like Cartagena, any effective reorganization of the militia would have to not only incorporate *pardos* but also extend *fuero* rights to them. By joining the militia, then, *pardos* gained not only legal privileges but also access to symbols of status, such as uniforms and officer rank, which provided an escape from rigid colonial racial hierarchies.[7]

The *pardos'* influence in the city was replicated in the country-side. Caribbean New Granada was not an export-plantation society. Although some attempts were made to develop cotton and cacao plantations for exportation, New Granada's participation in the world market remained insignificant.[8] Thus, most haciendas produced foodstuffs and livestock for the local urban markets. A substantial subsistence peasantry surrounded these haciendas. Although wealthy landowners producing cattle, sugar, and *aguardiente* (sugar-based liquors) for urban markets might own slaves, most of the province's peasantry was free. Of the 118,750 habitants of the province of Cartagena in 1779, only 8 percent were slaves, 66 percent were free people of color, 10 percent were white, and 17 percent were Indian.[9]

Mompox and Honda, the other two important port cities on the Magdalena River, followed Cartagena's social and economic patterns. These cities had a white elite composed of merchants, crown officers, and hacienda owners and a large free colored population including artisans, small vendors, peasants, and *bogas* (river boatmen). At the bottom rung of society were the slaves, who composed only a small percentage of the labor force in both cities and rural areas.

Late Colonial Tensions

A rigid legal racial hierarchy framed social relations among the different sectors of Cartagena society in the late colonial era. Parish registries dutifully recorded the color and legitimate or illegitimate status of newborn babies. Privileged positions and access to universities were barred to those who could not claim white and legitimate status. Although white and *pardo* families manipulated the system, finding legal and illegal mechanisms to change the racial status of their relatives, they did so without challenging the ideology behind such classifications.[10] Yet in the last decade of the eighteenth century, a series of political and ide-ological changes began to fracture this racial hierarchy. On the one hand, the shattering events of the French Revolution and their radical manifestation in the Caribbean colony of Saint Domingue brought to the local political imaginary new ways of understanding social and racial relations. On the other hand, new Bourbon racial policies slowly began to erode the ideological bases of the colonial racial hierarchy. In the second half of the eighteenth century, the Bourbons sought to re-form colonial administration to ensure tighter political control and increase royal revenue. Within an imperial ideology that increasingly emphasized the need to boost the productivity and utility of American colonies, Spanish assessment of free people of African descent began to acquire more positive tones.

In 1795, the Spanish Crown published a royal decree that con-tained a list of some seventy-one royal waivers (*gracias al sacar*), with their respective prices. For 500 *reales*, it was possible for a *pardo* to buy his or her whiteness. This decree did not establish a new proce-dure but only regularized an earlier practice that allowed meritorious and wealthy *pardos* to acquire the legal privileges of whites through service to the Crown and a monetary gift.[11] The 1795 decree was one of a series of laws through which the Bourbons sought to adapt colo-nial legislation to the increasing demographic and economic weight of the *castas* (people of mixed racial descent). The earlier 1778 decree regulating marriages in America, changing policies toward Indian lands, and the creation of *pardo* militias had also reflected Bourbon attempts to confront, regularize, and legislate for the *castas'* newfound impor-tance.[12] New Bourbon policies toward *pardos* were not meant to chal-lenge racial hierarchies but merely to encourage *pardos'* loyalty to the Crown by providing them with access to symbols of honor and respect.

Notwithstanding their moderation, the Spanish concessions to *pardos* provoked strong opposition from the creole elite of cities with dominant *pardo* populations, such as Caracas and Cartagena. Although both enlightened creoles and Spaniards were aware of and sometimes sympathetic to new ideologies that prized merit over birth, they did not agree with their implications for the local racial hierarchy. On the contrary, creoles and Spanish bureaucrats tended to take opposite sides in *pardos'* claims, a difference that often reflected the tactical importance of *pardo* support in the increasing political conflicts between creole and peninsular Spaniards.[13] Creoles feared that the Crown's cautious racial policies in favor of *pardos* would eventually disrupt local hierarchies. Of equal importance, however, was their belief that Spanish support of *pardos* was a sign of their contempt toward creoles. A particularly sore point for creoles was the Spanish notion that American whites were rarely free from racial mixture, which justified the blurring of color distinctions in America.[14] This notion created a dreadful distance between creole and peninsular Spanish, further emphasizing the former's increasingly disadvantageous position. They had already confronted Cornelius de Pauw's and George Louis Leclerc Comte de Buffon's theories of Americans' natural inferiority. After the Bourbon reforms, they saw their economic and political autonomy increasingly challenged.[15]

Creoles strongly disliked the extension of the *fuero militar* to *pardos*. In particular, they bitterly resented losing jurisdiction over an important sector of the urban population and worried about the effect that their diminished social control would have on established social hierarchies. Spanish authorities tended to privilege corporate military interests over the maintenance of local social hierarchies in judicial cases involving *pardo* militiamen. Coastal town councils (*cabildos*) witnessed with dismay the actions of Spanish officials, who did not mind offending and attacking their authority vis-à-vis *pardo* militiamen.[16] Tensions were probably highest in Caracas, where creole authorities had to contend not only with Spanish military authorities but also with the Spanish-controlled *audiencia* (appeal court).

In contrast, for the Spanish authorities, the maintenance of local social hierarchies tended to take second place to corporate military interests, a sensible approach since their priority was imperial defense. Military commanders constantly emphasized the *fuero*'s value for the militia's morale and the *pardos*' crucial importance for imperial protection. According to New Granada viceroy Pedro Mendinueta, *pardos* were not only the most numerous coastal population but also the more robust and better suited to the local climate. The viceroy emphasized their loyalty to the king and their willingness to fight for him, not only in their own regions but also, unlike white creoles, in distant places.[17] *Pardo* loyalty became even more important as political instability increased in the viceroyalty. Fresh in the royal authorities' memory was the 1781 Comunero rebellion, when violent tax riots spread across the highlands.[18] They also remembered the important role of the coastal *pardo* militia in restoring order in the highlands.[19] Moreover, a recent republican conspiracy in Bogotá had revealed the disaffection of its creole elite. In 1794, four creole students and a Spaniard had posted lampoons against the tobacco monopoly and the *audiencia* on the walls of Bogotá. The apprehensive viceregal authorities began a full inquiry, which revealed that the prominent creole Antonio Nariño had translated and printed the "Declaration of the Rights of Man." Convinced of having unveiled a full-fledged republican conspiracy to overthrow the government, the Spanish authorities arrested many creoles and became suspicious of creoles in general, including the *cabildo* authorities. Although eventually authorities realized that no organized conspiracy existed, and most prisoners were freed, the authors of the lampoons were sentenced to perpetual exile and long years in prison overseas. Nariño and ten alleged accomplices were sent to Spain to receive their sentences. This alleged conspiracy had revealed deep tensions between creole and Spanish authorities, further convincing the viceroy of the crucial importance of coastal, and particularly *pardo*, support and loyalty.[20]

An examination of Spanish arguments in favor of *pardo* claims sustains creole fears that this Spanish support reflected contempt for creoles. For example, in 1794 in Cartagena, the issue of whether a mulatto novice should be allowed to become a regular nun tore apart the convent of Santa Clara in a conflict that involved the city's main civil and religious authorities. The nuns complained to the king that the mother superior and the convent's priest, with the support of the bishop and the governor, had subjected them to threats and arbitrary imprisonment for opposing the mulatto novice. According to the nuns, the mother superior and her patrons had imposed the mulatto nun against the congregation's laws and traditions, which required a majority vote to accept a new nun. While the nuns (probably mostly creole) rejected the novice for being the illegitimate daughter of a mulatto mother, the Spanish governor prized her high moral qualities. He argued that the accusations of illegitimacy were false and that her baptismal record did not refer to her as mulatto, only mentioning that she was the child of unknown parents. Significantly, he continued, "even if the nun were a mulatto, in this region this characteristic [calidad] has no relevance . . . , when you can see in the streets pardos and morenos who are Franciscans, which is the same order as that of the nuns."[21] Thus, for the governor, the mulatto novice deserved to be a nun not only because her moral qualities were more important than her race but also, and perhaps more importantly, because racial distinctions among Americans increasingly made little sense. A lawyer for the Consejo de Indias reasoned similarly in 1765, when he supported the right of the pardo Cristóbal Polo to practice law in Cartagena in spite of local white opposition. He argued that Polo should be permitted to practice because this befitted a city with a large mulatto population such as Cartagena.[22] Likewise, Viceroy José Espeleta, in support of a request by pardo militiamen to wear the same insignia as their white counterparts, noted that white militiamen, with the exception of officers, should not be considered properly white. Most of them were "blancos de la tierra [local whites], who in substance are mulattos a little closer to our race."[23]

Spanish notions of the coastal regions as mulatto societies could sometimes lead to the construction of powerful dichotomies that divided colonial society between loyal and useful *pardos* and proud, disloyal, and lazy creoles.[24] Thus, when the Spanish military commander of Mompox affirmed during the 1811 patriot insurrection that the lower classes (mostly *pardo*) were loyal, he was building on an established bureaucratic tradition. He argued that conspiracy came from "the feces of the peninsula and the idle creoles who find here protection, honor, and authority: their habits and manners cannot hide their origins. They have become vain with their wealth, which is the sad product of their crimes and rapacity."[25]

Given this, it should not be surprising that the creole elite responded with outrage to the 1795 decree of the *gracias al sacar*.[26] The petition the Caracas town council presented to the Crown opposing this policy provides one of the most articulate expressions of creole racial views at the end of the colonial period. It not only illustrates creole racial prejudice but also acutely reveals the importance of the tensions between creole and peninsular Spaniards over local racial relations.[27] The petition did not oppose the ability of some meritorious *pardos* to gain legal whiteness; rather, it argued that the 1795 decree made this procedure too simple and inexpensive.[28] In the words of the Caracas town council, it was necessary "to keep *pardos* in their present subordination, without any law that would confuse them with whites, who abhor and detest this union . . . and see it as an invention to discredit them under the false pretension that it serves the interest of His Majesty."[29] How could a white, whose family had carefully maintained its *limpieza* (racial purity) generation after generation, be equal to a *pardo*, who was tainted by illegitimacy and slavery? According to the council, the royal decree could only be the result of false and evil-intentioned reports from Spanish officers in the Americas who did not care about the welfare of Spanish American subjects (*españoles americanos*). The *cabildo* petition against the new law expressed the creole sentiment that the *gracias al sacar* was yet another arbitrary Spanish act intended to undermine creole authority and promote social chaos.[30]

Creole racial concerns resulted not only from Spanish policies in favor of *pardos* but also from *pardos'* active defense of their new prerogatives. They joined the militia, attracted by its offer of social advance and recognition; the access it granted to symbols of respect, such as arms, uniforms, and insignias; and the legal protection from creole authorities gained through the *fuero militar*. The importance Cartagena's *pardos* bestowed on symbols becomes apparent in their reaction to a new military ordinance that forced *pardo* militia officers to wear special insignia that would distinguish them from white officers.[31] Although they already had to wear uniforms that were different from those of white militia officers, they held dear the fact that they wore insignia identical to that worn by whites. *Pardos* soon submitted a formal petition against the new ordinance.[32] In addition, in 1794, disturbing rumors ran through Cartagena that *pardos* offended by the new ordinance were authoring lampoons that were apparently even more seditious than those that had appeared in Bogotá during the Nariño conspiracy.[33]

Although the viceroy wrote to the Crown that he doubted the truth of these rumors, he used them to defend his policy of ignoring the new ordinances. He had acquiesced to the *pardos'* formal petition, he said, because he considered it imprudent to humiliate the *pardo* militias, particularly in time of war with France and in the face of creole disaffection in Bogotá. He emphasized their loyalty, reminding the Crown of their past services, in particular their role in quashing the 1781 Comunero revolt. He used the seditious lampoons to warn the Crown about the dangers of unwise racial policies: the rumors betrayed local belief in the dreadful consequences of *pardo* dissatisfaction. Thus, the viceroy continued, seditious people could take advantage of any indication that the Crown could no longer count on *pardo* support and loyalty.[34] Faced with external war, increasing manifestations of creole discontent, and the nearby example of the Saint Domingue rebellion, local Spanish officers understood the importance of maintaining the loyalty of *pardo* militiamen.

For ambitious and relatively wealthy *pardos*, militia service also provided an effective way to rise above rigid colonial racial distinctions. Indeed, some prominent *pardos* used their service in the militia to improve their social status by ascending to positions legally reserved for whites. Wealthy *pardo* militia officers such as Pedro Romero, from Cartagena, and Pedro Antonio de Ayarza, from Portobelo, used their service to the Crown to give their sons access to university educations, a right reserved almost exclusively for whites.[35] In January 1795, Pedro Antonio de Ayarza, the captain of the *pardo* militia of Portobelo, petitioned the Crown to distinguish his family with the title "Don," so that his three sons could continue their higher education in Bogotá and receive university diplomas. The arguments with which Ayarza sustained his petition are indicative of the late eighteenth century's shifting notions of status, which, while still officially acknowledging the relevance of birth and origin as rightful determinants of social position, had begun to prize merit and education as legitimate avenues for social mobility.

This petition thus provides a concrete and detailed example of the workings of the *gracias al sacar*. Ayarza did not challenge colonial limitations on *pardos*. Far from denouncing the viceroy's decision to deny his son the right to obtain a university degree, he acknowledged that the viceroy had followed the law. His approach instead was to portray himself as an exceptional *pardo* who deserved to rise above his condition. He appealed to the king's clemency toward those whose lives were devoted to the service of God and the monarchy. Following the traditional tactics of the *hoja de méritos y servicios*, he reminded the Crown of his twenty years of service as captain of the *pardo* militia, during which he had always received praise from his superiors. He emphasized his willingness to sacrifice his life and wealth for the Crown, as he had demonstrated by donating his entire stipend to support the present war. He further sought to convince the Crown that he was an exception to his humble *pardo* class: "Although my birth has denied it [the title of Don] to me, divine providence has granted me enlightenment enough to acquire some esteem."[36] He defended his exceptionality, pointing to the good reputation he had gained in his trading activities with Cádiz, Panamá, and Cartagena. The definitive proof of his capacities was that the bishop had trusted him with the finances of Portobelo's church, and the Franciscan order had chosen him as their apostolic representative even though his town did not lack people of rank.[37] The members of the Bogotá elite who recommended Ayarza's sons echoed his arguments. According to Joseph Miguel Pey, the mayor of Bogotá, the fine behavior of José Ponseano (Ayarza's son) clearly demonstrated his excellent upbringing, winning him the esteem and consideration of people of repute "in spite of his *pardo* quality."[38] Ayarza's approach proved successful; the king approved his petition and removed his oldest son's *pardo* status—with the important caveat that this would not serve as a precedent for other *pardos*. Although merit and education could thus be officially used to counterbalance racial origins, this notion was still applied only to what were seen as exceptional cases that did not, and should not, alter established racial hierarchies.[39] Yet the argument that some *pardos* deserved special treatment because of their unique merits suggested the radical notion that legal and social status should not be based on race but on merit. Indeed, one stated purpose of Ayarza's petition was that his three sons should not be "judged for the humbleness of their class but only for their habits and behavior."[40]

By the 1790s, the Bourbons' gradual reforms were confronting a larger Atlantic world that provided new, radical examples for understanding political and social relations. The influence of the French and American Revolutions among white patriots is well known. New revolutionary ideas evoked interest and passion among creole patriots, who found in the revolutionary critique of despotism an ideological framework for expressing their mounting discontent with Bourbon colonial policies. Yet the influence of French and Haitian revolutionary ideas on the local racial imaginary is less clear. When Antonio Nariño published the first Spanish translation of the "Declaration of the Rights of Man" in 1794, not only had the French already executed their king and established a republic, but the revolution in their Caribbean colony of Saint Domingue had escalated into a terrifying slave revolt, which led to the declaration of full legal equality between blacks and whites in 1792 and the abolition of slavery in 1793. In 1804, six years before the establishment of the first patriot juntas in New Granada, Haiti declared its independence, becoming the second independent nation in the hemisphere and the first modern black nation in the world. The Spanish authorities in New Granada saw the slave revolts in the French Caribbean islands as a terrifying possibility that should be avoided at all costs. The correspondence of Spanish authorities reveals their careful attention to any suggestion of Haitian-inspired racial revolt in their possessions.[41] French-inspired revolts, too, met with exemplary repression.[42]

Fear and repression, however, were not the only responses to the Haitian Revolution. One of the most learned men of the viceroyalty, the wealthy and powerful Cartagenero José Ignacio de Pombo, questioned the soundness of established racial hierarchies in a memorandum to the king dated 1804. Influenced by new political and economic theories, Pombo reasoned that radical reforms were the only way to secure the peace and loyalty of the Americas. He suggested certain changes for the economic development of the American colonies, including measures to stimulate the growth of an abundant and industrious population. He proposed the immigration of Catholic Europeans, who would contribute to the exploitation of New Granada's abundant natural resources. Moreover, he argued that the only way to save the Americas from revolution was to abolish slavery and promote interracial marriage: "It is necessary to promote by all possible means the union and mixture of castas, so there will be but one type of citizens among commoners." Those who showed their worthiness and knowledge should be rewarded with positions of authority in their towns.[43]

Pombo's proposal was a skillful attempt to reconcile traditional hierarchies with enlightened beliefs about the value of an industrious and unified nation. The equality he proposed was to be applied only to commoners, thus leaving intact the privileges of the aristocracy. Yet the values Pombo privileged were quite modern, implying a radical reconsideration of the ideology that up to then had organized colonial society. He prized national unity, expressed in the homogeneity of citizens, over slavery and racial hierarchy, although he considered the latter necessary to prevent unrest. And he believed in the advantages of valuing merit over birth to promote industry and knowledge. Although Pombo's views were still exceptional, similar racial ideas would become common among the creole elite after 1810 patriots took control of local politics.

A more radical project for altering race relations in Spanish America had earlier appeared in the program of the Gual y España republican conspiracy of 1797. This conspiracy was planned in the port city of La Guaira in Venezuela. The conspirators translated into Spanish the 1793 version of the "Declaration of the Rights of Man," adding a "preliminary speech to the Americans."[44] They also wrote two revolutionary songs, the "Caramañola Americana" and the "Canción Americana," and a forty-four-article ordinance, meant to regulate the government of the new republic. These documents combined republican ideology with more traditional grievances against local taxes, Crown monopolies, and corrupt Crown officers. Of particular relevance here was the conspirators' radical republican notion of racial equality. Article 32 declared, "The natural equality between all the inhabitants of these provinces and districts demands that the greatest harmony reign among whites, Indians, *pardos*, and blacks, regarding one another as brothers in Christ, equals in the eyes of God, seeking to better one another solely in merit and virtue, which are the only true and real distinctions between men and the only ones that shall be present in our republic."[45] Articles 33 and 34 abolished the Indian tribute and black slavery—after compensation to owners. Although the articles eliminated color distinctions, they left political control in the hands of landowners, Article 6 declaring that only they could be elected as members of the temporary Junta Gubernativa (Government Board). The ordinance did not clarify how the independent government was to be organized, although Article 8 invited all citizens to submit their ideas in writing.[46] Finally, Article 44 declared that, "as a symbol of the union, harmony, and equality that shall reign among all the inhabitants of Tierra Firme, the emblem will be a cockade with four colors: white, blue, yellow, and red, . . . which stands for the four colors of its reunited patriots, who are *pardos*, blacks, whites, and Indians." These four colors would also represent the four provinces—Caracas, Maracaibo, Cumaná, and Guyana—and the four fundamental rights of man—"equality, liberty, property, and security."[47] Like Pombo, then, the Guaira conspirators sought to abolish racial distinctions by declaring legal equality and the abolition of slavery and proposing merit, rather than birth, as the means to distinguish among citizens. Yet these republican conspirators did not limit racial equality to the commoner class. They went further, centering national identity, as symbolized in the cockade, around racial union. For the first time in the viceroyalty of New Granada, racial equality and republican patriotism were intrinsically linked. The connection among republican virtue, nationalism, and racial equality present in this document would later become the mainstay of patriot racial rhetoric. Yet in 1797, it still belonged to a radical and marginal political imaginary.

This conspiracy was also distinctive because of its multiethnic composition. Of the six main leaders, two were Spanish, three were white creoles, and one was a *pardo* artisan and militia member named José Cordero.[48] Cordero's involvement in this conspiracy illustrates the interest of black artisans in the new political ideas circulating around the Atlantic. He had heard that the prisoner of state Juan Bautista Mariano Picornell was being held in the local jail; curious about his crime, he asked the jailer to allow him to visit. In his conversations with Picornell, Cordero learned about his participation in the Madrid republican rebellion against Spanish tyranny. Cordero and Picornell agreed that Spain did not have the right to conquer and colonize the Americas and that "class" (racial) differences and slavery were irrational. Picornell asked Cordero to participate in a conspiracy against Spain that he was organizing with the support of important creoles. Cordero's subsequent involvement was important enough that the Spanish authorities listed him among the main conspirators. Significantly, he had the task of making a clean copy of the ordinances for the new republic.[49]

Creole conspirators also made a conscious effort to attract other *pardo* militia members, one of whom later betrayed the conspiracy to the Spanish.[50] The subsequent criminal investigation uncovered eighty-five suspects from all classes and professions.[51] The large degree of *pardo* and white involvement was probably a consequence of numerous opportunities to learn about French revolutionary ideas. Intense trade and smuggling between Venezuela and the Caribbean islands facilitated the arrival of news about the revolutionary events in the Atlantic. Sailors and slaves traveling with their owners brought back firsthand accounts of black freedom and equality in the French islands. Spanish authorities apprehensively reported talks between free and enslaved blacks about following the example of Saint Domingue, fearing the attraction that "seditious ideas" held among slaves and people of color.[52] Spanish fears became a reality when in 1795 the "law of the French" inspired a major slave revolt in the Coro region of Venezuela.[53]

It is unclear what impact, if any, the Gual y España republican conspiracy had in Cartagena. News of the conspiracy arrived in Cartagena with a merchant ship less than a month after its discovery.[54] Given the close maritime contacts between Venezuela and Cartagena, it is likely that Picornell's translation of the "Declaration of the Rights of Man," and the conspirators' "preliminary speech to the Americans" —printed in Guadeolupe and sent as propaganda to the coast of

Venezuela—also arrived in Cartagena. It may thus be no accident that Cartagena's 1810 electoral instructions closely followed the language of the Gual y España ordinances.[55] Significantly, when the independent government of Bogotá printed a Spanish translation of the declaration in 1813, it chose Picornell's version, including the "speech to the Americans."[56] Moreover, the multiethnic makeup of the conspiracy members was also a factor a few years later in Cartagena, where *pardo* artisans and militia members again cooperated with creoles in the various patriot conspiracies that emerged between 1810 and 1819.[57]

The similarities among the various patriot conspiracies in Venezuela and Caribbean Colombia derived from the regions' comparable demographic and social structures and from the contacts they had with each other and with the larger Atlantic world. Although Cartagena had no republican conspiracy or slave rebellion on the scale of Venezuela's in the 1790s, local *pardos* did have contact with the Haitian Revolution. Indeed, they had multiple opportunities to learn about the events of the Atlantic revolutions, sometimes through rather odd happenstance. In 1795, for example, colonial authorities witnessed with surprise the arrival of French privateers off the coast of Río Hacha. Not only did the privateers bring along a tricolor flag, which they intended to raise in the city fortress after the plunder, but their ship itself was named *Fantasía de un mulato* (Mulatto's Fantasy).[59] A few years later, in 1804, Spanish authorities discussed what to do when another French flag arrived on the Colombian coast, this time legally, when two French government commissioners from Saint Domingue and Martinique proudly displayed the tricolor flag in the house they occupied in Cartagena's lower-class neighborhood of Getsemaní.[59]

On occasion, contacts with Haiti had more violent connotations. In 1799, the city of Cartagena was shaken by a conspiracy of Haitian, African, and creole slaves to take over the city and kill all the whites. Although the alleged conspiracy was stopped in time, thanks to the denunciation of a member of the *pardo* militia, a group of slaves did manage to escape and burn a few nearby haciendas, leaving the local elite with a new source of anxiety in their already problematic relations with local blacks.[60] The Spanish authorities became even more alarmed after discovering another French-inspired conspiracy in Maracaibo a few months later. They began to fear an international conspiracy among French and Spanish blacks from various coastal regions of New Granada. Although these Spanish fears proved unfounded, one Carta-genero, José Diego Ortiz, did participate in both plots. Thus, even though grand international schemes were imaginary, contacts among blacks from these Caribbean regions were real enough.[61]

It is difficult to assess the influence the French and Haitian Revo-lutions had on local *pardos* and slaves in the region of Cartagena. As Aline Helg has noted, in spite of Spanish fears, the Haitian example did not result in a major slave revolt.[62] Yet it is safe to say that Haiti had entered the local popular imaginary. Its example would become a recurrent motif in local political conflicts between *pardos* and whites during the Wars of Independence and their aftermath.

In the last decades of colonial rule, most creoles in New Granada were little inclined to show any flexibility in their attitudes toward race, in spite of new enlightened ideologies that favored merit over birth. *Pardos* were usually supported by peninsular officers, who prized their economic and military contribution to the Crown and compared their obedience and loyalty to creole arrogance and discontent. Most coastal creoles saw Spain's cautious promotion of *pardos* as yet another metropolitan imposition, an attempt to debase American creoles and widen the increasing distance between peninsular and American Spaniards. Contemporaneously, however, a few creoles began to ques-tion the entrenched racial hierarchy. More radically, some creoles began to envision a republican America free from Spanish despotism, slavery, and racial inequality. Following we will examine how this radical vision, supported by a few creoles, became the dominant racial ideology among Colombian patriots.

A Republican Myth

of Racial Harmony

IN THE EARLY decades of the nineteenth century, the newly independent Spanish American countries decreed racial equality among free men and constructed powerful nationalist notions that linked racial harmony and equality to national identity. The significance of this step tends to be explained as the result of creole tactics to attract non-whites during the Wars of Independence and elite attempts to avoid racial conflict and ensure white domination in the republican period. This explanation is certainly valid: contemporaries used just such arguments to convince recalcitrant creoles. Yet this argument implies a predetermined relationship among race, republicanism, and equality that obscures the uncertainty about the future of race relations that characterized the early years of the independence period.

Blacks' support could arguably have been secured without such overhauling legal changes. Moreover, promises of equality could have been reversed, as happened in the United States following Reconstruction.[1] In addition, as the South African experience shows, nonwhite majorities can be dominated without legal equality. Indeed, when creole elites decreed racial equality, they relinquished well-established mechanisms for maintaining social hierarchy and instituted a new racial system whose implications were far from clear or reassuring. Furthermore, in the contemporary political imaginary, modernity and racial equality were not necessarily linked. The United States had shown that racial inequality could be compatible with republicanism. In spite of this, Spanish American elites agreed on the notion of racial equality to a surprising degree. While the creole elite fought long and bitter wars over issues such as federalism and church-state relations, consensus over racial equality was reached in the early years of the struggle for independence.

During the struggle for independence, full citizenship for people of African descent thus shifted from being the goal of a few American and Spanish radicals to becoming one of the main issues dividing Spaniards from American patriots. The years 1810–12 were crucial for this transition. They witnessed the emergence of patriot conspiracies in which Afro-Colombians and elite creoles joined together to depose Spanish authorities. In Cartagena, these conspiracies led to a formal declaration of racial equality. Further, during these years, the gathering of the Cortes (Spanish parliament) at Cádiz gave rise to the Spanish world's longest, most detailed, and most passionate debates on the citizenship rights of people of African descent. It was at Cádiz that racial equality became emotionally linked to American patriotism, thus making this a foundational moment for the history of modern race relations in Spanish America. Racial equality could easily have become an issue dividing radicals from conservatives regardless of nationality, as had happened during the French and Haitian Revolutions.[2]

Instead, the linkage made equality a patriotic cry that clearly separated Americans from Spaniards. This association with patriotism gave racial equality its force. After Cádiz, to oppose racial equality was to be unpatriotic and un-American.

Citizenship and Racial Equality

The 1808 French invasion of the Iberian Peninsula and subsequent imprisonment of the Spanish king, Ferdinand VII, sparked a series of events that would have dramatic political consequences for the Spanish Empire, eventually leading to the independence of most of its American colonies. In the following years, the Spanish Empire would witness extraordinary changes in its political imaginary as modern notions of nation, representation, and citizenship began to replace traditional ones.[3] By 1810, the notion prevailed that in the absence of the king, sovereignty returned to the people, who were the original source of legitimacy. Following this principle, cities in Spain and the Americas began to organize locally based forms of government called juntas that would rule in the name of the imprisoned king. This shift in sovereignty brought to the fore questions about the nature of the relationship between Spain and its overseas territories. The issue was particularly acute in the Americas, where the creation of juntas tended to take governmental power away from Spanish authorities and place it in the hands of the creole elite. The Spanish solution to the apparent vacuum was to call for a gathering of the Cortes, which—with the participation of representatives from all regions, including the Americas—would draft a constitution for the Spanish monarchy.

In 1810, while a French army occupied most of the Iberian Peninsula, the Cortes was summoned in the free city of Cádiz, where some of the most brilliant and liberal men of the Spanish Empire gathered with the task of modernizing Spanish political and legal institutions.[4]

Among the sweeping transformations enacted at Cádiz, the restructuring of metropolitan-colonial relations was of special importance for Spanish American race relations. On October 15, 1810, the Cortes confirmed an 1809 decree that abolished the colonial status of overseas territories, declaring them an equal and integral part of a single Spanish nation.[5] This change was only the beginning of a series of questions and debates. How would equality manifest itself? Would Americans have equal representation? How would equal representation be defined—by an equal or a proportional number of deputies? Given the demographic weight of nonwhites in the Americas, the debates soon acquired racial connotations. If representation were proportional, would it be proportional to the number of whites; of whites and Indians; or of all free Spanish subjects, including blacks? This became one of the thorniest issues at the Cortes, forcing Spanish Americans to develop notions of race and citizenship that they could not have foreseen a few years before. From this moment forward, American representation became tied to discussions of racial equality.[6]

At the core of the debates was the question of how a racially heterogeneous society would be represented in a constitutional parliament —whether all the races should enjoy the same type of representation and, if not, on what bases different rights of representation would be organized and justified. Since the number of deputies was proportional to the number of citizens, the issue of citizenship for people of Indian or African descent would determine the proportion of American deputies. After some debate, Indian citizenship was quickly recognized. As James King has noted, Indians' legal freedom and nominal equality were overtly grounded in Spanish legislation.[7] The situation was quite different for people of African descent. The question of whether they could be citizens sparked one of the most passionate and heated debates between Spanish and American deputies. Because few *castas* could prove they were free from any African ancestry, counting people of African descent would mean that Americans would outnumber Spanish deputies and dominate the Cortes. Since Americans had been formally granted equality, and the official Spanish nationalist rhetoric promoted harmony between Americans and Spaniards, Spanish deputies could not openly express their fears at being outnumbered. They had to focus their attack instead on *pardos'* qualification for citizenship. This was of enormous significance: it tied American representation to *pardo* citizenship and thus linked full racial legal equality to patriot nationalism.

Pardo equality did not become an intrinsic part of patriotic discourse overnight. The Cádiz debates over the rights of people of mixed descent began in January 1811, focusing on the issue of whether American representation should be discussed immediately or wait until the drafting of the constitution. Some deputies still drew upon a traditional notion of representation in which every estate was distinctly represented in parliament. Indians should represent Indians, creoles represent creoles, and mestizos (individuals of mixed Spanish-Indian background) represent mestizos. This corporate concept of representation had been used in Venezuela during its first revolutionary movement, but when the Caracas town council first deposed local Spanish authorities on April 19, 1810, a creole was nominated as deputy of the *pardo* guild.[8] Eventually, the idea of racial representation along corporate lines did not prevail: it was at odds with prevalent notions of representation that sought to abolish all vestiges of feudal society, including traditional representation by estates.[9]

Even if American deputies tended to favor liberal notions of citizenship, however, they did not immediately promote *pardos'* equal rights to representation. Most liberal deputies believed in an idea of nation and sovereignty that privileged unity and homogeneity over division and difference. Fundamental to this notion was the idea that the nation had a collective interest that should not be divided by factions or parties.[10] In the January debates, Spanish deputies used this idea to contrast a racially homogeneous and harmonious Spain with an America rife with racial diversity and rivalry.[11] To the Americans' request for equal representation in the Cortes constitutional debates, Spanish deputies responded that American racial heterogeneity was a complex and little-understood phenomenon that required further study before adequate legislation could be passed. The debate over American representation thus needed to be held later, when the constitution was drafted. This was a challenging argument for American deputies, since they shared with the Spaniards a notion of citizenship that favored homogeneity. Their strategy in January was therefore a hesitant compromise: they acknowledged the problem and, by requesting only the explicit acceptance of Indian and creole representation, left it to be solved during the constitutional debates. At the same time, they sought to discredit Spanish representations of America as a society torn by racial conflict. The Spanish had used the frightful example of Haiti to warn Americans about the dangers of conceding citizenship to *pardos*. Americans responded with images of a harmonious society of benign slave owners and peaceful blacks, one that had nothing in common with Haiti, where the cruelty of French masters had fostered bloody revolution.[12] Eventually, however, the Spanish attacks on American heterogeneity would force Americans to adopt a defensive position and create a series of arguments in defense of racial diversity.

When, in September 1811, the constitutional commission presented a draft of the new Spanish constitution to the Cortes, American deputies were obliged to develop a firmer defense of their racially heterogeneous society. By declaring that all free men were Spanish, the constitution officially included free people of African background as members of the Spanish nation. Yet Article 29 declared as citizens only those Spaniards whose origins could be traced to Spain or America, but not to Africa. In addition, parliamentary representation was to be proportional to the number of people whose origins went back exclusively to Spain or America—once again including creoles, Indians, and mestizos but excluding many people of mixed racial descent with some degree of African background. This formula greatly diminished American representation, calling into question official Spanish declarations of American equality.[13]

Still, in spite of their opposition to *pardo* citizenship, liberal Spanish deputies could not create a rigid barrier between black and white citizens. They shared the Christian notion of intrinsic equality among men and the enlightened belief that merit rather than origin should determine social status. More important, they did not wish to completely alienate the *pardo* population in America, who for the most part continued to remain loyal to the Spanish. They explained African Americans' racial difference as a result of their "regrettable origin and lack of education." In the less euphemistic words of one Spanish deputy, blacks, having originated in Africa, "belonged to a nation of irreligious and immoral habits." Even those born and raised in America, he continued, had learned African habits from their parents.[14] Therefore, Spanish deputies argued, the incorporation of people of African descent had to be a slow process. The Cortes would grant citizenship on an individual basis to those *pardos* who could prove their merit and virtue, along the lines of the *gracias al sacar* principle of 1795. With the incentive of citizenship, people of African descent would assimilate to Spanish culture, and eventually the desired harmonious society would be achieved. To American accusations that the Spaniards' exclusion of people of African descent from citizenship was inconsistent with their proclaimed liberal principles, a Spanish deputy responded by citing the examples of Great Britain and the United States. Nobody could deny the progress, enlightenment, and liberal laws of these countries, he claimed, yet they had not granted citizenship rights to free people of African descent. How then could Spain, which was only beginning its path toward liberty, take that innovative and dangerous step?[15] Spanish deputies accused Americans of denying racial antagonism only out of political expediency, challenging them to give *pardos* not only the right of representation but also the right to serve as deputies. Counting on the strength of creole prejudices, they thought that fear of *pardo* participation would make creoles desist from promoting *pardo* citizenship.[16]

To defend their position, Spanish deputies built upon the ideas of Jean-Jacques Rousseau, arguing that it was necessary to "establish in all citizens the moral unity that is essential for the government to promote the general good without the hindrance of divergent habits and opinions."[17] Since both American and Spanish deputies agreed on the notion that a nation's citizens should share common interests and values, Spanish deputies had to prove that people of African descent were hostile and different, while their American counterparts had to present a racially harmonious picture of America. Thus, Spanish deputies used racial segregation in American parish registries and the offense creoles took at being mistaken for mulattoes to prove that racial antagonism divided Americans. They appealed to the lengthy catalog of elite creole racial prejudices—for example, the creole notion that people of African descent were immoral and tainted by vice and illegitimacy—to remind creoles that Spaniards had traditionally been *pardos'* allies and protectors.[18]

During the September 1811 debates on Article 29, American deputies, with one exception, closed ranks in favor of the right of *pardos* to be represented, which would determine the number of American deputies in parliament.[19] Yet they divided over how this representation would take place. The most conservative deputies were willing to grant people of African descent the right to vote but not the right to be elected. In the words of Guatemalan deputy Antonio Larrazabal, this approach was fair because "the hierarchies present in heaven prove the presence of hierarchies on earth."[20] Most American deputies, however, did not share this traditional understanding of a naturally hierarchical society. Like Spanish deputies, they thought that education and merit would gradually enable people of African descent to enjoy all citizenship rights. Yet the American threshold for merit was considerably lower than the Spanish. American deputies were willing to submit *pardos* to the same citizenship requirements that the Cortes had decreed for all Spaniards. Most shared the notion that people of African descent who had been born of free parents and who had a profession—including artisans—or who had enough property to sustain themselves independently should be citizens.[21] They also held that all men who met the required constitutional qualifications should enjoy the right to be elected, regardless of origin.

To defend *pardo* citizenship, American deputies had to do something innovative: construct an image of racial diversity that would not be at odds with the contemporary ideal of a nation in which all citizens shared common interests and values. They thus had to prove that harmony rather than conflict characterized racial relations in Spanish America and, therefore, that bestowing citizenship rights on *pardos* would not divide the nation. Moreover, since they wanted *pardo* citizenship and representation to be enacted immediately, they had to prove that these harmonious relations were not a goal for the future but a current reality. According to one deputy's idyllic picture, whites and blacks, nursed together by black women, learned to love one another from childhood.[22]

American deputies also worked to overturn the curse of illegitimacy that had traditionally characterized discourse about people of mixed racial descent. Interracial sexual relations were now presented in a positive light, as proof of harmony. The deputies argued that pervasive racial mixing had developed strong ties between creole and black families that should not be broken by exclusionary laws. Moreover, since many members of the creole elite were racially mixed, mulattoes passing for whites had long successfully occupied positions of authority, thus proving their political abilities.[23] American deputies admitted the existence of racial prejudices that led people to seek all legal and illegal means to hide their mixed racial descent. Yet they argued that these means were only the product of despotic and barbarous laws, such as the regulations on *limpieza de sangre* (purity of blood), which fostered racial conflict and division.[24] It followed that the constitution's exclusionary laws were not an adequate remedy for a society riven by conflict; rather, they were the continuation of despotic laws that fostered conflict in a society naturally characterized by harmony.

American deputies also had to develop arguments against the Spanish exclusion of *pardos* from the national body politic. Spanish deputies argued that people of African descent were outside the original social pact created during the conquest among Spaniards, creoles, and Indians and that therefore they had not contributed to the constitution of the nation.[25] American deputies presented a different notion of nationality, in which social contribution to the *patria*, birth, and education prevailed over origin. Building on Abbé Emmanuel Joseph Sièyes's reevaluation of productive work, American deputies defended the idea that those citizens who performed useful work constituted the nation—a notion that the Cádiz Constitution admitted for all members of productive classes except those of African descent. American deputies reminded Spaniards that in the Americas, *castas* constituted the majority of the productive classes. American deputies extolled at length *pardos'* toil as agricultural laborers, their contributions as craftsmen, and their invaluable role as militiamen.[26] One deputy went as far as to say that "our *castas* are the depositories of all our happiness."[27] Their contribution to the wealth and welfare of the nation rightfully entitled them to citizenship.

American deputies emphasized an idea of nationality that privileged birth, culture, and love for the fatherland over origins. According to one deputy, *pardos* "were Spanish by birth; from their cradle they had suckled the Spanish religion, language, customs, and concerns."[28] Another deputy argued that people of African descent who had been born in America were "shaped by the land," which they loved as their fatherland. To deprive them of the right to citizenship was to condemn them to a punishment reserved only for Jews: to forbid them to belong to the nation in which they were born.[29]

Pardos *and the* People, *Cartagena,* 1810–11

While parliamentarians debated American representation and *pardo* citizenship at Cádiz, in Cartagena, events were taking a faster pace. As in other cities of the Spanish Empire, creoles in Cartagena had deposed Spanish authorities and established juntas, invoking the sovereignty of the people. "The people," however, was not merely a rhetorical invention to legitimize a creole government. The Cartagena creole elite asked certain men and women to join the patriot movement, and many armed themselves and gathered in plazas to give legitimacy to patriot declarations. In a region like the province of Cartagena, where free people of African descent constituted the majority of the population, the entrance of the people as a political protagonist acquired special racial connotations, opening the crucial question of the racial and social limits of modern political participation.

The solution to this question was neither simple nor immediate. For the Mompox town council, for example, the inconvenience of calling an open town meeting (*cabildo abierto*) derived from uncertainty about the appropriate way to convene it: "If only the nobility is called, the inferior classes would be offended at their exclusion. . . . If only honorable and educated *pardos* are called, the rest would argue that poverty is not a crime. There are several reasons to fear this outcome that you are aware of and that prudence forces us not to mention."[30] It was not clear who had the right to participate in local political decisions. Moreover, an official rhetoric setting the limits and characteristics of political citizenship had not yet been developed.[31] Contemporary revolutionary ideology provided a range of examples, some more inclusive than others, and it was unclear for the moment which would be the safest and most convenient to follow. It was uncertain whether race or poverty could be a factor of exclusion.

Notwithstanding their apprehensions, the creole members of Cartagena's town council—mostly merchants and lawyers—could not successfully depose Spanish authorities without first securing the support of the local lower classes.[32] In May 1810, for example, the Cartagena town council began to conspire against the province's Spanish governor, Francisco Montes, a task facilitated by his unpopularity. The governor had openly expressed his distrust of creoles. Moreover, he had stopped defense construction projects, not only leaving many artisans without employment but also making him vulnerable to accusations of treason for ignoring defense needs in a time of war against France.[33] According to one local witness, the town council sought the support of specific persons close to the common people before taking the momentous step of deposing the governor. For the artisan and *pardo* neighborhood of Getsemaní, town council leaders chose Pedro Romero and Juan José Solano. Romero was a successful *pardo* artisan and militia member who worked with his sons in the arsenal shop. Thanks to his support and Solano's, Getsemaní sided with the town council.[34] On June 14, 1810, having also secured the cooperation of the creole-led Fijo regiment, the town council deposed the governor, as men armed with machetes and a crowd of local people of all classes surrounded his palace.[35] This event reveals the importance of early patriot alliances between the creole elite and *pardos*, particularly the crucial importance of prominent *pardos* in securing the support of lower-class neighborhoods. Such alliances, of course, were not unique to Cartagena. In the nearby city of Mompox, the *zambo* (half Indian, half black) José Luis Muñoz played a part in 1810 town council conspiracies against Spanish authorities. According to the Spanish military commander Don Vicente Talledo, winning back Muñoz's support was vital because of his influence with mulattoes and *zambos*.[36] This pattern of securing *pardo* support for urban patriot conspiracies continued until the very end of the struggle for independence. In 1819, for example, Spanish authorities discovered a patriot conspiracy in Mompox that involved members of the creole elite and *zambo* artisans.[37]

The alliance between white and *pardo* patriots was made official during Cartagena's first elections, which incorporated *pardos* into the people. Without awaiting legislation from Cádiz, the new junta of

Cartagena granted equal citizenship rights to people of African descent. The December 1810 electoral instructions for the Suprema Junta of the province of Cartagena included all races: "all parishioners, whites, Indians, mestizos, mulattoes, *zambos*, and blacks, as long as they are household heads and live from their own work, are to be summoned for elections." Only "vagrants, criminals, those who are in servile salaried status, and slaves are excluded."[38]

The patriotic alliance between *pardo* and creole patriots was also represented in original patriot narratives of the period, which began to extol the new social and racial unity and contrast it with Spanish colonial practices. One contemporary witness described the alliance between creoles and *pardos* to depose Governor Montes as the birth of a new revolutionary people unencumbered by colonial social hierarchies. In exalted revolutionary language, he narrated the transit of Cartagena's people from darkness to light. In becoming free, the people of Cartagena had left behind divisions between nobles and plebeians, the arrogance of birth and riches, and the vilification of mechanical work.[39] This writer's account of the interview between the town council leader, José María García de Toledo, and the *pardo* artisan Pedro Romero can be read as a compelling allegory of that process. The first was a prominent and enlightened patriot, the second a respectable *pardo* who enjoyed the confidence and support of his humble fellow artisans. The narrative tells us that when Pedro Romero was first asked to support the movement against the governor, he saw it as an extremely odd and altogether impossible action to take against a magistrate of His Majesty. This initial reaction was explained as the natural result of his education in false political notions. Like most Americans, he was ignorant of his political rights. However, García de Toledo convinced him of the project's justice, and Romero agreed to cooperate, with all his goods, his family, and his influence. Together the two joined forces to defend the fatherland.[40] This narrative was strengthened by junta accounts of patriot actions against the Spanish that praised the deeds of *pardo* and white militia and patriot battalions.[41]

Given *pardos'* active participation in support of Cartagena's junta, it should not be surprising that Cartagena declared independence after receiving news of the Cortes's denial of citizenship to *pardos* and, as it was interpreted, equal representation to the Americas.[42] When the news from Cádiz arrived, the junta had already conferred equal legal rights on all races, and a nationalist rhetoric that associated racial hierarchy with Spanish despotism had begun to emerge. When the constitutional congress of the fledgling First Republic of Cartagena published its constitution in 1812, two *pardo* deputies signed it. One of them, Remigio Márquez, was a member of the Republic's Congress.[43]

The Congress of Venezuela

Although the debates of the Cartagena junta about *pardos'* citizenship rights have not survived, the debates on *pardo* equality that took place at the 1811 Venezuelan constitutional congress provide an example of the arguments used for and against *pardos* in a region with similar racial and political characteristics. In July 1811, the first congress of republican Venezuela debated whether to include in the constitution an article that would explicitly revoke any legal distinctions between *pardos* and whites. As in other parts of Spanish America where blacks and mulattoes constituted an important percentage of the population, *pardos* in Venezuela had been an active and decisive force in the struggles between royalists and patriots.[44] While in the region of the Llanos (the Venezuelan plains), the *pardo* alliance with the royalist army was crucial to Spanish victories, in revolutionary Caracas, urban *pardos* had become increasingly involved in republican politics. On October 22, 1810, led by their creole junta deputy, *pardos* requested reprisals against Spaniards for the massacre of creole patriots in Quito. A few months later, *pardos* became active members of Caracas's patriotic society, a radical political group that vigorously pressured Congress. According to a contemporary witness, the patriotic society had fostered *pardos'* awareness of their political strength and stimulated their egalitarian desires.[45] When the parliamentarians first debated the article on *pardo* equality, on July 31, 1811, they did so with a keen awareness of *pardo* political activities.

Unlike the Cádiz deputies, Venezuelan deputies did not debate *pardos'* right to citizenship. The issue was whether the constitution should explicitly eliminate any racial distinctions between blacks and whites.[46] Congressional discussions did not question the legitimacy of the proposal but focused instead on the political expediency of approving such an article. Deputies debated whether this would foster harmonious racial relations or create additional conflicts, a question that became linked to debates about federalism as the General Congress discussed whether it should impose the article on the other provinces of Venezuela or leave them to make their own decisions. Deputies who opposed the article referred to the United States, where the determination of civic categories was left to the individual states. They argued that although Caracas might be ready for such a declaration, this sudden change would only spur conflicts in other provinces.

Deputies in favor of the article argued that the issue of racial equality was too important to be left to the discretion of individual provinces. If racial equality were left up to the provinces, how would the central government respond to racial conflicts spurred by *pardos'* aspirations to equality? Only uniform racial laws could address this predicament: the issue was fundamental and had to be decided collectively. To avoid doing so would only produce chaos and anarchy. These deputies also argued that the U.S. example was not valid for Venezuela. In Venezuela, blacks and mulattoes far outnumbered the white population, and whites were divided between royalists and patriots. Moreover, the clock could not be turned back. Despotic laws that promoted discord among Americans were gone for good. Blacks' and mulattoes' eyes had been opened; they had learned about their rights. They knew that by birth they were sons of the country, possessing rights and obligations no less than their white compatriots. To deny their equality would only promote conflict. Further, the course of the wars had shown that in places where liberal laws guaranteed racial equality, patriots could count on *pardo* support. Eventually, the article was approved, the Venezuelan Constitution of 1812 decreeing the derogation of "all the ancient laws that degraded a section of the free population of Venezuela known until this moment as *Pardos*. . . . To them are restored all the inalienable rights that correspond to them as to any other citizens."[47]

Pardos' *Rights Are Patriots' Rights*

Patriot nationalism consistently gained power and cohesion by setting itself in sharp contrast to Spain.[48] Spain symbolized corruption, despotism, and the past, while America represented enlightenment, virtue, and the future. Patriot racial constructs fitted neatly within these dichotomies, linking racial hierarchies to Spanish despotism and making racial discrimination a sign of un-Americanness. This dynamic is clearly at work in the "preliminary speech to the Americans" included with Juan Bautista Mariano Picornell's 1797 translation of the "Declaration of the Rights of Man," republished in 1813 in Bogotá.[49] By examining at length what republicanism meant in America, this document adapted contemporary liberal ideas of nation and citizenship to Spanish American racial reality, carefully elaborating the notions of republican virtue that underlay most official racial discourse in early republican Colombia. Employing rhetoric found in other revolutionary materials, Picornell presented a sharp distinction between a colonial, despotic past and the new era of republican virtue, seeking thereby to educate Spanish Americans on the differences between a corrupt monarchy and a virtuous republic.[50]

Among republican virtues, unity had special implications for early republican racial discourse in Colombia. Picornell argued that in a monarchy, vassals cared only about their individual needs; color, lineage, customs, and education divided them. Each had his own interests and ambitions. The only shared ambition was the lust for gold, which excluded merit and talent and produced only vice and crime. Men were selfish, living in isolation, oblivious to the welfare of their fellows. Such a society, Picornell argued, "is in constant conflict, and its members are united only by the chains that oppress and fasten them. In a true Republic, it is the opposite, the body politic is one, all citizens have the same spirit, the same feelings, the same rights, the same virtues: reason alone commands and not violence; obedience derives from love not fear."[51] Unity's relevance to race relations becomes evident in Picornell's explanation of how this ideal should be achieved in America: "The most perfect union must rule between whites, Indians, *pardos*, and blacks." Despotic Spanish kings had introduced odious and unnatural distinctions that made Americans see one another as different rather than interrelated, in order to keep them enslaved. Picornell claimed that only Americans' vices stood between them and their liberty and asked his fellow Americans "to remain always bonded to virtue, so that the most perfect unity reigns among us." The moment had arrived for "fraternity to reign among us all," in place of the hatred, scorn, and hostility of the past.[52] Here contemporary republican notions of unity and fraternity acquired strong racial connotations: republican virtue and racial harmony had become one and the same.

This association of despotism with racial division did not necessarily have to become a marker of distinction between Spaniards and Americans. Indeed, Picornell was himself a republican Spaniard. Even as late as July 1810, Joseph Blanco White, the editor of *El Español*, argued that people of African descent would fare better under a reformed Spanish monarchy than under an independent Spanish America. Blanco White favored abolition and racial equality. Like Picornell, he considered that differences among classes of people were "fatal for the union and prosperity of America."[53] Yet he argued that there were compelling reasons to believe that such racial reforms were more likely under the Spanish monarchy than in an independent America. Experience had shown that creoles were very attached to their racial prerogatives; thus, a creole government would likely increase rather than diminish distinctions between blacks and whites. The U.S. example seemed to confirm this prediction. In the United States, anxieties concerning blacks and mulattoes had increased following independence to such a degree that the country's last president had proposed expelling people of African descent to avoid the "contamination of Virginians' blood."[54]

Only a year later, Blanco White's argument would be impossible to sustain. The Cádiz debates had made racial equality a distinctively American characteristic. What began as a tactical attempt to secure a larger number of American representatives had become a powerful nationalist construct. The evolution of the debates, the ways in which they set Americans and Spaniards against each other, and the publicity they received gave to *pardo* citizenship a strength and emotional appeal that could hardly have been predicted a couple of years earlier.

The Cádiz debates were widely followed throughout Spanish America.[55] Newspapers, particularly the London-based *El Español*, were crucial opinion makers about these debates. While the Cádiz deputies were discussing the citizenship rights of people of African descent, *El Español* published a long article on black intellectual abilities.[56] Translating and commenting on the abolitionist William Wilberforce's "Letter from Liverpool," the writer for *El Español* presented a thorough defense of black intellectual abilities that vehemently attacked the major arguments of contemporary racism, arguing that there was no proof that physical differences had any connection with spiritual and intellectual ones. To the idea that miscegenation caused degeneration in humans, he responded that all nations, including European ones, had mixed throughout history. To the argument that Africa's lack of civilization proved African inferiority, he replied that England had been just as uncivilized in Roman times and that, since civilization developed through contacts with other peoples, Africa's historical isolation explained its condition. *El Español* also summarized the Cádiz debates on black citizenship, emphasizing the inconsistencies of Spanish opponents and applauding the arguments of American supporters.[57] Americans read in *El Español* that the *castas'* labor was crucial to the welfare of the Americas and that their contribution rightfully entitled them to full citizenship rights.[58] *El Español* thus not only familiarized its Spanish American readers with the latest scientific racial debates but also associated the defense of racial equality with the American cause.

Although whites wrote most of the commentaries on the Cortes of Cádiz, at least one political pamphlet was written by a *pardo*. Its title was "Political and Moral Reflections of a Descendant of Africa to His Nation, in Which He Manifests His Amorous Lamentations to His American Brothers."[59] This pamphlet sought to demonstrate that the Cádiz laws lacked any moral, religious, or political basis for discriminating against people of African descent. The author developed two main arguments: he insisted that social hierarchies are not natural but are the product of force or necessity, and he argued that racial discrimination was unchristian. To discriminate against *pardos* was to contradict the notion that, as descendants of Adam and Eve, all humans were equal. Moreover, laws that discriminated against *pardos* violated a fundamental Christian principle: do unto others as you would have them do unto you. The constitution shaped at Cádiz thus contradicted both religion and nature. Mockingly, the author declared that until this moment, he had operated under the belief that only original sin was transmitted from generation to generation and that baptism eliminated it. But there was no absolution for being a descendant of Africans. He summarized his arguments in patriotic verse:

> The cause of causes that created the world
> To all men liberty gave,
> And of equal material Adam and Eve made;

Even if selfishness opposes it without reason
Then all men are equal without possible argument
Then *pardos* should not be excluded from the elections
Because any law established according to religion
Is for all and should make happy every nation.
May mine be justly granted, what others enjoy under the constitution.
When united in society we gave up our liberty,
It was to be happy like citizens,
For that reason we bestowed our rights on the king,
And leaving our land in wars we sacrificed ourselves;
But what advantages did we get?
To lack all knowledge from education,
Exclusion from employment by the constitution.
Fellow patriots, let us shed tears over our sad condition,
Which neither the fatherland nor the constitution could alleviate.

La causa de las causas que al mundo entero creó
a todos los hombres libertad les dio,
y de igual materia a Adán y Eva formó;
luego todo hombre por construcción aunque el egoísmo gima sin razón
en todo y por todo es igual a otro sin contestación,
luego los *Pardos* no deben ser excluidos de la votación,
porque toda ley establecida según religión
es para todos y debe hacer felices a cada nación.
Concédesela a la mía por justa razón, la que otros gozan por
     Constitución.
Cuando en sociedad reunidos nuestra voluntad coartamos,
fue para hacernos felices como son los ciudadanos,
por eso nuestros derechos en nuestro Rey renunciamos,
y abandonando la Patria en guerras nos sacrificamos;
pero que utilidades de nuestra sangre sacamos,
cuales son las felicidades que gozamos
el carecer de toda ciencia, y educación,

y estar privados de todo empleo por Constitución
infelices compatriotas lloremos nuestra situación;
sin poder hallar alivio, ni por la Patria, ni por la Constitución.

What makes this poem special is its use of commonplace liberal principles to support *pardo* citizenship rights. The poem argues that, because all men are created equal, *pardos* should be equal before the law and not excluded from suffrage. It invokes *pardos'* military service in defense of the Spanish Crown and laments that their only reward for their blood and sacrifice was a lack of knowledge, education, and employment. For this *pardo* author, citizenship represented an end to colonial laws that prohibited people of African descent from entering universities and practicing coveted professions. Happiness is the purpose of society, the reason why people renounce their natural rights to join in a political covenant. Yet *pardos* were denied the means to attain their rightful happiness. They could only "shed tears over [their] sad condition, / Which neither the fatherland nor the constitution could alleviate."

The pamphlet's author is not identified, but he was clearly educated. His text begins with an extensive quotation in Latin, a language that continues to appear throughout the text in citations of classical and Christian authorities. This show of erudition was probably not gratuitous. Most early nineteenth-century political pamphlets no longer used Latin, but here, used by a *pardo*, the language sent a clear political message to those who alleged that *pardos* lacked civilization and were naturally inferior. It is unclear where the author was from, but it matters little. Like the parliamentarians at Cádiz, he wrote as an American addressing the Spanish Empire.

"Political and Moral Reflections" is one of the more eloquent examples of *pardo* interest in the Cádiz debates, but it is not the only one. According to James King, *pardos* followed the debates with interest, paying particular attention to laws concerning their legal status.

Patriots thus effectively used the Cortes's denial of citizenship to Americans of African descent to win over the black and mulatto population.[60] This was apparent to one Spanish officer visiting the patriot troops of General José Antonio Paez in 1820. He reported that the soldiers, when asked why they sided with the patriots, replied that "the Spanish constitution does not suit them because it denies citizenship to those of African descent."[61] The importance of the debates in rallying *pardo* support for the patriot side is further exemplified in a speech José Francisco Bermúdez gave to black soldiers during the Spanish siege of the First Republic of Cartagena in 1815:

Remember above all, you men of color, how this conflict began; it can only call more strongly on your gratitude, your self-interest, and your honor.

In forming its government, Spain excluded America from its rightful share of representation; American governments opposed this arbitrary measure by force. Spain modified it by granting whites their rights but denying them completely to men of color; and the whites then cried out that they would defend with weapons in hand the rights that belong to you. Could you fail to respond to such a generous resolution?

No, the origin of this conflict was more yours than ours.

Come, let us unite and give Europe an example of fraternity; let our oppressors know what a people unjustly insulted is capable of doing.[62]

Acordaos sobre todo, hombres de color, del motivo de esta disputa en sus principios: él debe empeñar más a vuestra gratitud, vuestro amor propio, y vuestro honor.

La España en la formación de su gobierno excluyó a la América de la parte de representación que le correspondía; y los gobiernos que se hallaban en ella se opusieron con la fuerza a esta medida arbitraria. La España la modificó luego acordando sus derechos a los blancos, pero negándolos enteramente a los hombres de color; y los primeros entonces gritaron en alta voz que sostendrían con las armas en la mano los que os pertenecían. ¿Dejaréis vosotros de corresponder a tan generosa resolución?

No, la causa en sus principios ha sido vuestra mas bien que nuestra.

Venid pues, unámonos todos, y dando de este modo al mundo de Europa un ejemplo de fraternidad, hagamos saber a nuestros opresores de cuanto es capaz un pueblo cuando se le insulta injustamente.

To fire up the support of his *pardo* soldiers, Bermúdez portrayed the conflict as a struggle over *pardo* rights. Skillfully, he transformed the creoles' need for *pardo* support to defeat the Spaniards into the *pardos'* need for creoles to obtain their citizenship rights. According to Bermúdez, the war was not about creoles' rights of representation; the Cortes, after all, had granted them these rights. If the conflict persisted, it was only because altruistic whites were standing up in defense of their black American brothers' rights. It followed that *pardos* should not only support the patriot cause—which was, after all, their own—but also be grateful for the self-sacrifice of their white brothers.

Thus, racial difference was officially linked to Spanish oppression and despotism, and racial harmony to a new era of republican virtue. American deputies and patriots had turned colonial racial prejudices upside down, developing the major themes of what would later be known as the myth of racial democracy. While miscegenation had previously been associated with illegitimacy, and the *pardos'* role as craftsmen and militiamen with haughtiness and pride, now both were evidence of American harmony. Contemporary racial problems, including slavery, which remained legal, were dismissed as just another nefarious legacy of Spanish domination.[63] This discourse not only relieved creoles of all blame for current racial conditions, making whites and blacks joint victims of Spanish tyranny, but also associated the very notion of "Americanness" with racial harmony, a nationalist concept that would survive throughout the republican era.

After 1811, *pardo* citizenship and legal equality were not openly and officially discussed again. The 1812 constitutions of Cartagena and Venezuela both granted *pardos* citizenship rights. Ten years later, in 1821, the Cúcuta Constitution, which governed Gran Colombia, granted full legal equality to whites and blacks. Indeed, at Cúcuta, the issue was not even discussed. One important repercussion of this silence was that *pardos'* citizenship rights did not become a marker differentiating opposing patriot factions—as happened with issues such as state-church relations and federalism. Thus, after independence, racial equality was not associated with a particular political party, instead becoming a pillar of a shared nationalist discourse.[64] Yet this harmony would not last long: the end of the wars did not prevent conflicts over the meaning and implications of racial equality from emerging. Nevertheless, the racial discourse constructed during these years had long-term consequences, influencing race relations for the next two centuries.

Racial Harmony

The notions of American racial harmony developed during the Cádiz debates were expanded and further popularized in later decades. Like today's myth of racial democracy, early republican notions of racial harmony linked it to national identity. Yet the ideological bases of this nationalist notion were shaped by contemporary political values that were quite different from twentieth-century ones.

Peninsular racial tolerance was not presented as a historical precedent to Colombian racial harmony.[65] On the contrary, the "Black Legend"—the belief that Spanish rule was particularly tyrannical and obscurantist—was crucial to early republican racial discourse. It allowed the erasure of racial conflicts between Americans, all fellow victims of Spanish tyranny, and permitted patriots to envision a new era of republican equality, free from Spanish rule. Public speeches, manumission ceremonies, and newspaper articles recounted a history of Spanish despotism and violence that oppressed Indians and blacks and divided fellow Americans. Already in 1817, Bolívar contrasted republican equality with Spanish despotism, under which "*pardos* were degraded to the foremost humiliation, being deprived of everything. The state of holy priesthood was forbidden to *pardos:* it could be said the Spanish had even barred them from heaven."[66] The Spanish, another speaker announced, "after depopulating our country with fire and sword, were compelled to commit the equally horrible crime of re-populating it with slaves."[67] Even internal bureaucratic correspondence repeated the story of Spanish guilt and patriot innocence. In 1822, the governor of Cartagena, Mariano Montilla, wrote to the national secretary of war about the reestablishment of local militias, "but without the class distinctions that Spanish tyranny had introduced to foster divisions among Americans."[68]

The Black Legend also shaped contemporary attitudes about slavery. Unlike racial equality, abolition had received only scant attention at Cádiz, most American deputies tending to ignore the subject.[69] The 1812 Constitution of Cartagena had abolished the slave trade but left slavery untouched. Thus, the burning issue of abolition still loomed over the new independent state when a constitutional convention gathered at Cúcuta in 1821. Manumission became the subject of some of the gathering's most intense and heated debates, yet it must be emphasized that not even the most vocal champions of slaveholders defended slavery as an institution.[70] It was officially agreed that slavery belonged to the past and should not taint a modern and enlightened nation such as Colombia. The question was when and how abolition would take place. Planters' supporters argued that property rights would be violated and the economy dramatically damaged if slaves were suddenly manumitted. After long and passionate debates, the 1821 congress decreed a free-womb law, which ensured that no more slaves would be born on Colombian soil. *Libertos* (children of slaves, born after 1821) would have to work for their mother's owner until the age of eighteen to pay back the alleged maintenance costs their owner had spent raising them. In addition, the congress established *juntas de manumisión* (manumission boards) in every town, intended to accelerate the manumission process through the creation of a fund to buy slaves born in captivity.

During the 1821 debates, manumission was officially declared a nationalist and republican virtue.[71] A medal of "Benemérito de la Humanidad" (Benefactor of Humanity) was proposed for those manumitting more than ten slaves. In the heat of the debates, six congressmen manumitted all their slaves amid public applause. The president of the congress stated that Colombia had exceeded in virtue the ancient republics of Rome, Sparta, and Athens, because its representatives did not merely content themselves with an easy, theoretical love for justice but took pleasure in following its mandates.[72] Moreover, with the creation of the new manumission boards, the Colombian state established a crucial space for spreading its notions of race, nation, and citizenship. Historians have characterized the *juntas de manumisión* as ineffective institutions that tried to hide the crude reality of slavery, and indeed, they manumitted very few slaves.[73] Yet they were important, not because they manumitted many slaves but because they associated manumission with Colombian nationalism, linking slavery to Spanish tyranny, and freedom to republican virtue. Prominent citizens were asked to demonstrate their patriotism by contributing to the juntas' funds. Contributors' names and donations were duly mentioned in manumission ceremonies and published in local newspapers, and individual slave owners made private manumissions on official commemorations of independence. Thus, acts that had been previously presented as evidence of Christian charity were now portrayed as signs of "love for national independence and the republican constitutional system."[74]

Indeed, the manumission law of 1821 decreed that juntas should manumit slaves during national celebrations.[75] These were elaborate occasions. For example, in 1825, independence festivities in Cartagena began with a Te Deum, immediately followed by the manumission of four slaves in the "Temple of Liberty," a splendidly adorned shrine with Doric columns and a cupola crowned by a Liberty bust.[76] The year before, in Mompox, a manumission ceremony took place on a damask-dressed stage, the chosen slave wearing a Liberty cap. The ceremonies were accompanied by vehement speeches that officially recognized the debased nature of slavery. Colombians, however, were declared innocent of this crime against humanity. Spanish greed and violence had brought slaves to America. Although Colombia could not solve this inherited problem overnight, its measures against slavery surely made it one of the most enlightened and philanthropic nations in the world. America, one speaker claimed, "had been the first to show the world the path to end slavery."[77] A year later, another speaker echoed these sentiments, stating that because of Cúcuta's 1821 free-womb law, "the sun would see only Colombians [free citizens] born."[78]

The Black Legend's linkage of Spanish rule and racial inequality also affected the question of representation. When the Colombian Congress gathered for the first time in 1823, a group of *pardos* from Caracas asked if it was legal for all their provincial representatives to be white. The congressional response was telling: deputies explained that the electoral college's only criteria for selecting representatives was to favor the most enlightened citizens. If all deputies were white, this was only because the Spanish, who despised *pardos*, had failed to provide them with the education that would give them the necessary knowledge and enlightenment to be elected.[79] Like slavery, then, blacks' electoral underrepresentation derived not from contemporary discrimination but from the unfortunate legacy of Spanish despotism.

The idea of unity also played a key role in early nationalist notions of racial harmony. Early republican authorities believed they had the daunting task of creating a unified nation out of a region beset by regional and racial divisions. Most analyses of the "illusion" of unity have focused on attempts to control regional divisions.[80] However, this illusion was as much a matter of racial as of regional integration.

As Bolívar told legislators in Angostura: "Unity, Unity, Unity, must be our motto in all things. The blood of our citizens is varied, let it be mixed for the sake of unity: our constitution has divided the powers of government, let them be bound together to secure unity."[81] This statement evidences a broader political dichotomy that privileged unity over factionalism, drawing inspiration from Rousseau's belief in the inherent antagonism between unity and factions.[82] For Rousseau, a perfect state was one ruled by the general will, which represented the common interest of society. However, because individual interest often conflicted with the common interest, the sum of all the various particular wills did not necessarily reflect the general will. The tension between individual and societal interest was magnified when individuals ceased to act as individuals and began instead to vote as members of factions. Rousseau believed that factions represented the emergence of specific group interests, which ultimately could lead to the destruction of the state.[83] In Rousseau's vision, virtue would be possible and factions would disappear in a society ruled by the general will—a society in which reason had overpowered passion and men had reached their full potential; in which all men were, and desired to be, what they ought to be.[84]

Racial differences were inscribed in these notions. Race facilitated the emergence of factions, which made it difficult to achieve the dream of a society ruled by virtuous citizens. From this perspective, Bolívar's notion of pardocracy represented the triumph of a particular faction, that of *pardos*, over the unity of the nation. It followed that racial politics equaled factional politics and as such constituted a threat to the nation. As long as Colombia continued to be divided by race, virtuous politics would be impossible. It is significant that when the introduction of trial by jury was proposed to the 1825 Senate, Colombia's "heterogeneous and scattered population" was one of the arguments presented opposing the project.[85] In early republican political ideology, citizenship and race were incompatible; the first stood for union and equality, the second for division and antagonism. Thus, this period's racial policies must be understood as subsumed within this overarching goal of eliminating any cause for racial conflict and division and fostering a nation of citizens, which is to say, a nation of men with equal interests and values.[86] Significantly, legislation to attract the immigration of Europeans followed a secret session on the threat of race war in Colombia. Such immigration was considered an "effective remedy" to the "dangers that the Republic might experience over time due to the difference of races."[87]

Another element of the new republican racial ideology was interracial mixing among Europeans, blacks, and Indians. European immigration was a fundamental aspect of this project. As early as 1819, Bolívar proposed that national unity could be achieved through racial mixing.[88] As a path to national unity, it also played a key role in one of the first independence histories of Gran Colombia. Drawing parallels between Spain and Spanish America, this history highlighted how the expulsion of the "Moors" from the Iberian Peninsula had been achieved not by "the aborigines" but by "a distant generation of mixed blood" whose "right to recover the independence of their country no one had questioned." The same had happened in Spanish America, but with the difference that "we have not had the time to prevail over the heterogeneous elements and condense a new mass, like the Spanish did in 1600 years."[89] Several elements of this narrative foreshadow later ideologies of *mestizaje* (racial mixing): the notion that people of mixed descent embody the nation and the idea that racial mixing leads to the creation of a "new mass," a new type of people. A less neutral view of racial mixing was proposed by Gerónimo Torres, who sought to "extinguish the black race" by sending vagabonds and prostitutes from regions with lighter-skinned people to live in regions populated mostly by blacks. This measure, he believed, would accomplish the double objective of mixing blacks and whites and contributing to Colombian population growth.[90]

Such projects could be interpreted only as racist attempts to eliminate Colombian racial diversity, but that would not help us understand the political values and ideologies that gave coherence to early republican racial policies. This is not to say that racial prejudices were absent among the elite. On the contrary, Torres was not afraid to express his negative views of free and slave blacks. Moreover, these projects did not envision racial mixing in neutral terms but were part of a conscious attempt to whiten the country. Nevertheless, racial policies must be understood in relation to broader contemporary notions of citizenship, which could not imagine difference and diversity in positive terms. For example, one government scheme to bring European immigrants to Colombia mandated a proportional number of immigrants from every nation so as to avoid any "spirit of domination or partiality."[91] Differences in culture and values were expected to bring difficulties even among Europeans. Revolutionaries at various ends of the political spectrum tended to see racial differences as a problem. In the words of the *pardo* intellectual Juan García del Río, "heterogeneity was a malefic principle."[92] Significantly, he linked heterogeneity to hierarchical colonial caste divisions; to eliminate one was to eliminate the other. Quoting Buffon, he stated, "Man is not strong without union and is not happy without peace."[93] Therefore, he only hoped for the Revolution to "exert its beneficial effects" and "fuse our population."[94] This idea influenced his assessment of the Colombian population: he praised those who were willing to assimilate and criticized those who were not. Del Río lamented indigenous peoples' attachment to tradition. In contrast, his view of the *pardo* population was optimistic. He believed that the "the people of color, although quite ignorant, are more capable of improvement." The Revolution, he added, "has assimilated them into the privileged classes; the government in its justice has promoted to honor and employment those who have distinguished themselves; there is no doubt that as this class continues to educate itself, public opinion will give up its color prej-

udices."[95] For him, as for other Colombian intellectuals and politi-
cians, to imagine Colombians was to imagine citizens with similar interests and values. Confronted with citizens of different colors, early
legislators could think either in terms of blending, mixing, and assim-
ilating or in terms of exclusion.[96]

The Americas provided various models for solving the supposed
conflict between racial difference and national unity. The United
States had developed a white man's country imaginary that excluded
blacks from citizenship, either through schemes for expatriating ex-
slaves or by withholding full citizenship rights from free blacks.[97] Haiti
had initially resolved conflicts between blacks and mulattoes by declaring all its citizens, regardless of color, black by constitutional decree.
When, in 1804, its constitution declared that "Haitians will be known
under none other than the generic denomination of blacks [noirs],"
including in this measure Haitians of all shades, even whites, Haiti
was also following an ideological belief in the necessity of a homogeneous citizenry, of eliminating color as a cause of conflict.[98] Colombia
followed yet a different path: blending. This solution skillfully adapted
Colombia's peculiar social and political reality to contemporary notions of nation and citizenship. The war had made the political and
legal exclusion of *pardos* impossible, both because of their military
power and because of the link between racial equality and patriot nationalism. Racial mixing, like education and legal equality, thus became part
of the larger project of creating a unified nation of Colombians.

Interior Minister José Manuel Restrepo, in his report to the 1823
Congress, summarized the approach early republican projects were
taking to eliminate racial conflicts and promote a homogeneous citizenry. He predicted that, within sixty years at most, *castas* would disappear, and Colombia would be inhabited only by free men—a "most
pleasing and comforting" perspective. Thus, one of the new government's priorities was to pass laws that eliminated racial differences
through cultural and physical amalgamation, which they hoped would
gradually eliminate the colonial legacy of racial conflict and division.[99]

First and foremost, it was necessary to abolish colonial laws that fostered racial inequality and antagonism. Restrepo welcomed the eradication of practices that humiliated and debased one sector of the population, such as the public whipping of Indians.[100] The central government eliminated racial identification from parish registries, military records—including promotions—and judicial records.[101] The free-womb law was the most controversial racial legislation. Restrepo told legislators that no law would have a larger impact on Colombians' future than the free-womb law or the law granting citizenship to Indians. Although he acknowledged the economic problems that could derive from the free-womb law, he asserted that these were much lesser evils than the inevitable race war that would follow if slavery were maintained.[102] Manumission was also explicitly considered an antidote to race war, and eliminating racial conflict was the guiding principle behind this officially promoted practice. If manumission's goal was a racially harmonious citizenry, then former slaves had to become Colombians with full legal rights.[103] This notion was publicly represented in manumission ceremonies, which signified the rebirth of slaves as citizens. During these ceremonies, slaves took an oath to defend the constitution and the laws, and Colombians were asked to "recognize them as compatriots, Colombians, and fellow citizens." In return, ex-slaves were asked to live as peaceful, law-abiding citizens to show their gratitude to a country that had fought a long and bloody war for their freedom.[104]

Controlling the manumission process in order to secure social order was the other side of government policy to eliminate racial conflicts. Thus, the long apprenticeship of *libertos* was justified as a defense of both property rights and social order. *Libertos* were expected to work for their owners until the age of eighteen not only to compensate the owner for the alleged expense of supporting a child but also to avoid the dangers of providing sudden liberty to people unaccustomed to it.[105] The *juntas de manumisión* were also intended to help with the maintenance of social order. The 1821 manumission law decreed that owners should contact these juntas when their slaves' children turned eighteen, informing them about their conduct and character, so that the juntas could help find them a useful profession.[106] If slaves were going to be free, their freedom had to be organized and controlled, a process whose conditions the state defined. This intention is evident in the Cartagena junta's 1832 rejection of a petition for compensation from an owner of a slave who had joined the government party in a recent civil war and then refused to abandon his regiment to return to service.[107] The members of the *junta de manumisión* vigorously refused to use their funds to manumit this slave. This was not the purpose for which the juntas had been created, they argued. Slaves could not just be manumitted at any moment: "It is one thing to free specific slaves on certain chosen days, and with certain formalities . . . and quite a different thing to free undeserving slaves, when there are worthier ones."[108] Two issues were at stake here. The junta's manumissions could not be random and improvised; they had to be accompanied by magnificent ceremonies that would lend glory to Colombia. Further, slaves who were to be freed had to have certain attributes. The junta reminded Cartagena's governor that according to the 1821 Cúcuta law, juntas should favor the most industrious and honest slaves. The junta's purpose was to elevate to the rank of citizen those slaves "who had earned it by a long and heavy servitude. . . . Let us not be mistaken: he who is a bad slave is an even worse citizen."[109] The members of Cartagena's junta were particularly disturbed by the image of slaves taking their freedom into their own hands. They argued that it was one thing to award freedom to slaves who had joined the great patriot army in the fight for independence. It was another to award freedom to any slave who took up arms in the multiple conflicts that plagued the country. This would reward delinquent slaves over law-abiding ones, disrupt the social order, and plague society with vicious freedmen.[110]

Education was another pillar of the state program for creating a nation of homogenous Colombians out of a racially diverse population. Legislative projects sought to educate all Colombians, including blacks and Indians, by bringing schools to all corners of the Republic.[111] The 1814 Constitution of Mariquita, for example, explicitly declared that "no school shall make any distinction between whites, *pardos*, or any other class of people. Talent and progress in learning shall distinguish youth in the Republic."[112] The 1821 Constitution was not so explicit, but the 1823 Congress clarified that it was unconstitutional to discriminate against *pardos* in university or seminary admissions.[113] These laws were meant to eliminate yet another source of conflict and resentment. Perhaps more important, inclusion was part of a larger project that sought to unify the mores and values of Colombian citizens and foster the progress of the nation through an educated and industrious citizenry.

By the 1820s, racial harmony had become so attached to Colombian nationalism that to deny its desirability was tantamount to opposing republicanism and favoring the Spanish monarchy. To oppose the notion of harmony and equality was to be incapable of one of the most important forms of patriotic love—love of your Colombian brother; to be incapable of "melt[ing] in pleasure" at the sight of Indians and slaves being transformed into fellow citizens and Colombians.[114] This is not to deny that some people opposed this notion, just as some remembered with nostalgia the peace and order of Spanish authority and sought to reestablish monarchical rule. However, expressing such notions involved a high political and personal cost; they could easily lead to weighty accusations of treason and sedition.

The First Republic
and the *Pardos*

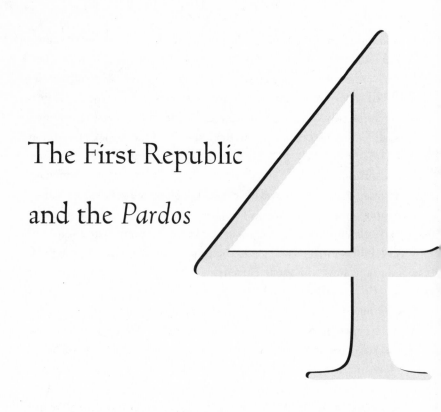

OFFICIAL DESCRIPTIONS of Cartagena's struggle for independence extolled the unity and patriotism of its people. According to the patriot junta of Cartagena, "the people's general clamor" had forced deposition of the Spanish governor and the establishment of the new government. It was the people who abhorred despotism and the tyranny of the Spanish governor.[1] This glorious narrative conceals the deep social tensions that characterized the emergence of modern politics in Cartagena. In particular, it silences anxieties over the nature of popular participation in the new regime now that *pardos* had joined the patriot movement. This problem would divide Cartagena, during the five years of the short-lived First Republic, into two distinct political camps: the "demagogues," or Piñeristas, and the "aristocrats," or Toledistas.[2]

The participation of *pardos* as fellow patriots confronted the elite with the predicament of how to deal with lower-class political action in the new regime. The ambivalent nature of *pardo* involvement in the patriot movement made the resolution of this problem all the more complex. On the one hand, the creole elite had called people of African descent to support their political actions against the Spanish. These actions were then glorified by patriot rhetoric as the righteous attempt of the people to recover their freedom and sovereignty. This crowd, as the people, had helped legitimate the creoles' seizure of power. On the other hand, the creole elite feared that blacks and mulattoes might escape their political control.[3] Although abstract, the constant rhetorical references to the people as protagonists of historical and political change fired up listeners' imaginations. Men from Cartagena were not only convoked as witnesses but were also told that they were agents of revolutionary change. This rhetoric would have long-term consequences, as the lower classes deployed it to legitimate political initiatives that went beyond the elite's initial intentions.[4] *Pardos* read their embodiment of sovereignty, as the people, as a legitimization of any type of mass political action. At issue was the limit of such actions' legitimacy. This was not merely a matter of political theory; rather, it spoke to the crucial question of whether or not the creole elite would maintain its traditional political and social control.

The legal and electoral system upheld the notion that sovereignty had indeed returned to the people, including both blacks and whites, without racial distinction. The December 1810 electoral instructions for the Suprema Junta of the province of Cartagena included all races: "All parishioners, whites, Indians, mestizos, mulattoes, *zambos*, and blacks, as long as they are household heads and live from their own work, are to be summoned for elections." Only "vagrants, criminals, those who are in servile salaried status, and slaves are excluded."[5] This law not only helped secure *pardos'* essential support for the patriot cause, leading to the participation of a few influential *pardos* in the government, but also conformed to the liberal notion—to which most patriot creoles adhered—that political power should be in the hands of men of merit, regardless of origin. Providing equal legal rights to all races and sharing congressional seats with a few outstanding *pardos* did not imply a loss of traditional elite political power. A few *pardos* might become part of the constitutional assembly and the parliament, but they would still be a minority in the government.

It was quite a different matter, however, to allow an uncontrolled crowd of black and mulatto artisans to determine the political future of the city. Yet the novelty of the electoral process and the notion of the people's sovereignty led to ambivalence over the legitimacy and extent of street political actions. For example, during the election of a new expanded junta in August 1810, a crowd led by an Afro-Colombian militia officer gathered in front of the government palace to press for the election of José María García de Toledo, a prominent creole patriot, as president of the junta. García de Toledo vehemently rejected their expression of support, explaining to the crowd that this election "did not belong to the people but to their representatives."[6] Moreover, he made sure to have a personal conversation with their leader, reproaching him for his audacious initiative and obtaining his word that he would not again muster a crowd when the representatives gathered to elect the junta's president. To García de Toledo's satisfaction, "not a soul was in the plaza" when the junta elected him president on August 14.[7] This event reveals the fluidity of the notion of elections at this time. Here, the issue was not who would be elected, but how and by whom. Would the president be elected by the crowd, by the representatives with the support of the crowd, or exclusively by the representatives? The people in the crowd had acted under the assumption that they were entitled to express their choice directly.[8]

Although in this situation, creole leaders solved their conflict with *pardo* patriots to their satisfaction, the contrary was often the case. *Pardos* tended to take anti-Spanish rhetoric to an extent not intended by the junta. Fears and tensions caused by mass political participation began to spring up even before the Declaration of Independence. Nine months after the deposition of the Spanish governor, the Spanish soldiers of the Fijo regiment conspired to overthrow the junta. They were defeated by recently created *pardo* and white patriot militias and by crowds of lower-class people who filled the streets in defense of the junta. However, these lower-class patriots were not content to express their patriotism by merely defeating the Fijo regiment. Without waiting for the junta's authorization, crowds of blacks and mulattoes began to attack and plunder the houses of wealthy Spaniards whom they considered accomplices of the regiment. The junta, which had not yet declared independence from Spain, strongly disapproved of these attacks. Yet it could do nothing to stop them. Not only was it hard to control the hundreds of armed men who filled the streets, but, more important, it was difficult to justify the repression of a crowd that was acting not as a riotous mob but as the patriot defenders of the junta.

Manuel Trinidad Noriega, a lieutenant of the patriot *pardo* battalion, provided a description of these events that clearly illustrates the dimensions of the predicament.[9] His account, a rare example of a narrative written by a patriot *pardo*, is one of the most vivid descriptions of revolutionary events in Cartagena. In this personal letter, Noriega described his attempts to protect the house of Don Juan Incera, his patron's peninsular son-in-law, from being plundered. Noriega's description supported the official narrative about harmony between the junta and the *pardos*, but his portrayal of *pardo* participation placed in their hands a larger degree of autonomy, initiative, and aggression. These days, in his account, were marked by tumult and violence; traditional authorities had lost all control, and only the junta enjoyed authority. Noriega compared this episode to the Last Judgment: "fury ran unbridled," he remarked, as patriots plundered and attacked Spanish houses; "the whole night was a revolution." While the junta deliberated for an entire day and night, "more than three thousand people patrolled the streets."[10]

Noriega's account reveals the shifting notions of authority that characterized this revolutionary moment and the lower-classes' perception of their own political legitimacy, their right to engage in revolutionary action as the people. Noriega described the arrival at Incera's house of four hundred men armed with machetes, pikes, and axes. The bishop of Popayán, who was passing by, tried unsuccessfully to restrain the multitude. Seeing this, Noriega confronted the men, asking them to save the house to which he owed his life. Ultimately, he succeeded where the bishop had failed. His achievement was based upon his identity as a patriot; a son of the country; a "brother, friend and defender of all of you."[11] In order to save the house, however, he also had to promise to hand over Incera that night. He was forced to write and sign a bill that read: "I oblige myself before the people to deliver Incera before the junta tonight at seven. If I fail to honor this, I will answer with my head."[12]

The identification between this motley crew and the people becomes explicit in Noriega's letter. Commoners saw themselves as the rightful defenders and representatives of the junta, yet they escaped its control. Although that night the junta decided to free Incera, the following morning the people once again requested his imprisonment. A group of two hundred armed *zambos* blocked Noriega and requested that he fulfill his obligation to hand over Incera.[13] Noriega convinced Incera that he could only save his life by jailing him and then "notify[ing] all the people" of his imprisonment.[14] This tactic indicates the degree of power the people in the streets had achieved. On the one hand, the people legitimated the assault on the Spanish authorities; on the other, the people's embodiment of sovereignty could be read as a legitimization of the crowd's political actions. For the first time, lower-class crowds had attacked the local elite not as members of a riotous mob but as legitimate political actors.

Significantly, the official press did not condemn the excesses against the Spaniards. An account of the event emphasized the prowess of the *pardo* and white militias and patriot battalions in the defense of the junta, thus contributing to the nascent rhetoric associating patriotism with racial equality.[15] However, the legitimization of crowd actions inaugurated political possibilities that did not have clear limits. Would the crowd become a legitimate actor that influenced local politics? Or would crowd actions be delegitimized as anarchic and demagogic, at odds with ordered and legal society?

These conflicts began to divide Cartagena's patriots into the two distinct camps mentioned earlier: the Piñeristas, or "demagogues," and the Toledistas, or "aristocrats." The leaders of the two camps, Gabriel Gutiérrez de Piñeres and José María García de Toledo, did not differ in social status. They both belonged to wealthy creole families that were among the most prestigious in the province, and they were both educated men who were familiar with the new political and philosophical ideas of their time. They did, however, belong to different generations. By the time of independence, García de Toledo was forty years old; he had occupied prestigious positions in the Spanish bureaucracy and acted as one of the *cabildo* leaders against the Spanish governor.[16] Gutiérrez de Piñeres, thirteen years younger, could anticipate a long political career in the new republican state.[17] Their main difference came in their approach to the political participation of the lower classes. Although the creole revolutionary junta had initially solicited the cooperation of *pardos* to depose the Spanish governor and had given equal legal rights to all races, its members had grown increasingly wary of *pardos*' political participation. Gathered around the president of the junta, García de Toledo, they tried to control local *pardos* and maintain political activities within institutional channels that they could oversee. They opposed the mob's attacks against Spanish property and saw the humiliation of prominent Spaniards at the hands of the *pardos* as an assault on social order. Gabriel Gutiérrez de Piñeres and his brother Germán, on the other hand, based their political power on the support of *pardo* artisans, an alliance that quickly earned them the label of demagogues. They were compared to the French revolutionaries Danton and Marat, and one of them even signed himself as "the fervent."[18] Not only were they unafraid to call black and mulatto artisans to the streets, but their revolutionary rhetoric emphasized the end of aristocracy and the equality of all men. They did not hold back from denouncing unpatriotic aristocratic manners and behavior among the local elite. The Piñeres brothers and their followers took the antiaristocratic rhetoric of racial equality to extremes unintended by other members of the elite. They linked anti-Spanish feeling with a revolutionary rhetoric that not only promoted racial equality but also favored the active participation of lower-class *pardos* in city politics.

The two groups were also sharply divided over the issue of how political change should take place, in particular the Declaration of Independence. Although García de Toledo supported independence, he was extremely concerned about when, and especially how, it would be achieved. He feared a tumultuous independence movement that would allow a riotous crowd to call the day. He strongly believed that independence should not be declared until the convention had been elected in January 1812. According to him, only the convention's deputies, as the representatives of the people, had the legal right to take such a momentous step.[19] Independence should only be declared by "the Convention in tranquility without demagogy, which was the legal, political, and convenient procedure."[20] If the convention declared independence, the Toledista elite who dominated the junta would maintain their traditional control. It would be quite a different matter if independence were declared in advance with the support—or under the pressure—of the new patriot militia, then controlled by the Piñeristas.

Ultimately, it was not the convention that declared independence but a helpless creole junta threatened by armed crowds of blacks and mulattoes. With the backing of *pardo* artisans and *pardo* patriot militias (the Lanceros de Getsemaní), the Piñeristas conspired to petition the junta to declare independence on November 11, 1811, establishing a republican government. Since local blacks and mulattoes left behind no records of their reasons for forcing the junta to declare independence, their motives can only be inferred. One possible explanation derives from the development of social and racial politics in both Cartagena and the Spanish Empire. As mentioned before, it was probably not a coincidence that Cartagena's independence followed the Spanish refusal to grant citizenship rights to people of African descent in the new 1812 Constitution.[21] Patriots used Spanish opposition to African American citizenship to gather the support of *pardos*, constructing a rhetoric of harmony that considered racial conflicts and divisions a legacy of Spanish despotism.[22] The way racial equality became associated with republican antiaristocratic rhetoric may help explain the *pardo* artisans' support for the Piñeres conspiracy in favor of independence.

It is also telling that the conspiracy centered around the *pardo* artisan neighborhood of Getsemaní. The main leaders of the republican conspiracy were all persons of influence among the artisans of Getsemaní, and the rebellion headquarters were in the house of the artisan Pedro Romero, a *pardo* officer in the Lanceros. The artisans of Cartagena had agreed to stop working on November 11. They followed the junta's deliberations from Romero's house, and when their agents reported that the junta was going to end its session without considering their petition for independence, they decided to march into the city. The patriot *pardo* militia took control of the city bastions, and a large crowd of people from Getsemaní went to the city armory and forced the door. Armed with spears, daggers, and guns, they went to the government palace. There, through their spokespersons, they requested that the junta approve their petition for independence. In spite of the crowd's belligerence and the junta's lack of military support, García de Toledo refused to comply. Irritated by this opposition, the crowd invaded the session hall, led by Gabriel Gutiérrez de Piñeres. Treating

García de Toledo with disrespect and violence, the crowd imprisoned him. Under duress, García de Toledo and the other members of the junta signed the Declaration of Independence.[23]

That day and the next, the defeated junta had to endure a city controlled by the crowd from Getsemaní. The royalist bishop of Santa Fé later described Cartagena's independence as "a species of revolution of the people, plotted by a handful of men with gratification to only a few people of color."[24] According to the bishop, the enemies of the Spanish were "men without knowledge, consciousness, or property and without any law other than ambition and licentiousness."[25] Unsurprisingly, García de Toledo later spoke of Independence Day as a "nefarious and dangerous day" and of the next as "a day of tears and scandal, not only for this city and its province but for the entire country."[26] In contrast with the harmony espoused in the official patriot narrative, Cartagena's declaration was fraught with violence between the "demagogue" and "aristocrat" patriot factions, the elite-controlled junta defeated at the hands of a riotous mob of blacks and mulattoes.

Following independence, the elite confronted the vital issue of whether or not they would recover political control. Cartagena was sharply divided between the patriot camps, and it was unclear who—if anyone—would control the city. Both sides were represented in government. Although a minority, the Piñeristas were represented in Congress, and the Piñeres brothers often occupied important offices. The military was also divided, the patriot militia supporting the Piñeristas, the Fijo the Toledistas, and the other corps oscillating between the camps.[27] Although the Toledista party counted upon the support of most of the creole elite, contemporary accounts constantly emphasize the political strength, influence, and belligerence of the demagogues during the following four years. Even if the junta remained in power under the control of a Toledista majority, it was the Piñeres brothers who "imposed their opinions, by hook or by crook, supported by the militias and the people of color."[28]

When Cartagena's constitutional convention met on January 21, 1812, the elite tried to control the growing power of the *pardo* militia. The creole elite dominated the convention, yet the government feared the patriot *pardo* militia would continue with their riots and disturbances in favor of the Piñeristas. During the independence upheaval, the patriot *pardo* militias had appropriated four cannons, and they now refused to return them. To force the issue, the president of Cartagena ordered gallows to be placed in the plaza. Afterward, he successfully demanded that the patriot *pardos* return the cannons.[29] Significantly, no one was executed, but the *pardos* were forced to return their arms. Neither camp could completely impose its will on the other.

It is impossible to provide for the First Republic of Cartagena the rich political details that are available for other contemporary revolutions. We do not know what, if any, republican political clubs and groups existed. Nor do we know the life stories of many of the Revolution's main protagonists. This said, it is possible to get a sense of the enormous transformations in political language and behavior that characterized Cartagena's early republican life, in particular the impression among contemporaries that they were experiencing an epochal change that would transform local politics and society. According to the royalist witness Fernández de Santos, it would have been extremely difficult after one year of independence to convert Cartagena's populace back to the royalist cause. Cartageneros had become "enchanted with promises of happiness and frenetic egalitarianism, and [were] contented with their poverty as long as their disorders [were] not corrected."[30]

It was year one of the Republic of Cartagena. Beginning with the introduction of a new calendar, the new republic emulated the rhetoric of the French Revolution.[31] Throughout the country, ceremonies and speeches announced the destruction of the old regime. Cartageneros read in the national gazette that people from the port city of Honda had petitioned against the shameful exhibition of the portraits of the Bourbon kings Charles and Ferdinand in the city hall, requesting a public ceremony during which the portraits would be put in the gallows for nine hours and then burned. Not only was this request granted, but the government also decided to officially publish it.[32] Cartageneros certainly approved of this patriotic act: they themselves had burned the Inquisition's instruments of torture in the plaza.[33] A royalist bishop who refused the Republic's authority went into exile and was replaced by the presbyter Juan Fernández de Sotomayor y Picón, who not only supported the new regime but had written a political catechism to instruct local people about republican principles.[34]

Republican institutions seemed to confirm the promises of equality. Previously, a white Spanish and creole elite had controlled the institutions that governed Cartagena. Now, not only were the Spanish out of power, but the new laws guaranteed equal political rights to free *pardos* and whites. The 1812 Constitution eliminated legal color distinctions; guaranteed suffrage to all free men but vagrants and servants; and, although it did not abolish slavery, outlawed the slave trade. In addition, *pardos* of modest origin became members of the constitutional assembly, the war council, and the parliament.[35] The dismantling of the Spanish military system also favored *pardos'* influence. Following the deposition of the Spanish governor, the junta had organized *pardo* and white patriot militias, and the Fijo regiment, after its failed conspiracy against the junta, had been purged of its pro-Spanish elements. Furthermore, after independence, the leading officer positions were opened to blacks and mulattoes.[36]

Political language also changed dramatically. Revolutionary concepts became the staple of local politics, announcing the rule of the people and a new era of liberty and equality. Patriots proclaimed their commitment to republican virtue, and antagonistic parties framed their conflicts according to republican notions of tyranny, despotism, demagoguery, and aristocracy. Songs against the royalist bishop mockingly announced his transformation into a Jacobin.[37] Social interactions also changed. Behavior considered "aristocratic" was not to be tolerated. For example, a Piñerista pamphlet accused García de Toledo of being too proud and snobbish with the people. In a revealing response, he vehemently denied the accusation and went on to vindicate himself at length by clarifying that he had not made distinctions among classes and colors. He explained that he did not allow any person, regardless of class, to use the honorific "Your Highness" with him. In his house, he offered a seat to people of all classes and danced with women of all classes, treating everybody with kindness and politeness. On festive days, he let all types of people into his home, permitting them to wander throughout without saying a word. He welcomed invitations from everyone and to every place and did not accept preferential seating, except in church. How then, he asked, could anybody accuse him of being conceited? That García de Toledo, the president of the junta and one of the leading creoles in the region, had to thus publicly defend his egalitarian social behavior is indicative of how the Revolution had momentarily changed social customs. The rigid hierarchical etiquette of colonial times had given way to revolutionary egalitarianism. In the words of Gabriel Gutiérrez de Piñeres, "In a popular government, no man should be superior to another; if Toledo enjoyed too much recognition and esteem, it was necessary to level him."[38]

Not only did Cartageneros have to get used to seeing *pardos* serve as congressmen and watching *pardo* mobs imprison and mistreat wealthy white Spaniards with impunity; they also had to adapt to a new type of foreigners arriving in the city. In desperate need of funds, the government had transformed Cartagena into a haven for Caribbean corsairs in 1812, and French and Haitian sailors now became a common sight. Cartageneros and Haitians sometimes joined together as pirates, and Haitians served as sailors in the new republic's navy.[39] During the defense of Cartagena in 1815, a fifty-man garrison was formed exclusively with Haitians.[40] Although we cannot access the conversations that took place between these Haitians and Cartageneros, we can imagine that they shared stories about the Haitian Revolution, which likely fired up the political imagination of local *pardos*. Venezuelan soldiers further added to these years' cosmopolitanism. In 1812, members of the defeated Venezuelan revolutionary army found refuge in Cartagena. From them, local residents probably heard stories about José Tomás Boves's campaign, the emancipation of the slaves who had fought for the royalists, and their bloody treatment of the Venezuelan elite. It was in Cartagena, with a predominantly Haitian following, that Antonio Nicolás Briceño prepared his Venezuelan *guerra a muerte* in 1813.[41] And again in 1814, these men returned defeated, with additional stories to tell.

Descriptions of these years often focus on events that forced the elite to endure acts in which *pardo* patriots showed little inclination to give up the power they had achieved, thinking they rightly deserved this power as the people in whom sovereignty now resided. For example, following independence, Antonio José de Ayos, a member of the junta and an ally of Toledo, decided to leave the city in order to avoid retaliation by the Piñeres faction for his participation in the repression of the nearby city of Mompox. Although he obtained a passport to leave the city, when he arrived at the Santo Domingo gate, he was forced to return. The people had decided to guard the gate of their own will. They tore up his passport and forced him to return, telling him that they were in charge now.[42] This was not the first time Ayos had faced an angry populace. He had earlier given refuge to the daughter of Spanish exiles. When she was abducted by a lower-class man, José de Cabarcas, Ayos had denounced this unsuccessfully to the judiciary authorities. While Ayos was in court, the abductor arrived with thirty other men and decided to whip him in front of the judge. Ayos had to flee and was followed by a mob until some neighbors managed to beg that he be forgiven.[43]

In an attempt to improve their relations, Piñeristas and Toledistas asked Manuel Castillo, who had been away from the city and therefore excluded from partisan politics, to take charge as military commander of the city. He accepted, but it soon became clear that he favored the Toledistas. As during the Fijo conspiracy and the independence movement, controlling anti-Spanish feeling and controlling *pardo* crowds and militias became closely related issues. At stake now was the treatment of Spanish prisoners. Apparently, the *pardo* troops in charge of watching the prisoners had imposed unauthorized punishments on them, the prisoners insulted and mistreated while toiling on Cartagena's public works.[44] Castillo changed this policy, turning custody of the Spanish prisoners over to veteran troops and punishing excesses committed against prisoners. More important, he sought to clean up the army by punishing and expelling soldiers whom he considered dangerous elements.[45] Moreover, he counterbalanced the *pardos'* power in the patriot army by reincorporating Spanish soldiers and officers who declared their loyalty to the Republic.[46] In spite of Castillo's reforms and his antagonism to the Piñeristas, the latter continued to challenge the power of the Toledistas, who remained alert in defense against political initiatives that might undermine their traditional authority. When, for example, the Piñeres brothers conspired with a Venezuelan officer to solve the city's economic problems by confiscating the property of the rich, both Spanish and creole, Castillo learned of the conspiracy. He prepared the city to defend itself against the Venezuelan officer, who was soon imprisoned and sent to Bogotá to be judged. However, Castillo could do nothing against the Piñeres brothers. He tried to convince the junta president of their guilt and of the need to imprison them, but the president refused. His advisors dissuaded him from taking action by conjuring up images of the popular disturbances that would surely follow such a measure.[47]

The greatest challenge to the Toledistas came in December 1814, during the election of the governor. On December 17, the Republic's electoral college gathered to vote for the new governor. García de Toledo won, with fifteen votes, while Gabriel Gutiérrez de Piñeres came in second, with ten.[48] In spite of his victory, however, García de Toledo would not become governor. Those in the galleries interrupted the electoral process, shouting their rejection of Toledo and demanding the election of citizen Piñeres because that was the will of "the people." The crowd, which nominated themselves as the people, was described by the Toledistas as not "the household heads, the honest neighbors, or the virtuous patriots of Cartagena, but the scum, a throng of obscure men with nothing to lose."[49] Some Piñerista members of the electoral college joined forces with the crowd. Ignacio Muñoz accused García de Toledo of pro-Spanish sentiments, while Germán Gutiérrez de Piñeres defended his brother's candidacy, stressing his sacrifices for independence and his popularity as "the idol of the people." Piñerista deputies also denounced an electoral system in which the electors were all friends and clients of García de Toledo, explaining that the tumult in the galleries was the natural result of ignoring the will of the people. Toledista deputies responded that the electoral college had lost its freedom and was muzzled by fear, declaring that any decision made that day would be invalid. They proposed to end the session and wait for things to calm down, but those in the galleries would have none of it. Armed with machetes and cutlasses, they closed the doors and forced the electors to continue the debates and make a final decision. After long debate, Gabriel Gutiérrez de Piñeres proposed a compromise: nominating both García de Toledo and himself as consuls with equal power. This was not enough for the people in the galleries, who shouted that they wanted "Gabriel without crutches." After some Piñerista deputies explained the reasons for this agreement, those in the riotous galleries accepted it. Before allowing the session to end, however, they requested an official declaration stating that their conduct did not merit indictment and persecution. Gabriel Gutiérrez de Piñeres tried to convince them of their righteousness, stating that they had committed no crime and therefore needed no pardon. In spite of his influence, he failed to persuade them; the galleries did not calm until they had obtained an official pardon.

The tumult at the electoral college received much attention from contemporaries—for good reason. It exposed the weakness of the creoles' political control and, perhaps more important, the lack of an authoritative, established discourse that could provide automatic answers to such crucial questions as who constituted the people and who had the right to represent them. In spite of the lack of established political rules, conventional republican rhetoric did set limits, if not on political actions, at least on the ways in which these actions could be framed and understood. All political actors had to avoid accusations of demagoguery, aristocracy, anarchy, and tyranny, framing their actions in terms of virtue, freedom, and equality. Yet what these political terms meant in Cartagena was hotly contested. This tension—between a shared and established republican rhetoric of political virtue and the fluid and conflictive political reality—characterized republican politics during the independence period.

For the Toledistas, the tumult in the electoral college was the culmination of the anarchy, violence, and turmoil that had afflicted Cartagena under the rule of the Piñeristas. The crowd had attempted to replace a constitutional representative government with a despotic and dictatorial one.[50] If the electoral college did not recover the freedom lost to seditious men, disorder and anarchy would triumph over legal and constitutional order.[51] However, to argue that the crowd had no right to impose its will on elected representatives was not enough. The Toledistas had to demonstrate that the riotous galleries, and the Piñeristas as a whole, were not the people. To do so, they appealed to those elements of the republican imaginary that would help them delegitimize crowd actions. Piñeres, they said, was not the idol of the people but a demagogue who based his popularity on his ability to corrupt *zambos* with money and liquor.[52] According to the Toledistas, the men in the crowd were not the people; they only claimed to be the people. These men had no right to representation; they were merely "scum, men without house and family and nothing to lose." Nor were they "real patriots"; rather, they had taken advantage of their situation to subject respectable Cartageneros to three years of insults and vexations.[53]

The Piñerista narrative of these events was, of course, completely different. The Piñeristas' perspective was expressed in a published pamphlet that defended their actions in the electoral college.[54] Although this pamphlet shared the early republican discursive framework utilized by the Toledistas, it differed in its interpretation of what constitutes demagoguery, aristocracy, factions, and anarchy. Piñeristas claimed to be following the laws of the Republic, accusing the Toledistas of destroying all that independence and republicanism stood for. According to them, the election of Toledo went against the constitution, which guaranteed a government for the common good of the people, not for the benefit of a man, a family, or a particular class. Toledo wanted to impose his aristocratic ideas on the people, without concern for the suffering of humanity or the perdition of the fatherland.[55] The Piñerista rhetoric emphasized the antiaristocratic nature of the independence movement, linking this struggle to the struggle against the social divisions of the old colonial regime. "Independence," the Piñeristas declared, "destroyed the basis of aristocratic pride, opening the door to merit and virtue alone, and its liberal system sanctioned legal equality. That is what displeases these so-called nobles."[56] Toledo had betrayed his pro-Spanish sentiments by publicly declaring November 11—Independence Day—to be sad and nefarious. He had also placed the government in the hands of his clients. These actions were proof of his aristocratic inclinations. It followed that his rule would annihilate the people. Citing Cicero and the Bible, the pamphlet defended the legitimacy of rebellion in order to save the fatherland. It rejected the notion that the tumult at the electoral college was an attempt by the rabble to hinder the freedom of the electoral system; instead, this was a patriotic act through which the people had saved the liberty of the Republic.

A few days later, both Gabriel Gutiérrez de Piñeres and García de Toledo renounced their positions as cogoverning consuls. By January 5, the governorship was in the hands of Pedro Gual. The Piñeristas were strengthened by the fact that the Toledista military commander, Manuel Castillo, had left the city in order to conduct a campaign against the royalist stronghold of Santa Marta, leaving the military government in the hands of a Venezuelan military commander who favored Piñeres. When news of the Piñerista revolt against the electoral college reached Castillo, he prepared to reconquer Cartagena. From a nearby town, with the support of provincial towns requesting respect for their rights of representation, Castillo asked Governor Gual to imprison and exile the Piñeristas.[57] At first, Gual refused, believing that it would be possible to reestablish order without alienating the numerous patriots who sympathized with Piñeres. Yet a series of conspiracies against his government and his life convinced him that reestablishing harmony among patriots was now impossible.

Recent conspiracies were even more threatening than the attempt to replace Toledo with Piñeres. According to the Toledistas, the plotters sought to kill the governor and other honorable men and put the *pardo* Pedro Medrano in charge of the government. If accomplished, this would have fulfilled creoles' worst racial and social nightmare: that the independence struggles might unleash a race war, thus repeating the events that had recently transformed the French colony of Saint Domingue into the free black nation of Haiti. The Toledistas closed ranks. Mariano Montilla entered the city, and the Public Health Committee, headed by Toledo himself, decreed the expulsion of the most important Piñeristas, including Pedro Medrano.[58] It is far from clear whether the Toledistas' fears had any basis. Yet the menace of race war served to justify the expulsion of prominent *pardos* who had been worthy patriots and allies but who had now acquired too much political power and recognition. This strategy would continue to be used during the 1820s, with long-term implications for the evolution of race relations and ideology in Colombia.

Following the expulsion of the Piñeristas, the creole elite prepared to celebrate victory. Commemorative acts were orchestrated that portrayed the role of prominent creoles in saving the city from "chaos" and "anarchy." Tales of creole heroism would be painted in the Senate chamber and narrated in the books of meritorious citizens; the names of the heroes would be inscribed in golden letters to immortalize their glory.[59] These commemorative acts were among the first attempts to invent an official narrative of independence that erased the participation of the lower classes, even though the events themselves were too recent to be so easily forgotten. Thus, the still-remarkable actions of the lower-class elements were depoliticized, their actions rewritten as attacks on law and order. *Pardos'* patriotism and support for independence were now presented as a sordid pretext that concealed seditious and factious intentions. *Pardos* were portrayed as a "faction who had taken hold of government under the shield of independence."[60] The uproar at the electoral college had revealed their intention to continue "their horrible projects of plunder, murder, and desolation."[61] Virtuous and law-abiding citizens had endured the insults of factious and seditious men who had replaced law and order with tumult and riot. Creole patriotic history thus made raucous bandits of Afro-Colombian patriots.

The creole plans to commemorate their victory over the Piñeristas erased the debates over the meaning of modern forms of representation that had characterized the early years of independence. The Piñeres brothers, radical leaders who enjoyed the support of the lower classes, were delegitimized with the label of demagogues. Piñerista support of a notion of sovereignty that proclaimed the right of the lower classes to participate in politics outside electoral channels was constructed as chaos and anarchy.

Elite difficulties in controlling lower-class politics and imposing a particular vision of republicanism were inscribed in a complementary discourse of illusion. In the midst of the Piñerista-Toledista conflict, for example, the Cartagenero Miguel Díaz Granados wrote to his brother-in-law that he was extremely displeased "at having to stay in this Babylon. . . . A better acquaintance with the purposes and lack of order and morality in the prevailing system made me soon desire to separate myself from an illusion which, like Plato's Republic, only existed on paper."[62] For this Cartagenero, the alleged virtues of republicanism were only good on paper. The Republic had actually brought disorder and immorality. Significantly, what made republicanism an illusion, in this view, was not the indifference of the lower classes toward modern politics but their excessive participation. By inscribing lower-class participation in a discourse of disorder, this Cartagenero disconnected the lower classes from republican politics, transforming the Republic into an elite illusion that could not be adapted to local reality.

Such contemporary attempts to inscribe the antiaristocratic republican activities of *pardos* in a discourse of chaos and demagoguery had a lasting impact on independence narratives. Either victims of or obstacles to modernity, the lower classes were expunged from the political sphere. They became the perennial subjects of pedagogical projects that sought to educate them in modern forms of political participation. Then as now, these master narratives of Colombian independence concealed multiple readings of, and conflicts over, republicanism and democracy.

Alas, glorious creole victory would not be possible; elite political control would yet again be challenged. In July 1815, the creole elite simultaneously confronted an alliance between local *pardos* and Haitian soldiers and the return of the seditious Piñeristas who had been exiled by the Public Health Committee. Conflict began when a group of patriot *pardos* from the artillery and marine corps decided of their own initiative to kill a large number of Spanish prisoners who had recently been captured.[63] When the military governor learned of the massacre, he requested the immediate imprisonment of its authors, putting Remigio Márquez, a *pardo* congressman, in charge of the process. Most members of the marine and artillery corps were blacks and mulattoes from Getsemaní and nearby towns, and they soon expressed their outrage at the possibility of seeing their comrades sent to the gallows solely for "killing a few *chapetones*."[64] They wrote a petition to the governor in defense of their companions' actions, opposing the government's priority on maintaining order and enforcing authority. They acknowledged that the law had been broken and regretted this; however, this concern came second to the defense of independence. The petition argued that internal sympathizers with the royalist cause had threatened the city and that the three hundred Spanish prisoners had almost outnumbered the members of the local garrison. It had been a patriotic duty to put them to death. If those patriots who killed the prisoners were executed for taking the law into their own hands, they would face death with pride and happiness for having protected the patria.[65] When the military commander found out about the discontent among the patriots from Getsemaní, he sought the support of Haitian soldiers to guard the imprisoned *pardo* patriots. However, the Haitians joined with local *pardo* troops, stating that their only duty was to fight the Spanish.[66]

At around the same time, half of the dangerous Piñeristas who had been exiled to Jamaica returned to Cartagena. The governor of Jamaica had refused to accept them. The returned men petitioned the government for their freedom, reiterating their patriotism and loyalty to the government. The members of the Public Health Committee restated their opinion regarding the disorderly and insubordinate nature of these men, so the government decided to send seventeen of them to prison and put eighteen under house arrest until the judiciary had made a final decision about their case. Before a decision could be made, however, news of the imminent arrival of Pablo Morillo, the new leader of the Spanish military forces in New Granada, reached Cartagena. Morillo's force had left Spain in February 1815 and, after conquering Venezuela, had started for New Granada in May of the same year. Faced with the organization of Cartagena's defense, the government decided to free the *pardo* patriots—the returned exiles and those who had massacred the Spanish prisoners. The patriot army needed their skills and cooperation. In his memoir, Manuel Marcelino Nuñez, a prominent Piñerista, recalled how Toledo's closest ally, Ayos, had come to him in jail and, with an embrace, asked him to forget all their previous differences and unite with him in defense of the patria.[67]

The First Republic of Cartagena had begun when an angry mob of *pardos* forced the elite creole junta to sign the Declaration of Independence. After four years of constant struggle, the creole elite had managed to regain political control of the city, imprisoning radical Piñeristas. Yet now Morillo's siege forced the creoles to free these dangerous *pardos*, rallying their support by reviving the discourse of reconciliation, patriotism, and unity against the Spanish. The scenes that began and ended the First Republic of Cartagena are emblematic of the political paradoxes of the revolutionary period. Elite backlash against *pardos* would ultimately not be possible, at least among patriots. The struggle against the Spanish would continually force creoles to reiterate notions of racial harmony and equality. Every year of struggle, and every battle in which *pardos* and the creole elite fought together under the banner of republican equality, further consolidated nationalist notions of racial equality.[68]

After a long siege, Morillo's army reconquered Cartagena on December 5, 1815. Morillo entered a desolated city in which thousands of people had died of hunger. Until 1821, when patriots reconquered it, Cartagena remained under Spanish rule. The official policy of King Ferdinand VII, back on the Spanish throne, aspired to turn back the clock. Ferdinand eliminated the Cádiz Constitution and sought to return to the politics and culture of the Old Regime. In New Granada, the behavior of Morillo's army increasingly weakened what support the royalists enjoyed. In city after city, hundreds of patriots were sentenced to death. Indeed, according to Viceroy Francisco de Montalvo, seven thousand people belonging to New Granada's most prominent families were sentenced to death.[69] Moreover, the underfunded royalist army constantly requisitioned goods and money from the region's already impoverished inhabitants. This, along with Spanish soldiers' open distrust and low opinion of Americans, further exacerbated anti-Spanish feelings in New Granada. When the patriot army returned in 1819, it could rely on the anti-Spanish feelings of the local population. After the Battle of Boyacá on August 7, 1819, patriots began a successful campaign that culminated with the conquest of Cartagena in 1821. A few royalist forces continued to fight, but with

Antonio José de Sucre's victory at Ayacucho in 1824, the wars in South America were over.[70]

Cartagena was one of the cities most adversely affected by the wars. It had lost numerous lives and economic resources during the long siege of 1815. Local funds had been further depleted when Cartagena became the seat of the Spanish government of New Granada. Nine prominent creoles, including García de Toledo, had been executed. Some *pardo* and white patriots had escaped death and prison by fleeing Cartagena in thirteen corsair boats. Some managed to survive, finding refuge in Haiti.[71] A group of these exiled patriots would accompany Bolívar in the reconquest of New Granada. Gabriel Gutierrez de Piñeres, suffering exile in Jamaica at the time of Morillo's conquest, would join them and die fighting in Barcelona, Venezuela.[72] By the time the independence struggles were over, several *pardos* had become officers—even generals—in the patriot army. The question now was what role these men would play in the new republic.

Life Stories of

Afro-Colombian Patriots

IN ADDITION TO descriptions of faceless crowds, we have access to the lives of a few Afro-Colombian patriots whose stories have survived because at some moment they found themselves in court. Occasionally, their encounters with the law were the results of their own attempts to seek justice from republican courts. More often, however, their political activities provoked the anger or fear of local elites. Sometimes, court records provide abundant information, allowing for a rich description of their lives. At other times, they provide only legal summaries that highlight the most threatening aspects of their political activities. Yet all these records shed light on the characteristics of racial conflict during the independence period. Analysis of these trials allows us to examine a wide range of patriots' political aspirations and the ways in which the new republican rhetoric of freedom and equality inspired some to press for the realization of justice and equality. The records also reveal the ways in which the creole elite sought to control the activities of politically dangerous blacks and mulattoes.

The trials examined here took place during the years 1811–28—foundational years of revolutionary fervor during which expectations and fears ran high. These were years of constant war and political change. Not only did Colombia shift back and forth from republican (1811–15) to Spanish (1815–19) to republican rule, but it also thrived with political and legal innovation. Newspapers flourished, as did constitutional writing. Colombia witnessed three national constitutional conventions (Angostura, Cúcuta, Ocaña), and from 1811 to 1815, various regions of the country even constituted themselves as small republics with their own laws and constitutions. The actions of Colombians must thus be understood as part of a political atmosphere that could foster fervent belief—warranted or not—in the possibility of revolutionary change.

Justice

On February 13, 1811, the *zambo* Buenaventura Pérez landed in jail. He was accused of organizing a *juntica* (small council) in opposition to the whites. Pérez was a master gunpowder maker, and this was not the first time—or the last—that he had to face the consequences of provoking the rage of the Honda elite. He had already suffered the humiliation of being struck by a municipal officer, and he would later be accused of insulting "people of honor" in his usual pretentious manner.[1] Indeed, the records paint a portrait of a man not easily cowed by threats or imprisonment. Jail did not seem to intimidate him, and he confronted the authorities who interrogated him with shouts and accusations of injustice, of using their political authority to vent personal antagonism toward him. In the words of these authorities, Pérez uttered "proud words of a haughty character."[2]

Pérez's conspiracy came at a critical political moment, when Colombian cities abounded with revolutionary juntas that had taken the government away from Spanish authorities and placed it in the hands of the creole elite. In July 1810, a junta had overthrown the viceroy in Santa Fé, and in June of the same year, a junta had deposed the governor of Cartagena with the support of local *pardo* artisans. Unlike those in Santa Fé and Cartagena, however, Honda's town council had a reputation for being pro-Spanish: Pérez would later refer to it as a "Cabildo de Chapetones." The Honda town council had expelled two prominent creole patriots and was in conflict with the nearby patriot town of Ambalema.[3]

Buenaventura Pérez was imprisoned after a fellow artisan, twenty-seven-year-old blacksmith Vicente Castro, accused him of conspiring to support the revolutionaries of this nearby town. According to Castro, Pérez had stopped by his shop and told him not to fix any firearms for the people of Honda. This was unwise, he said. Then Pérez invited Castro to join in "a *juntica* against the whites," saying that "if they did not take charge, the whites would screw things up." He asked Castro to go to his house, where he would give him further details.[4] Other artisans confirmed Castro's accusations, testifying that Pérez had invited them to a meeting outside the city where they would learn more about his plans.[5]

Pérez's role in the conflict between Spaniards and creoles is unclear. He might have been an intermediary between creole patriots and artisans. As we have seen, in Mompox and Cartagena, the creole elite sought the cooperation of influential artisans to secure the support of the urban lower classes. According to the artisans' testimony, Pérez did mention counting on the support of important friends. Moreover, he had openly expressed his opposition to the expulsion of "outstanding and noble Americans."[6] Pérez and other patriots might have thought that an alliance between local artisans and creole patriots from Ambalema could overthrow the pro-Spanish junta and put local government in the hands of American patriots. Yet it is not clear where the initiative for this alliance lay. Pérez's declaration that "they" (*pardos*, artisans) should take charge to keep the whites from ruining everything puts the future of the Revolution squarely in artisans' hands.[7]

Pérez's trial exposes a long history of confrontation between Pérez and the elite over the administration of justice in Honda. During the trial, Pérez bitterly mentioned how the local elite had once opposed his attempt to seek justice from the viceroy. The tradition of seeking arbitration from the central government went back to colonial times, when the king was seen as a source of justice in confronting the arbitrariness of "evil" local authorities. This notion had long been an intrinsic part of colonial legitimacy, and humble people, including slaves, regularly appealed to the central government, often with success.[8] Thus, when a member of the local elite refused to pay him for his work, Pérez had sought justice—but to no avail. He earned only the public humiliation of being struck by a town officer. Moreover, the mayor broke into his house and stole his petition to the viceroy.[9]

This event had apparently left a profound mark on Pérez. When the struggle for independence began, his loudest cry against local authorities was of injustice. He had reputedly ranted against the local town council—in charge of the local administration of justice—going so far as to say "se cagaba en el ilustre cabildo" (he shit on the illustrious town council). There was no justice to be had in Honda, he said. Although he denied having uttered such violent remarks, during his interrogation, he declared, "Though I had not told anybody there is no justice in this town, I now say so, because it is true that there is none; whoever wants to can beat me and steal my labor."[10]

To Pérez's satisfaction, a month after his arrest, a new patriot government replaced the pro-Spanish junta. The new patriot authorities were sympathetic to his cause and set him free. This confirmed his belief that patriots would bring needed justice to his town, and he wasted no time in seeking additional redress from the new government. Having been freed was not enough for Pérez: he wanted to be compensated for the economic losses he had suffered in jail. He wrote a vitriolic letter to the junta vice president, seeking monetary compensation from the members of the old town council who had kept him unjustly in jail. Fully immersed in the patriot rhetoric of liberty against despotism, he ranted against the former junta: "Buenaventura Pérez, resident and property owner of this town, master maker of gunpowder, . . . says that during the previous government, formed by the oppressors of this town's liberty, I was denounced by a satellite of the Spanish tyrants of the town council, and sent to prison by the obdurate Don Nicolás Pérez, the selfish Don Tomás Gartero, the haughty Don Ignacio Camacho, supporters of the greed and tyranny of the barbarian and schemer president of the old junta."[11] After adding up all the economic damages he had suffered, he reminded the new republican magistrate that "he [the magistrate] had been sent by the supreme government of Santa Fé . . . to administer justice to all the patriots oppressed by their mandarin despots."[12]

Pérez's letter illustrates how he worked to take full advantage of the new political situation. He began by validating his place in the new body politic, his status as a *vecino* (townsman) with property and a profession—the new requirements for enjoying active citizenship. He used revolutionary rhetoric to impugn the social authority of his enemies, accusing them of pride, barbarism, despotism, and greed— all alleged characteristics of the despised Spanish enemy. Finally, he advanced the notion that being a virtuous although humble patriot was more important than being a prominent *vecino* with royalist inclinations.

As can be expected, the members of the old town council used a very different tactic in their defense, appealing not to patriotism and justice, like Pérez, but to the social order. They referred to the new political system only to confirm their allegiance to it. They reminded the junta that they had taken an oath to the constitution and that as good, honorable, and useful citizens who contributed with their patrimony to the state, they enjoyed the protection of the supreme government in Bogotá. Choosing to emphasize Pérez's low condition and unbecoming behavior, they argued that he could not have written the legal suit alone, that somebody important must have been supporting him. Yet the inventory of his property shows not only a book but, more important, an inkwell.[13] They portrayed Pérez's conduct as disruptive and potentially dangerous. His attempts to use the law against them were merely a sign of "his usual pretentious character." Calling his suit libelous, they declared that, if he was "not stopped in time," he would "continue insulting people of honor, stirred up by the support of his followers."[14] The former junta members thus sought to transform Pérez's long struggle for justice into a mere sign of the passionate and dangerous nature of somebody who did not know his place. Their letters reveal profound indignation that Pérez had not only escaped punishment but had managed to put them on the defensive against the new authorities, who were taking his accusations seriously.[15]

Initially, Pérez seemed to have won. The new junta declared the president of the old junta guilty of subjecting Pérez to an illegal trial and responsible for covering his court costs.[16] However, the former *cabildo* president appealed to Bogotá's judicial authorities, who annulled the decision of the Honda judge and released the previous junta president from any economic responsibility.[17] Although Pérez did not have all his grievances addressed, the new authorities were clearly treating him differently from the old ones. His trial revealed that patriotism was now more important than social status in determining a person's position. Pérez probably gained enormous satisfaction when the old town council was deposed and found guilty, while he was freed and declared innocent. So far, events seemed to prove that justice was now administered more fairly.

Pérez was not alone in his belief that the new system would curb elite abuses. A few years later, in 1819, Juan José Mexia shouted to his neighbors in Camarones, "Long live the patria; now, boys, your backs will no longer suffer the lash of Juan Gutiérrez."[18] Like 1810, 1819 was a turbulent year in which power was rapidly changing hands. The royalists had controlled New Granada since 1816, but now the tide was turning in favor of the patriot army. According to his neighbors, Mexia had signed up with the patriot troops when General Gregor MacGregor briefly captured the city of Rio Hacha earlier that year. He then became an ardent advocate of the new system, voicing his beliefs to anybody who cared to listen. One witness said that Mexia had told him, "We will be relieved; we won't be oppressed like we were under the old government."[19] Another said that Mexia had declared, "*Compadre*, it's about time I get even for all they've done to me and despotically [con despotiquez] taken away from me in the name of the king."[20]

The documents do not specify the grievances of Juan José Mexia, a forty-four-year-old peasant, although we can infer that he resented the rule of Juan Gutiérrez, who was probably a local boss. Yet his words are quite telling in another way: they reveal the familiarity that peasants such as Mexia had with patriot language and terminology. Mexia closely followed patriot dichotomies that distinguished between a despotic colonial past and a republican future free of injustice and oppression. He did not merely repeat patriot slogans, however: not only was his language very colloquial, but, more important, he adapted broad patriot concepts to his local concerns, in particular his anger toward the regional boss.

Seven years later, in 1826—two years after the end of the wars in South America—an artisan from the city of Honda appealed to the central authorities, denouncing the persistence of despotic Spanish practices in his city. Although the wars were definitely over, the nature of social and political relations in the new republic was as uncertain as it had been during the First Republic. Frustrated by the situation, Cornelio Ortiz, who described himself as a poor but honest shoemaker, decided to "complain constitutionally against Mr. Ponce for beating him" during public festivities in the plaza of San Francisco.[21] The events were simple. When Cornelio Ortiz walked by the entrance of a house where Dr. Ponce, a local judge, and his wife were watching the festivities, Mrs. Ponce's dog tried to bite him, and he defended himself with a stick. Mrs. Ponce found this highly impertinent and complained to her husband, who went after Ortiz and beat him with his club until it broke. As a result, Ortiz had to endure many days recovering in bed.

Ortiz could have accepted his beating with resignation, learning his lesson of being careful not to offend powerful men, but he did not. In the shifting political and social landscape of the early republican period, Ortiz's appeal to the central authorities tested the issue of whether local authorities could treat artisans however they wished, with impunity. In arguing his case, Ortiz skillfully used the early republican nationalist rhetoric that proclaimed the arrival of a new era of equality and justice. He flattered the central government for its justice, saying that he had kept silent for a few days, doubting whether local authorities had the right to use violence against the citizens under the new system. Having learned that similar excesses had already been punished, however, he had decided to exercise his constitutional rights and protest the abuse.[22] He further characterized Spanish rule as tyrannical and despotic. Ponce's despotism, he said, "was a natural element of his peninsular character."[23] Because of him, justice had not yet arrived in Honda, where he controlled the town council and people were afraid of antagonizing him. Ortiz himself had been coerced into signing a false declaration. Justice could only be achieved if the central government took charge of the case. Fittingly, Ortiz ended his letter by protesting the acts of "violence and oppression" to which he had been subjected. He asked the central authorities to protect the rights of "honest citizens," on which "Colombia's public health depended."[24]

Ortiz, like Pérez and Mexia, hoped that the new republic would curb abuses of power by the local elite, that his new citizen status would free him from the lashes of local bosses. And at first, the new republican authorities seemed to fulfill these expectations. Although the records do not tell us how Ortiz's case ended, the prosecutor did side with Ortiz. Citing the new law regulating complaints against public officials, he demanded Ponce's suspension and requested his presence in the capital.

Slave or Citizen?

If for some *pardos* the Wars of Independence represented the possibility of fulfilling an old desire for justice, for many slaves they opened new avenues to achieving their freedom. Some slaves took advantage of the royalist and patriot armies' policy of freeing slaves who joined them; others took advantage of contemporary political chaos to run away.[25] The case of the slave Tomas Aguirre, alias Tomasico, illustrates how the Wars of Independence had altered power relations between slaves and their owners, forcing slaves to adapt their political strategies to the new revolutionary times.[26]

From the beginning of the independence conflict, Tomasico's political behavior was determined by his desire for freedom. During the turmoil caused by the wars, he revolted with the slaves from his hacienda and ran away to the mountains nearby. He then allied himself with royalist troops and, in 1816, helped to take the city of Honda by surprise, capturing two patriot captains and delivering them to the royalist army. The Spanish then rewarded Tomasico with his freedom.[27] Like many other slaves from New Granada, forced to choose between the king's troops and the creole forces, he sided with the king.[28] This strategy was quite understandable, considering that the king was traditionally seen a source of justice vis-à-vis local slave owners.[29] Moreover, during the first years of the wars, it likely made more sense to slaves to trust the king's ability to free them, rather than that of the insurgent army. Throughout the rest of the wars, Tomasico and the slaves he had escaped with remained in control of the hacienda, removed from political developments. They never supported the patriot army, yet the patriot victory involved political changes that Tomasico could not ignore.

Once the wars were over, a new owner cheaply bought the worthless hacienda and its insubordinate slaves, who, according to the opinion of the local elite, "besides being evil, continually express their hatred and enmity to the whites."[30] Witnesses reported them singing "blacks on top, whites below," testifying that they had never served anyone willingly. The recognized leader of these slaves was Tomasico. Both he and the new owner of the hacienda were fully aware of the crucial importance of their initial steps toward each other and toward the other slaves; these first moves would determine who would dominate the hacienda. The instability brought by the long years of war gave Tomasico considerable weapons in negotiating with the new owner, who tried to gain the slaves' favor with philanthropic tactics, summoning all the slaves and holding a lottery, the two winners receiving their freedom. Tomasico refused to attend this ceremony, probably because it would have entailed recognizing the new owner's authority and renouncing the freedom he had gained while fighting for the Spanish. He decided instead to negotiate his own freedom individually. In contrast to the conciliatory liberal and nationalist language he would later use with the government, he now requested that his owner recognize his freedom as he held a machete in his hands. Cunningly, his owner neither accepted nor refused this demand. He instead wrote a certificate of freedom that the overseer would give Tomasico if he behaved faithfully and peacefully for one year—a clever tactic, since this acknowledged leader's faithful behavior would reestablish order and discipline on the hacienda. Tomasico, however, did not comply. He continued to encourage acts of disobedience among the slaves and stole the certificate of freedom from the overseer, an act that eventually landed him in jail.[31] On one of his trips to Honda, the governor of Mariquita imprisoned him in the military garrison.

Tomasico's wife, a free woman, took his case to court.[32] The establishment of a new republican system had radically affected Tomasico's and his wife's understanding of freedom. While fighting for the king, Tomasico had seen the possibility of freedom as either a special reward for his services or the de facto result of running away. This was freedom within a slave society. However, the new republican era changed this concept radically. Now the dominant abolitionist political discourse considered slavery a momentary but necessary evil, incompatible with a modern and civilized nation such as Colombia—an evil that would soon end.[33] Since Tomasico's owner could not openly oppose this liberal philanthropic rhetoric, he chose a different strategy. He asked respectable citizens to testify regarding Tomasico's well-known rebellious character and his enmity toward whites. One after the other, members of the elite complied.[34]

In his petition to Congress, however, Tomasico (or his lawyer) took full advantage of the new political language. Tomasico argued in defense of his rights as a citizen, demanding that the central government stand by its principles of liberty and equality. He denounced the fact that he had been taken prisoner by the military for running away as an affront to his personal guarantees as a citizen and a free man.[35] Gone forever in his rhetoric were the rights of owners to take the law into their own hands; gone forever were the differences between libertos and white men. This rhetoric proved successful with the commission that examined Tomasico's case; it determined that his owner's arbitrary acts had transgressed his rights as a citizen.[36] While the documents are silent about the case's final outcome, ending with Congress's decision to send the case back to the Supreme Court, the conflict powerfully demonstrates the extent to which the wars had affected power relations. The elite's coercive power had greatly diminished, and a new liberal ideology had shaken their traditional legitimacy. Power relations now had to be renegotiated, and nobody knew with certainty how this would happen or what the outcome might be.

A *Seditious* Pardo *Justice*

On May 22, 1822, Esteban Sampayo, a resident of Majagual, a small town in the province of Cartagena, wrote to the provincial authorities warning them against the new justice (*alcalde de segunda nominación*), Valentín Arcia, who allegedly harbored a "criminal aversion toward whites."[37] According to Sampayo, Arcia had gone so far as to state that "the war [for independence] will never end because a new and bloodier war against the whites will start, just as it had in Guarico [Haiti], and he eagerly waited for that moment to join in the fight against them."[38] Arcia, Sampayo continued, had set himself the task of fracturing the union, peace, and tranquility in which the town had lived. If he was not stopped, "the government would be attacked, its laws trampled, and homes condemned to bitter mourning."[39]

Arcia, the object of these serious accusations, was a successful thirty-one-year-old *pardo* carpenter who, as a small merchant, sometimes traveled from his hometown of Majagual to Popayán, in the far south. He was married with children and had recently been elected justice of Majagual. As such, he enjoyed political power over local rich white *vecinos*, and he expected to be treated as their social equal. Arcia was also concerned with national policy and was fond of writing about political issues.

Yet things did not flow as placidly as he may have wished. As a representative of the state, he enforced military recruitment and faced lower-class desertion, but as a *pardo* mayor and carpenter, he confronted the hostility of the local elite. Indeed, from 1822 to 1824, the white elite of Majagual and the nearby town of Algarrobo simultaneously accused Arcia of promoting a race war and exceeding his power as an *alcalde* (judge) in his attempt to enforce enlistment. His predicament illustrates the political culture surrounding literate *pardo* artisans, revealing the various meanings that such terms as *republicanism* and *independence* acquired among competing class and race interests and showing how the threat of race war was used in local conflicts.

In May 1822, Valentín Arcia went to the house of another town council member to discuss some administrative matters. Perhaps proud of his latest written work—a dialogue between a *pardo* mayor and a *labrador* (peasant)—he decided to read it at the gathering. According to Arcia, this dialogue was based on a real conversation that had taken place between himself and a local peasant. It therefore offers a rare opportunity for understanding the concerns of small landowners and peasants at the end of the independence wars. Although written by a republican official, the dialogue at moments becomes a harsh denunciation of postwar conditions, describing how the decline in commerce had increased the town's hardships. The *labrador* protests government requisitions and military conscription. The *alcalde* complains of the difficulties he confronts as a humble craftsman made justice; his poverty prompts people to accuse him of charging the fees attached to his position with unusual exactitude. Finally, both lament the degree of inequality to which people of color are still subjected. While the man who denounced Arcia claimed he had threatened "a new and bloodier war against the whites," the witnesses' depositions, including Arcia's, indicate that Arcia's words were a bit less threatening. He had only said, "If people of his rank are as ill-treated in the rest of Colombia as they are in Majagual, God forbid, a new war against the whites may start."[40] Nevertheless, this dialogue prompted Sampayo's accusation. Arcia was arrested, and a trial that would last three years began.

Arcia's denunciation of racial discrimination—"contempt toward *pardos*"—was thus immediately linked to race war. Arguably, this panicked reaction was representative of a postwar environment in which elites felt a novel sense of social vulnerability and some *pardos* felt a new sense of empowerment that allowed them to express their concerns openly. In his letter to the judicial authorities, Arcia argued that his enemies had criminalized what was only an informal conversation. Apparently, far from promoting race war, he had merely intended to denounce racial discrimination and warn the local elite of the danger of continuing with such unrepublican practices. He claimed that the elite had criminalized his innocent conversation only because they were "uncomfortable with having him as a judge and being under his command, because he belonged to the class of *pardos*."

Indeed, the records of the trial reveal a long conflict between Arcia and members of the local elite over Arcia's role as an official. According to Arcia, they disliked him simply because he had attacked their corrupt practices. Mayor Acevedo disliked Arcia because he had put an end to his practice of taking bribes. The town treasurer disliked him because he had refused to falsify a certificate to free a deserter. Esteban Sampayo, his accuser, and his nephew opposed him because they disliked lending their property for government use. The vicar of a nearby town supported Arcia's version. According to him, Arcia had won enemies because since he had tried to enforce the laws of the Republic. His zeal sharply contrasted with the practices of the traditional elite, who disliked the new system and often refused to publicize the orders of the central government. These accusations of corruption sound all too familiar, fitting with what is known about local cliques and corruption in colonial times. It is likely that the Majagual elite had been waiting for an occasion to get rid of Arcia, an outsider, a *pardo*, who had taken his political authority too seriously.

As can be expected, elite accounts of the conflict were quite different. They presented Arcia's actions as proof of his antagonism toward whites. If Arcia had jailed a white man, this was not because he had broken the law but because Arcia hated him just for being white and wanted to humiliate him by sending him to jail, escorted by two armed soldiers. Similarly, when Arcia publicly rebuked two male members of the white elite for ignoring his demand that the entire town gather after mass, they described this as an excessive humiliation that could only derive from Arcia's racial animosity.

There was more at stake in this conflict, however, than the efforts of an elite clique to use race war as a pretext to rid itself of an overzealous official. The language of race war was not just a pretext but a sign of how much social relations seemed to have changed. It is probably no coincidence that the examples forwarded to prove Arcia's criminality centered on his use of symbols of authority. The power to wield such traditional symbols as the ability to summon people to the plaza, the use of state military force, and the right to rebuke and humiliate individuals in public was now in the hands of a *pardo* carpenter and could be used against the white elite. At stake, then, were the meaning and implications of revolutionary change for social and racial relations in Majagual.

Yet from Arcia's perspective, social relations in Majagual had not changed enough. When he read his dialogue and complained of the ill treatment people of his "class" received in Majagual, whites responded by asking what more they could possibly want than to have a *pardo* justice. Yet Arcia's discontent was not based on limits placed on his political ambition: he was a justice, which was one of the highest available local positions. Rather, his complaints reveal that he aspired to nothing less than being recognized as a social equal by the white creoles; he expected to receive the honorable social treatment that until then had been the sole prerogative of the white elite. Men of African descent had been excluded from colonial notions of honor, based on nobility, legitimacy, and whiteness—characteristics that were supposed to determine a person's character and conduct. *Pardos* were tainted by slavery and by the illegitimacy that colonial society associated with people of mixed descent. For this reason, *pardos* like Arcia embraced republican notions of honor that privileged merit and virtue over birth and race.[41] The conflict between Arcia and the white elite, therefore, tested the question of whether or not *pardos* would be entitled to honorable treatment and status. Arcia took offense when wellborn white women highlighted his humble origins, denying him the polite treatment appropriate to a gentleman. He mentioned with bitterness one instance when a white woman had not offered him a

chair in a social meeting she was hosting. Likewise, Arcia strongly resented elite attempts to undermine his right to wield power like any
white official.

Despite his disenchantment, however, Arcia remained a convinced
supporter of the new republican system. Indeed, the prosecutor, members of the local elite, and Arcia did agree on one thing: under the
new system, people like Arcia had gained tangible benefits impossible
under Spanish rule. But the elite feared the supposed radicalism of
Arcia's republicanism. Both Arcia's support for the new government
and his radicalism can be seen in his proclamation exhorting the people of Majagual to be good patriots and enlist in the army:

> Awaken Majagualeños; don't be lethargic.
> Be aware, he who has enemies, should not sleep. . . .
> There is no place for despotism anywhere in Colombia;
> *Americanos* with their bayonets must root it out.
> The tyrant's yoke shall not be seen in Majagual;
> Otherwise, you can expect
> a deserved death on our doorstep.[42]

Arcia's proclamation sought to reach those Majagualeños who did
not share his republican convictions—those for whom the Republic
meant little. The war, with its economic and human suffering, was
their real concern. Their solution—to run to the wilderness and pru-
dently wait for a Spanish or American final victory—was what Arcia
lamented in his proclamation: "You fill yourselves with confidence;
you say I have always run to the hills to avoid serving Colombia. . . .
Some people will say: Men, let's take things easy, step by step. Maybe
the present government will not last, and then we will have a hard time
with the Spanish. I believe, sirs, that all these people are wrong."[43]

Although his obvious intention was to recruit soldiers for the republican army, the proclamation's violent tone seemed too dangerous

for a *pardo* mayor. A rumor spread among whites that Arcia was trying to organize the colored classes against them, revealing the elites' fear of the potential political ramifications of having a *pardo* invested with authority. Indeed, the man who denounced him explicitly mentioned the power that Arcia had acquired as a representative of the state, fearing his influence among others of the *pardo* class. In Arcia's hands, acts of political zeal and authority became acts of disruption and disorder.

Eventually, however, Arcia was set free. The judicial authorities in Bogotá believed that he had not intended sedition and that the three years he had spent in jail waiting to be tried served as more than enough punishment for whatever strong words he may have uttered. Clearly, if for one section of the population the establishment of a republican government was inconsequential, for others it meant real change. The elite faced the possibility of being governed by a *pardo* craftsman "with no more means of subsistence than his tools."[44] The lower classes saw that they might be governed by one of their own. At stake in Arcia's trial was how much further these changes would go— whether the "Arcias" of New Granada would have to be satisfied with a bit of political power, without its correspondent economic power and social recognition, or whether conflicts would escalate to the point of race war. At the time, either option seemed possible.

Arcia's trial also illustrates the construction of a new republican discourse of social disruption. In their condemnation of Arcia, the local elite and Cartagena's prosecutor used novel republican and nationalist notions to transform his racial grievances into antipatriotic acts. Sampayo's letter of denunciation presented Arcia as a promoter of factions that sought to disrupt the harmony (*maridaje*) in which the town had lived until that moment. In his interrogation, Cartagena's prosecutor reminded Arcia of the benefits that the new system provided to people like him, scolding him for protesting against the government's requisitions. He told Arcia that instead of complaining, he should use his writing to explain the need to make sacrifices for independence, which would guarantee people of his background (*calidad*) freedom and equality. He reminded Arcia that the Spanish had confirmed in their constitution their intention to keep *pardos* in their previous state of "abjection" and "nullity." Since Arcia could not be a royalist, the prosecutor concluded, his lack of support for the new government could only derive from his desire to destroy public order by promoting racial conflict. Thus, the patriotic rhetoric of harmony and equality that had helped secure the support of *pardos* was now being used against Arcia. His denunciation of racial discrimination was transformed into an unpatriotic and ungrateful promotion of social division, an act of sedition.

A Senator under Trial

At forty-four, Remigio Márquez, a *pardo* colonel from Santa Marta, may have felt proud of his long and prestigious military and political career. From the early days of the patriot movement, he had occupied positions of responsibility. During the First Republic, he had served as an elector, a prefect of the convention, and a senator. Following the Spanish reconquest, he had suffered exile in Jamaica but continued to support the patriot cause, helping other patriot exiles, contributing to the financing of military expeditions, and sponsoring the printing and distribution of patriot literature.[45] Later, in 1822, the republican government appointed him general commander of the city of Mompox. The available documents provide little information about his personal life, although we know that he was a widower. The only outside description of his personality comes from a witness who described his "majestic tone of voice, which he always uses, even in the banquets destined for enjoyment."[46] Another personally revealing description comes from his own account of his political conflicts and life in Mompox, in which he writes of reading the work of Benjamin Constant in the peace of his home.[47] We know that before the Revolution, he was a pharmacist in the city of Santa Marta.[48] And we can infer that when the Revolution began, he was a man of some property because he mentions owning houses in Cartagena and Santa Marta and was able to contribute funds to the patriot cause. His wealth probably explains why he obtained important political positions during the First Republic. Márquez's wealth and education presumably made the creole elite comfortable enough to include him in their circles of power, as he was less likely to threaten their social and political control. Significantly, when Cartagena became divided between Piñeristas and Toledistas during the First Republic, he sided with the creole elite. Yet none of these factors would save him from the elite's eventual political hostility. In 1823, Márquez was accused of sedition, the subversion of public order, and the promotion of conflict between citizens and was subjected to a much-publicized trial before Congress.

When Remigio Márquez arrived as its new general commander, Mompox was the most important city of the lower Magdalena. It was the center of all commerce between the coast and the highlands, and as such it housed a rich merchant elite who profited from legal—and more often illegal—commerce. Its strategic location on the Magdalena River also made it a gathering place for ten thousand *bogas*—free colored boatmen—who enjoyed a large degree of mobility. Their travels allowed them access to news from the coast and the highlands, and, unlike other lower-class mobile men such as sailors and soldiers, they were not subject to a disciplinary regime. They were known for their unruliness and opposition to regimented labor; their desertion was a common problem with which travelers had to contend.[49] Again and again, the government tried to pass legislation that would discipline these boatmen, almost always unsuccessfully. In 1823, the interior minister asked Congress to pass severe laws to control the *bogas*.[50] Nevertheless, the boatmen did not change their "corrupt" habits, and the issue was again presented to the Senate in 1827.[51] Mompox was also the home of many artisans, mostly *pardos*, some of whom had made the city famous for its craftwork in precious metals. At the bottom rung of society were the slaves who worked in the city and on the nearby haciendas. The artisans and boatmen had actively participated in the patriot conspiracies of 1810 and 1819, and when the patriots took control of the national government, they used the laws of the Republic to refuse to pay a traditional colonial tax, the *real de navegación*, arguing it had not been instituted by Congress.[52]

One year after his appointment, Remigio Márquez was simultaneously accused of illegally confiscating merchants' property, attacking people of honor, fomenting racial division, and promoting disobedience toward the government.[53] According to his opponents, Márquez had ignored the legal and constitutional rights of local merchants, who had seen their property confiscated without any respect for legal procedures. In addition, they accused him of stealing merchandise.[54] As in most port cities in Spanish America, smuggling was a common practice in Mompox, and powerful merchant and political cliques had formed around it.[55] Apparently, Márquez, familiar with traditional smuggling practices, had used a strong hand to control them.

Had Márquez been white, this would be just another case of conflict over contraband between a local merchant clique and a government official. However, because he was a *pardo*, issues of race war and social control overshadowed the initial dispute. Márquez, after a long and prestigious military career, found himself confronting grave accusations of sedition. Clearly, more than contraband was at stake. "All respectable men have suffered some vexation from Márquez," his opponents lamented.[56] They seemed particularly upset at having a *pardo* governing them, controlling and disrupting their longstanding practices. His attack on smuggling was thus constructed as racial enmity, a manifestation of his seditious intent to promote racial division, anarchy, and disorder. Márquez's opponents went so far as to accuse him of sowing "discord and chaos and drawing attention to the existence of *pardos* and whites" in a city that had previously been characterized by "peace and fraternal union."[57] According to military reports, Márquez's government had bestowed far too many liberties on the populace; under his rule, Mompox had become a place of "insolence and licentious-ness."[58] Its inhabitants, the reports continued, had grown accustomed to "weak governmental indulgence" and were under the assumption that "they could serve the government as they saw fit."[59]

Márquez vehemently rejected the accusations, arguing that they were simply part of a conspiracy against him. He defended himself by asserting that he had only protected the interests of the Republic by forcing local merchants to pay all their taxes and proving that he had not stolen any merchandise. These false accusations, he declared, had been constructed by his enemies, who wanted to tarnish his name and rid themselves of his irritating presence. Márquez presented numer-ous reference letters from members of the Mompox *cabildo* and other regional authorities, praising his loyalty to the Republic and his law-abiding nature.[60] He managed to gather enough evidence of his inno-cence to convince Congress of his version. He was declared innocent, the victim of a group of conspirators who wanted to destroy his repu-tation because of his zeal in attacking smuggling.[61]

Even if the accusations against Márquez were mere machinations, as they seem to have been, the question remains of the extent to which they reflected racial conflict in Mompox. The elite accusations failed to acknowledge any degree of lower-class autonomy, providing few descriptions of the political characteristics and aspirations of the lower class. Yet it is necessary to ask whether threats of race war resulted from the adherence of some local *pardos* to radical racial and republican ideas. Having a *pardo* as the city's highest authority might have had an impact on local *pardos*—the *bogas* and artisans mentioned earlier; having a *pardo* in command of their city might easily have shaped their perception of the nature of the new republican government.

Indeed, although Marquez's opponents presented him as the sole cause of local disruptions, when a commandant more sympathetic to the interests of the local elite replaced Márquez in April 1823, social control did not improve. To the surprise of military officers, Mompox's populace continued to be ungovernable. One of the first manifestations of lower-class unruliness was their refusal to respond to calls for enlistment. In 1822, when a new royalist rebellion threatened the coastal city of Santa Marta, Márquez had managed to reorganize Mompox's military garrison, which he had found in ruins. He had trained a three-hundred-man militia and armed five war *bongos* (riverboats).[62] The new authorities, in comparison, were not so successful. To the dismay of military officials, only government employees and merchants responded to their calls for enlistment; perfectly able-bodied men continued to walk the streets without fear of the authorities. According to the new military authorities, the impunity enjoyed by the masses under Márquez had made them "bold and criminal."[63] However, enforcing enlistment was not simple. Mild methods—giving special privileges to enlisted Momposinos, promising that they would not be taken away from their region and that their service would not last for more than one month —met with little success. Coercion also failed. When a military patrol attempted to impose itself on the lower-class Barrio de Abajo neighborhood, it was ejected with stones and machete blows. The government found it impossible to get into a neighborhood where "neither political judge, nor military commandant, nor anybody else is obeyed." Moreover, the military officers feared that stronger military presence and repression would only result in people fleeing to the wilderness.[64]

When Márquez returned to Mompox in May, on his way to the Senate in Bogotá, opposition to military enlistment apparently escalated to new levels. According to military reports, Márquez's arrival provoked "disorder and anarchy among the lower classes [*pueblo bajo*]."[65] Every night, members of the "lowest class" (*última clase*) visited Márquez, playing drums on the doorstep of his house. Every night, masked men strolled in the streets; every morning, threatening anonymous broadsides for and against Márquez appeared on the walls. One of these broadsides has survived, providing a splendid and rare example of the unofficial political imaginary of the times.

The tone of this broadside, the military report complained, was typical:

> Señor juez político[:]
>
> Won't you tell me why the broadsides have not continued? Well, I'll tell you.
>
> It is because the damn whites learned . . . that the people want Mr. Márquez, and they fear the chop of the machete.
>
> You don't want Mr. Márquez to be the political judge because it deprives you of rum. Mr. Robledo doesn't want to leave his command because his robbing the troops would cease. . . . In the end, you will all be screwed because blood will run like in Saint-Domingue.[66]

> Señor juez político[:]
>
> No me dirá usted porque no han seguido los pasquines? Pues yo se lo diré.
>
> Es porque han sabido los blanquitos de mierda . . . que la gente quiere al Sr. Márquez y temen que ande el machete carájo.
>
> Usted no quiere que el Sr. Márquez sea juez político porque se le quita la chupadera de aguardiente. El Sr. Robledo no quiere cortar el mando porque se le quita el robo con la tropa. . . . al fin Vs se han de joder porque correrá sangre como en Santo Domingo.

How should we interpret this broadside and the complaints about Momposino unruliness? A closer reading of the available documentation suggests that descriptions of disorder and race war simplified and negated a complex conflict over local political rule.

It is notable that, as the broadside claims, the "people wanted" Márquez. It is possible that lower-class support of Márquez expressed a strong view on how the new republican authorities should rule. Members of the lower classes may have identified with a *pardo* governor who participated in their dances (*tamboras*). Márquez's political power may have symbolized the claimed end of racial discrimination proclaimed by the Republic. Márquez, however, insisted that his popularity was not based on his race but on the fact that the people had enjoyed "the delights of a liberal government" under his rule.[67] For him, the *tamboras* were not a sign of unruliness but a joyous expression of popular support. The people may have indeed approved Márquez's style of administration: the broadside applauded his confrontation of elite corruption, accusing the new military commander, Robledo, of robbing the troops. The lower classes no doubt also approved of Márquez's leniency: government officials, complaining that the masses had grown accustomed to "a weak governmental indulgence," stated that they were "under the assumption they could serve the government according to their own free will." Momposinos presumably did interpret the new republican liberty as granting them the right to live under a government that did not control but was controlled by the populace. It may not be too far-fetched to conclude that Márquez's government actually was—or at least was believed to be—different. Marquez, after all, was a revolutionary, a *pardo* who had suffered exile and sacrificed his property for the Revolution. Like Bolívar and other patriots, he could have embraced the revolutionary ideology identified with his career, and this characteristic may easily have affected the way he ruled.

The broadside also illustrates the importance of talk of race war in local politics. In addition to insulting whites and threatening them with the machete, it also made explicit reference to repeating the violence of the Haitian Revolution. More than a simple oddity, this reference reveals the importance of race-war images in general, and Haitian images in particular, in the contemporary popular imaginary. This is not to say that Márquez promoted race war. On the contrary, he unceasingly denied such charges, accusing his opponents of merely using them as a tactic to get rid of him. Still, talk of race war had become a recurrent element in conflicts between *pardos* and local elites over the meaning of revolutionary change during the early decades of the republican era. The conflict over Márquez's rule was thus part of a larger struggle over the concrete implications of revolutionary change in Mompox. His position as the town's principal authority represented the fulfillment of the revolutionary promise of legal racial equality. If, in addition, his government was felt to provide greater justice to the lower classes, the promise of ending despotism was also seen to be fulfilled. *Pardos*, therefore, may have interpreted the elites' attacks on Márquez as a rejection of republican justice and equality. Faced with the white elite's unwillingness to accept republican changes, some of them perhaps found comfort in language that played with the possibility of continuing the war to the point of abolishing not only Spanish but also white rule. On the other hand, the elite found in the language of race war a way to express their distress at seeing public authority in *pardos*' hands. Márquez's defense even suggested that his opponents had written the broadside to tarnish his name. Regardless of its author, it makes clear the importance of the language of race war in expressing social tension between *pardos* and the elite.

This tactic would continue to haunt Marquez. When news of his appointment as military commander of the city of Santa Marta arrived in Cartagena in 1831, the local authorities again used the threat of race war to express their discomfort. Manuel Romay wrote to Vice President Domingo Caicedo that "he saw much risk in that resolution; because of his natural inclination and his position of power." Márquez, he continued, "was proud and domineering, particularly among the good families, all of which, along with some aspirations among people of color, leads me to conclude that Márquez could cause great prejudices."[68] Regardless of his personal political conduct and loyalty, then, Márquez's mere presence as a *pardo* authority made him threatening.

Constitutionalism and Racial Equality

In 1828, Admiral José Prudencio Padilla, a *pardo* sailor who had become a general during the Wars of Independence, was one of the most influential men in Cartagena.[69] As a man with power and prestige, he corresponded with the most important men in the country, including Francisco de Paula Santander and Simón Bolívar. Moreover, he could count on the political support of Cartagena's lower classes, in particular the *pardo* neighborhood of Getsemaní. During the 1826 elections in the city of Cartagena, Padilla contributed to the success of Santander's candidacy for reelection as vice president.[70] According to contemporary descriptions, Padilla was a tall and imposing man who liked to dress well. Although generous and sociable, he was an implacable enemy who did not forget an affront.[71] A French traveler described him as a demagogue like Danton, a powerful Homeric figure.[72]

Padilla's career provides an example of the possibilities opened by the revolutionary wars for *pardos'* social and political advancement—and the tensions and conflicts caused by these advancements. Padilla also exemplifies the contact that numerous coastal *pardos* engaged in maritime activities may have had with the Atlantic revolutions. Born in the port city of Río Hacha, Padilla became a cabin boy in the Spanish Royal Navy in 1792, when he was fourteen years old. Eventually, he managed to become a boatswain, a high position for a *pardo*. In 1805, he participated in the Battle of Trafalgar and was taken prisoner by the English. Padilla remained in England until the peace of 1808, when he returned to Cartagena. By this time, his travels had no doubt made him familiar with stories of the French Revolution, the Haitian Revolution, and English abolitionism.

During Cartagena's first independence movement, Padilla supported the patriots, gaining recognition for his military talents as a sailor.[73] In 1815, after the fall of Cartagena, he took refuge in the Haitian port of Les Cayes, later returning with Bolívar to continue the fight for independence, thanks to the support of President Alexandre Pétion.[74] In 1821, he played an important part in the patriot siege of Cartagena.[75] In 1822, he was elected senator of Colombia. He reached the peak of his military career when he became a national hero for his decisive role in the 1823 republican victory at Maracaibo, for which he was awarded the prestigious title of Benemérito de la Patria. In

1824, he was back in Cartagena as commander of the navy. In spite of his successes, however, or perhaps because of them, Padilla was soon subjected to scorn and suspicion. Already in 1822, the commander general of Cartagena, Mariano Montilla, was trying to get rid of him, accusing him of favoring radicals and stirring up the "*zambos of Getzemaní*," who were now requesting his appointment as commander general of Cartagena.[76] This was a sore issue: Padilla enjoyed more popularity and at least as much military glory as Montilla, a white Venezuelan. As in the First Republic, the divisions between radical patriots and their elite enemies reflected conflicts over the extent of racial and social changes. At stake was not only whether *pardos* like Padilla would be granted the same promotions as their elite counterparts but whether they would also be granted the same honorable treatment.

Between 1823 and 1824, Padilla's honor was attacked two more times. As in Justice Arcia's case, colonial notions of honor excluded men of African descent, who were considered tainted by slavery and illegitimacy. Colonial concepts of honor further tainted *pardo* women, who, like most lower-class women at the time, tended to live in free unions, unable to conform to notions of honor that prized sexual purity and marriage.[77] Padilla challenged all of these notions. Separated from his allegedly adulterous wife, he lived with Anita Romero, a *pardo* woman who was the daughter of Pedro Romero, a well-to-do artisan and one of the leaders of the independence movement. Padilla took personal offense when the rich merchant Juan de Francisco did not invite Anita Romero to a ball he was hosting. Such disrespect fitted with traditional relations between elite men and their *pardo* mistresses, which reinforced colonial racial hierarchies by dishonoring *pardo* women— excluded from the honorable role of legitimate wives—while keeping white men's honor intact. Men's honor was linked to their legitimate white wives and children; it was marriage to *pardo* women, not extramarital affairs, that dishonored them. Padilla and other radical republicans disrupted these hierarchies by granting *pardo* women the same status and treatment as elite women. Indeed, in a private letter to Santander, Montilla denounced marriage between elite men and *pardo* women as a sign of dangerous republicanism.[78] Moreover, Padilla's union with Anita Romero did not follow traditional hierarchies established between elite men and their mistress. Not only was she a *pardo* like Padilla, but she was also daughter and sister to two *pardo* republican leaders. Thus, according to traditional codes of honor, to dishonor her was to dishonor Pedro and Mauricio Romero. Padilla refuted the claim that Anita Romero had been excluded from the ball because of her illegitimate status as a mistress. According to him, she had not been invited because of her color: "Everybody knows the class to which she belongs, and the desire to humiliate and degrade this class has been the only intention of the paterfamilias."[79]

Padilla and Anita Romero's union was again subjected to public scorn in 1824, when an anonymous open letter denounced Padilla's "immoral" abandonment of his wife and cohabitation with another woman. Since his enemies were unable to attack Padilla's military prestige, they skillfully questioned his ability to behave in the traditionally honorable way expected of men with military and political power. Padilla defended himself by publishing a broadside addressed to "the Respectable Public of Cartagena," denouncing the aristocratic values of his enemies and appealing to modern notions of honor and virtue. According to Padilla, his enemies failed to comply with the republican value of equality; they wanted to degrade and attack the *pardo* class and restore the aristocratic dominion of the old families. Turning colonial notions of honor upside down, Padilla suggested that the old families should be ashamed of their past, not proud, because they were the descendants of "ferocious Spaniards" who had "accumulated riches through their atrocities against unfortunate Indians." While he had earned his position defending the fatherland, his enemies were indifferent to the Republic, if not treasonous. They wanted to "undermine the holy edifice of the people's freedom and equality" and "replace the republican ways with their old privileges and the exclusive domination of a small and miserable portion of families over the great majority of the peoples."[80] For Padilla, the elite attachment to traditional notions of honor and hierarchy was fundamentally antirepublican.

In 1828, the long-standing conflict between Padilla and Montilla escalated to new heights. At this time, Colombian politics gravitated around the Ocaña Convention, a constitutional congress in charge of replacing the 1821 Constitution. The country was divided in two blocs, as was the convention. The first, led by President Bolívar, believed that contemporary political problems were the result of the excessive liberalism of the 1821 Constitution and that a stronger state was needed. The second, led by Vice President Santander, opposed a powerful central government and wanted to further liberalize the 1821 Constitution.[81] As one of Cartagena's leading personalities, Padilla was expected to take sides in this debate. Doing so, however, was not easy: his correspondence with Santander and Bolívar reveals his futile attempts to reconcile the men.[82] He had served under Bolívar, whom he respected and admired. Yet he was not afraid to express to the Libertador his friendship for Santander and his dislike of the new constitutional project, an opinion that he would maintain until the end.

Nevertheless, events in Cartagena soon forced Padilla to choose a side. Cartagena's principal military and political authority, Padilla's rival General Mariano Montilla, was a firm supporter of the pro-Bolívar bloc. He had recently renounced his office as commander general in order to be eligible to serve as a deputy at the convention, but in spite of his power and prestige, he lost the local election. Montilla's defeat followed a national trend, pro-Bolívar candidates throughout the country losing to pro-Santander ones. In Cartagena, as elsewhere, the pro-Bolívar bloc reacted to their defeat with a campaign to thwart the success of the convention, writing *representaciones a la convención*—threats to the convention's elected representatives.

The tumult in Cartagena began on February 29, when a group of military men from the Tiradores battalion refused to sign the *representaciones a la convención*, asking Padilla for his protection. Padilla responded promptly and firmly in their defense. That night, he and his followers ran into their opponents at a café called Matosi, where they debated the problems and merits of the *representaciones* in front of a racially and socially mixed crowd. Argument soon led to insults and threats. Padilla and his followers called the anticonvention faction "servile, ambitious, and base" and made toasts with "hurrahs to the *liberales* and death to the *serviles*." Padilla offered his sword in defense of the convention and told his followers not to fear because he would use all his influence, and if necessary his life, to defend them from any retaliation.[83]

In the following days, tensions escalated throughout the city.[84] On March 5, local conflicts reached a turning point when the artillery battalion made explicit its opposition to both the convention and the pro-Santander bloc. They cheered the Libertador and declared "death to Santander," alarming local liberals, in particular writers and journalists, who tended to favor the convention. Faced with this blatantly anticonstitutional act, Padilla requested the resignation of the local commander general, who was a close ally of Montilla. Following the advice of other city officials to avoid further violence, the intendant agreed to replace the commander with the judge of the military court, who was a neutral figure.

When Montilla refused to recognize the new commander in chief, ordering local troops to secretly leave the city, events took an unexpected and radical turn.[85] With no government and no army in the city, Padilla asked the intendant to gather the population in the church of Saint Agustin, then proceeded to arm local men (of the lower classes, according to his enemies) to back up the militia. Padilla also went with Dr. Ignacio Muñoz, a local liberal, to Getsemaní, where he addressed the crowd and accepted the position of commander in chief. By not calling the town council to approve his nomination, Padilla shifted the center of power to Getsemaní, placing local sovereignty not in the hands of elected authorities but in control of local *pardos*.[86] The elite witnessed subsequent events with alarm: armed proconvention soldiers strolling in the streets, masked men appearing at night.

They were probably dismayed, too, to hear that Padilla had armed the artisan neighborhood of Getsemaní.[87] With local *pardos* armed and in charge of deposing and nominating local authorities, rumors of race war began to spread throughout the city, interweaving racial antagonism with the Bolívar-Santander constitutional conflict. In the subsequent criminal investigation, several witnesses reported having heard discussions about the possibility of massacring the whites. Although such testimony should be taken with caution, as it was given under the intimidating and perhaps threatening environment of a criminal investigation, it nevertheless reveals the political culture of the times. Regardless of the witnesses' veracity, they had to build on the available political imaginary. Both *pardos* and whites used the language of race war to express social and political tensions. One witness reported having overheard someone in a group of five to six persons, "whose clothes reveal their belonging to the people," saying that "this would be a good night to finish off the whites."[88] Another reported two corporals saying, "finishing off the whites is going to be necessary."[89] A Venezuelan *pardo* officer, Captain Ibarra, who had lived in Haiti and was considered by some white officers a danger to the city, had allegedly stated that "he feared that people would turn in the last resort to declaring war on the whites."[90] Although Padilla's followers supported liberal institutions, which they held to be the product of their efforts and sacrifice on the battlefield, it is possible that, for a sector of the *pardo* population, defending these institutions was not enough. Liberty could not be enjoyed as long as the whites were in power, and some aspired to establish a republic without whites. As two *pardo* soldiers were reported as saying during the unrest in Cartagena, "We ourselves had created the fatherland, we were its founders, but without destroying the whites, we would never enjoy our freedom."[91]

On March 8, Padilla left Cartagena. He had learned that Montilla intended to take control of the city, using a letter from Bolívar that authorized him to take command in cases of internal disruption. Padilla probably did not want be accused of rebellion or see his conflict with

Montilla transformed into an act of sedition against President Bolívar. He traveled to Mompox and Ocaña, writing letters to Bolívar, trying to present his version of events and obtain pardon. However, he did not succeed. In the eyes of Bolívar, always fearful of "pardocracy," Padilla's color, political stature, and ascendancy over the *pardos* of the Caribbean coast were too dangerous.

Padilla's political activities in defense of the convention, then, were quickly and effectively linked to rumors of race war. Further, he chose to oppose Bolívar's constitutional project, which most military men supported.[92] His behavior was thus set apart because of the tight interweaving of racial issues with the conflict between the pro-Santander and pro-Bolívar blocs. Divisions between the two groups over how to restructure the Colombian government were profound, ranging over a variety of topics, but at heart lay the fundamental issue of the central state's degree of power. The pro-Bolívar bloc favored centralism, a strong presidency, and a small congress. Some even toyed with monarchical ideas, while Bolívar himself advocated the institution of a life presidency. Although in favor of enlarging the franchise, they sought to control it by diminishing the number of electoral colleges and raising the property qualifications for electors. They considered themselves the party of order and stability and feared anarchy more than any other political problem. They labeled their opponents *exaltados*, Jacobins, demagogues, and anarchic. In contrast, the pro-Santander bloc distrusted a strong central state, arguing that it would easily lead to tyranny. They favored federalism, an elective and rotating presidency, and a strong Congress. They also favored wider enfranchisement, but their constitutional project lowered the property qualifications and increased the number of electoral colleges.[93] They called themselves liberals, labeling their opponents aristocrats, goths, *serviles*, and despots.[94]

Members of the pro-Bolívar, aristocratic bloc tended to belong to wealthy and powerful families from traditional regions that had enjoyed power and social recognition in the colonial era. They belonged to the social sector that had the most to lose from the breakdown of colonial hierarchies and the political incorporation of new social sectors. In contrast, members of the pro-Santander bloc tended to belong to the middle sectors of society, to regions beyond the colonial centers of power. They usually derived their political prominence from their participation in the struggle for independence and had unblemished republican credentials. Many members of the aristocratic faction, on the other hand, had been indifferent patriots, if not active opponents of independence, but had been raised to positions of power because of their education, wealth, and social prominence.[95]

The rivalry between Padilla and Montilla mirrored these broader divisions. The conflict between civilians and the military in Colombia —often phrased in terms of a regional antagonism between Granadinos and Venezuelans (who had tended to dominate the military)—has traditionally been explained in terms of elite prejudice toward men of obscure social origins who had risen to positions of power and prestige through their military careers in the patriot army.[96] This generalization, however, does not hold for Cartagena. Padilla was a *pardo* Granadino general who used nationalist civilian rhetoric against his Venezuelan white rival.[97] Montilla, a member of the Caracas white elite, linked his defense of the military to social control. Since the early days of the Revolution, he had distrusted patriot officers of obscure social origins, whom he saw as inclined to "robbery, murder, drunkenness, and disobedience," as the authors of all the "revolutions and disasters" in the army.[98] He believed in strong measures of social control that would restrain such men. A month after the events in Cartagena, he complained to Bolívar about the pernicious ideas that informed exalted passions in the city, suggesting the appointment of a harsh police judge (*juez de policía*) as a measure to restore peace and order in the city.[99]

Contemporary politics encoded the social and political differences between the pro-Santander and pro-Bolívar blocs into the aristocratic-Jacobin opposition that dominated much early republican discourse. At the Ocaña Convention, *liberales* often played the antiaristocratic card to combat their enemies—a tactic that earned Santander the epithet Mr. Égalite and his followers the label *sans-culottes*.[100] What probably attracted *pardos* like Padilla to the pro-Santander bloc was such powerful antiaristocratic rhetoric, which had been linked to racial equality since the days of the First Republic. This was not the first time Padilla had chosen to side with radicals: he had done the same during the earlier conflict between Piñeristas and Toledistas.[101] Revealing here is the fact that when Bolívar rejected General José Antonio Páez's suggestion that he follow Napoleon's example and crown himself, he used blacks' opposition as one of his arguments. According to Bolívar, "the height and brilliance of a throne would be frightful. Equality would be broken and the people of color would see all their rights lost to a new aristocracy."[102] Racial hierarchies belonged to the social divisions of the Old Regime, which emphasized origins over merit and virtue. Like other liberals, *pardos* like Padilla owed their political and social prominence to their service to the patriot cause. Moreover, *pardo* artisans, who had tended to side with patriots since the early days of the Republic, were more likely to have political influence if the number of electoral colleges was expanded and property qualifications lowered.

The actions of the pro-Santander block seemed to confirm the notion that radicals favored racial equality. At the Ocaña Convention, during discussions of Cartagena's tumults, radical liberals supported Padilla, reading aloud his self-defense. Francisco Soto, a radical liberal whom José Manuel Restrepo described as the most terrible demagogue, not only asked the convention to formally thank Padilla for his patriotic defense of republican institutions and accept his offer to defend the convention but also proposed a statue in his honor. Santander and most liberals accepted Soto's proposal. The convention, however, rejected this letter, voting for one that would only acknowledge receipt of Padilla's communication and approval of his sentiments toward the convention. The convention thus refused to take a stance on the crucial issue of whether Padilla was a defender of the institution or a lawless promoter of disorder.[103]

According to Montilla, Cartagena's *pardos* followed the convention's debates about Padilla with interest and felt reassured by liberal votes in his favor. The Piñeres family proudly supported Santander, and Vicente Piñeres asked the populace to remain loyal to Padilla.[104] From Ocaña, Santander courted his *pardo* followers in Cartagena. He wrote to Vives, one of the leaders of the revolt against Montilla, and to Calixto Noguera, whom Montilla described as an enemy of the whites.[105] Padilla's and other *pardos*' support for the *liberales* was probably based on the belief that their proposed political system offered *pardos* more political opportunities, a notion confirmed by *liberales*' acts in behalf of Afro-Colombians during the convention. In February, Padilla wrote to Santander, expressing his support for the convention, his rejection of the institution of a life presidency, and his conviction that the salvation of the fatherland could only rest on a popular representative government with an elective and alternating presidency. He "would rather die than be deprived of the rights that had cost so much blood and sacrifice."[106]

Padilla used similar rhetoric when speaking to the people in Getsemaní, although he emphasized the implications of the constitutional debates for *pardos*.[107] According to witnesses' accounts, he declared that "after the people had sacrificed themselves for the cause of liberty, Montilla aimed to destroy the laws and constitution, and to dissolve the convention." According to one witness, Padilla said, "General Montilla should die because his purpose is to subjugate the people of Colombia to tyranny." Another deposition claimed that Padilla had asked the people if they "would recognize him as their commander, and if they wanted to be slaves or free, obtaining the response of some that, yes, they indeed recognized him, and they wanted to be free." According to the testimony of a third witness, Padilla was reported as saying, "the Carta Boliviana [conservative Bolivian constitution] provides no advantages to the second class [the *pardo* or colored class; the *clase de colores*], who fought on the battlefields to suppress tyranny." These accounts reveal what Padilla believed to be the issues that could arouse the *pardos'* political interest: an emphasis on their active role in the construction of the Republic and the declaration that conservative institutions and a stronger state would not address the needs of the *segunda clase*.[108]

Padilla had not aspired to take power or promote a popular riot, but only to protect Cartagena's liberals against Montilla's pro-Bolívar bloc and establish a neutral authority that would guarantee the rights of local liberals, while reasserting *pardos'* right to social and political equality. He counted on the support of the navy and of the *pardos* from Getsemaní. He probably also expected the allegiance of local elite *liberales*. Seeking to maintain order in the city, he guaranteed foreign consuls that the property of their nationals would be respected. These cautious politics explain why several members of the Cartagena town council initially sided with him. When, on March 12, 1828, Montilla asked members of the town council to testify about the tumultuous and seditious nature of the recent events, he received less support than he might have anticipated. Not only did none of the councilmen agree that the earlier days in March had been characterized by disorder and sedition, but four even chose to remind Montilla that the law defined as factious those who opposed the system of liberty and independence. Those like Padilla, who defended the constitution and the laws, were following the duties of the citizens of any enlightened nation.[109] However, a month later, it had become clear that Padilla had lost the support of the central government and that defending him could lead to accusations of sedition. Subsequently, the fifteen notables whom Padilla's sister asked to testify against the proposition that the March events had disrupted public order refused to do so.[110]

The "race card" was a dangerous, double-edged sword. On the one hand, Padilla derived his political power to a large degree from his popularity among Afro-Colombians and his ability to rally their support through racial identification. Simón Bolívar and the interior minister, José Manuel Restrepo, were afraid of the potential threat of Padilla's revolt in the provinces of Mompox and Cartagena.[111] Bolívar constantly expressed in his private letters to his close ally Daniel O'Leary his fears of the social disruption that Padilla could cause in the region, bitterly complaining about those who did not take this threat seriously enough.[112] On the other hand, Padilla's race and his ability to gather the support of Afro-Colombians helped his enemies to deprive his political actions of any legitimacy. According to Montilla, Padilla's support for the convention was merely an excuse that hid his real intention to foment a race war (*guerra de clases*).[113] Padilla was guilty of the worst type of sedition: "fomenting the most implacable hatred among compatriots."[114] Montilla immediately started summary proceedings to prove Padilla's intention to start racial violence in Cartagena. By accusing Padilla of promoting race war, his opponents transformed his support for the convention into a seditious act. Montilla inscribed Padilla's political act in a rhetoric of tumult, disorder, and violence, of which race war was the most terrible manifestation. According to Montilla, Padilla's inability to secure the support of the prominent and respectable people of Cartagena confirmed the riotous character of his behavior. Only a "mob made up of slaves and sailors" had rallied in his support, while decent and respectable people had hidden in terror.[115]

Padilla paid a high price for the conflict. Probably too confident of the prestige and support he enjoyed, he returned to Cartagena, where Montilla imprisoned him and sent him to Bogotá for trial. There, his already precarious situation became even worse, as he was linked to the September 25 plot to assassinate Bolívar. Padilla was declared guilty of the tumult in Cartagena and of participation in the September 25 conspiracy. Most historians agree that Padilla did not participate in the assassination plot; indeed, his sentence places as much emphasis, if not more, on the rebellion in Cartagena.[116] Many contemporaries also considered him innocent of promoting unrest, much less racial war. Daniel O'Leary often wrote to the Libertador that the gravity of the Cartagena events had been grossly exaggerated. Yet these opinions did not save Padilla from execution. The message was clear: race was a dangerous card that could lead to fatal consequences. On October 2, 1828, Padilla was executed in the main plaza of Bogotá, wearing his general's uniform. When the sergeant in charge of the execution removed Padilla's epaulettes, Padilla said, "The Republic, not Bolívar, gave them to me." His last words were, "Long live the Republic! Long live Liberty!"[117]

Race War

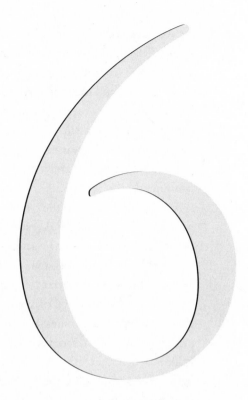

REFERENCES TO race war (*guerra de colores*) were an integral part of the political discourse of early republican Colombia. In 1823, the minister of the interior, José Manuel Restrepo, mentioned a number of conspiracies against whites in his private diary. He speculated, "It is most probable, and the Libertador always predicts it, that once the war with the Spanish is finished, we will have a new one with the blacks."[1] In its secret sessions, the 1823 Senate discussed "the dangers racial differences pose to the Republic if the problem is not conveniently solved."[2] In 1824, Vice President Santander wrote to the minister of the interior about the need to create more effective criminal laws to deal with blacks who were "developing projects of domination."[3] Such fears of race war were present not only among the presidency, Senate, and other central authorities in Bogotá but also among local elites.

As we have seen, from 1811 to 1828, race-war rumors surfaced in Honda, Majagual, Mompox, and Cartagena. Then, in 1832, there was a new racial scare in Caribbean Colombia. In January of that year, Juan Obredor and Manuel Silvestre Rios were executed in the city of Santa Marta for conspiring against whites, while their accomplices were banished from the region.[4] That same month, another *pardo*, Juan Antonio Avila, was executed in Mompox for conspiring to start a revolution of *pardos*, and a man and woman were banished for not denouncing the conspiracy.[5] Contemporaneously, race-war rumors spread in Cartagena, but the governor found no conspiracy. However, he did banish one *pardo*, Agustín Martínez, for two years, accusing him of writing and printing a seditious pamphlet against whites.[6] One year later, fifty *pardo* artisans were denounced for plotting a revolt against whites in Cartagena.[7]

The constant references to race war during this period pose some critical interpretative issues. We could try to explain why none of the period's many alleged racial conspiracies resulted in a full-scale race rebellion, or whether the *pardos* did truly aspire to establish black rule. In her analysis of Padilla, the most prominent and well-known Colombian *pardo* to face race-war accusations, Aline Helg emphasizes the relevance of patron-client relations between whites and *pardos* to explain the failure of Padilla's rebellion. According to her, such clientelistic relationships, in conjunction with the official rhetoric of racial equality, made expressions of racial identity unlikely and race-based rebellions prone to failure. That in Cartagena, as in most hierarchical societies, paternalistic relations helped reduce social tensions is not surprising.[8] However, Padilla's case was only one of a series of alleged racial conspiracies; we still need to explain the historical significance of the constant references to race war that characterized the revolutionary period and its aftermath. This requires analysis of several racial conspiracies, examining them as a group rather than in isolation, to allow the emergence of patterns that would not otherwise be apparent. The fact that none of these conspiracies resulted in a race rebellion does not diminish their historical relevance. On the contrary, their existence poses many questions: Why were rumors of race war so prevalent during this period? What do the rumors reveal about contemporary fears and expectations? When and why were rumors of race war most likely to emerge, and what impact did they have on republican racial constructs?

Although in some cases, the concrete origins of racial threats may be traced, such rumors usually seem to have been only the product of elite racial imagination. This begs the question of whether Afro-Colombians truly aspired to finish off whites and establish black rule. Yet rather than trying to determine the limits between imaginary and real threats, true or false aspirations (an issue that would probably never be satisfactorily resolved), it may be more helpful to simply try to determine the circumstances that led to the emergence of race-war rumors.

Analyzing the status of race war as a rumor allows an examination of its influence on the development of modern racial constructs.[9] One peculiar characteristic of this period in Colombia was the coexistence of an entrenched language of race war and a patriot discourse of racial harmony. At one end of the spectrum, the discourse of racial harmony was the language of the state: the language of patriotic ceremonies and military speeches. It provided official justification for racial policies, ranging from promoting European immigration, to eliminating racial categories in parish and judicial records. Crucially, this was also the language in which local whites and *pardos* addressed the state. Slave owners, elites disgruntled with the new *pardo* authorities, and *pardo* artisans all had to publicly express their allegiance to racial equality. At the other end of the spectrum was the language of race war: the language of threatening rumors and conspiracies, private and apprehensive letters, secret congressional sessions, and anonymous broadsides; the language of secrecy, deviance, and anonymity. The ambiguity and fluidity of racial speech during the independence period pose the question of how a hegemonic racial discourse was constructed. Pierre Bourdieu's emphasis on the social production of legitimate speech provides a useful theoretical perspective for approaching this issue.[10] It allows independence to be viewed as a moment of rupture, in which traditional authoritative discourses had been broken and new ones had yet to be established. Of particular interest are the times and spaces in which racial speech was produced—the who, where, when, and how of such speech. Some racial notions acquired enough legitimacy to be shared by *pardos* and whites, some were in conflict, and some were eventually eliminated from legitimate speech altogether.

Most scholars have assumed that *pardos'* tendency to avoid racial self-identification and open denunciation of discrimination was a direct consequence of nationalist declarations of racial equality.[11] However, a close look at the language of this period suggests that the erasure of explicit racial talk was not a necessary consequence of official racial equality but a sometimes violent process that demands explanation. When the nationalist discourse of racial harmony emerged, it did not necessarily preclude a language of racial grievance. Racial grievances could have been linked to racial harmony—as they were by *pardos*— as a necessary step toward achieving an ideal that was desired but not yet realized. Other republican ideals—abolition, literacy—were perceived in just this way. Indeed, during the early years of the Republic, it was not yet clear how and whether *pardos* could legitimately talk about their present difficulties and the persistence of racial inequality. The question was whether *pardos*, as *pardos*, could join together to fight for the implementation of the legally sanctified equality. The notion of race war played a crucial role in consolidating the boundaries of what was considered to be legitimate speech—in particular, the fluid area of racial grievances. This helped to silence the use of racial language as a language of denunciation, to silence public debate over whether race relations under the Republic were truly characterized by equality. Through a complex criminal and ideological process, a racial ideology emerged that allowed no gray space to exist between race war and racial harmony: racial grievances had to be fit into one category or the other. Thus, the airing of racial grievances—which could have been seen as a necessary step to overcoming the colonial legacies of slavery and discrimination—became associated with racial war and relegated to the arena of unpatriotic illegitimacy.

Rumors of Race War

Racial fears and rumors of race war were entrenched in the revolutionary environment of the larger Caribbean. The Age of Revolution had given birth to a racial phantom: Haiti, an independent black nation built by ex-slaves through the destruction of the white planter class. Since the beginning of the Haitian Revolution, the Spanish government had worried about its influence among local blacks. Republican authorities inherited this concern; they were just as worried, if not more so. In the words of Interior Minister José Manuel Restrepo, "Saint Domingue is an unfortunate example from which sparks of fire will come."[12] And although it was the most important, Haiti's was not the only Caribbean insurrection to inspire racial fears. The 1832 racial scare in Cartagena, Santa Marta, and Mompox coincided with news of the Christmas Rebellion in Jamaica.[13] In January 1832, the governor of Cartagena wrote apprehensively to the department of the interior in Bogotá about the news of a terrible slave rebellion in Jamaica. He explained, "This horrible event . . . keeps us in total anguish; there is great fear in the city because of rumors about an imminent race war."[14]

The rebellion in Haiti caused such local distress because circumstances there resonated with local reality. According to Vice President Santander, blacks' dangerous behavior and ambitions were "the result of ten years of revolution, during which the foundations of social order have been shaken, while the government has not been able to consolidate itself."[15] Slaves in particular were a cause of deep concern. Although slavery continued to be legal, the practice had been greatly disrupted by the wars. In the province of Cartagena, the number of slaves had fallen by 50 percent during the course of the Wars of Independence.[16] Slaves who had joined the patriot army were now legally free, and slaves who lived on the numerous haciendas that had been abandoned by their owners during the wars had grown accustomed to their de facto freedom.[17] The difficulties faced by the owners of Hacienda Santa Rosa del Arenal in trying to reclaim their property provide a telling example of elite problems in reestablishing control over land and slaves. When the owner of this hacienda tried to sell it in 1825, the slaves, one after another, began to claim their status as free men and women, then escaped to the bush to avoid being appraised.[18] Two years later, the slaves asked for and obtained from the judicial authorities confirmation of their free status.[19] The owner of Santa Rosa thus not only had to accept the loss of his slaves but also had to wait until 1829 to obtain legal recognition of his estate because the slaves had claimed the hacienda as their own.[20] The new opportunities slaves had to disrupt traditional social relations are also illustrated in the activities of a group of slaves from the city of Mompox. During the First Republic, these slaves took advantage of the precarious position of their peninsular owners, some of whom were under house arrest, coercing them into giving the slaves low-priced freedom letters by threatening to denounce them as royalists to the patriot authorities.[21]

The wars had also raised *pardos'* expectations and familiarized them with revolutionary ideas. In their town plazas, *pardos* often listened to political speeches that highlighted the advantages of the new regime, and *pardos* who served as soldiers heard multiple patriotic speeches about liberty and equality. In regions like Cartagena, *pardos* formed the majority of the patriot army's rank and file. Thus, notions of freedom, equality, the struggle against despotism, and the glory of patriotism were intrinsic to their political grievances and racial threats.[22] Members of the elite often interpreted *pardos'* political claims as a sign of their excessive ambitions. Bolívar made this point clear. In 1825, he warned Vice President Santander that "legal equality is not sufficient for the people, who want absolute equality, public and domestic; and later will want 'pardocracy,' which is their natural inclination, and to exterminate the privileged classes later on."[23] A few years earlier, the governor of Cartagena had expressed similar sentiments, referring to race-war threats as the result of the "ignorant ambition [of men who,] . . . not content with the advantages that the government and the public are providing them, march ungratefully toward their inevitable extermination."[24] For the elite, race war was an aberration, the Revolution turned sour, as had happened to French colonials in Haiti. They saw the specter of race war every time *pardos* attacked their social and political control.

Race war, however, was not just a phantom fear of the white elite; it was also part of the political imagination of local *pardos*. Colombian *pardos* had multiple opportunities to learn about events in Haiti through their contacts with Haitian sailors. Thus, it is not surprising that some Colombian references to race war explicitly mention Haiti's revolution.[25] In 1831, for example, Juan Antonio Barbosa, a Colombian passenger traveling from Cartagena to Kingston, overheard sailors' talk of race war. He informed the Colombian authorities about these conversations, providing them with excerpts from his diary and commentaries about what he had overheard. His transcription provides a rare and reliable window into the ways *pardos* spoke of race war—and the ways their notions of race war resonated with the elite imaginary.[26] Barbosa wrote in his diary, "Yesterday, I heard a lengthy discussion of great transcendence among the sailors about a conspiracy of blacks in Colombia." Two days later, he noted: "The discussion of the previous days continued. This talk, which is encouraged by any Colombian sailor, predicts another Saint Domingue in Colombia."[27] The sailors were mostly Colombian "*pardos* and blacks" (only one was white). Yet, Barbosa clarified, the sailors did not at any point express their own willingness to participate in such a revolution: "The conversation among the sailors was always expressed in a way that would not compromise them. Lamenting the upheaval suffered by the country, they commented that the blacks were very unruly, almost excepting themselves of such unbecoming conduct, thus concluding by judging that for these reasons there would be a conspiracy. All of which they always said with a disapproving tone."[28] Although Barbosa denied that such discussions provided grounds for prosecuting the sailors, he did think them capable of rebellion. More important, he thought that their conversations "showed the degree to which the notion of revolution was in the minds of all this type of people."[29]

Like the elite, these sailors associated political instability with social disruption and race war. Moreover, far from approving of race war, they excluded themselves from such unbecoming political activity. In spite of these similarities to elite discourse, however, references to race war had a different connotation in the mouths of *pardos*. If the elite saw race-war threats as a sign of *pardos'* excessive ambition and ingratitude, *pardos* saw race war as the natural consequence of elite failure to comply with the republican promise of equality. In the words of Mayor Valentín Arcia, "If people of his rank are as ill-treated in the rest of Colombia as they are in Majagual, God forbid, a new war against the whites may start."[30] Yet in spite of Arcia's "God forbid," and the sailors' disapproving tone, there seems to have been a sense of expectation in *pardos'* references to race war. Far from being seen as a nightmare or a republican aberration, the image of Haiti—of race war—was presented as a political alternative to a white-controlled Colombian republic. If race war was the only way for *pardos* to achieve their freedom and equality, it might be justified. As two *pardo* soldiers commented to each other during Padilla's revolt, "We ourselves have created the fatherland, we were its founders, but without destroying the whites, we would never enjoy our freedom."[31] *Pardos'* racial threats may have also derived from symbols of black radicalism that emerged during the Wars of Independence. Padilla was neither the first nor the last black Colombian general to be accused of fomenting race war by trying to use racial grievances to gain the support of local *pardos*.[32] The importance of these black generals as symbols of black resistance can be appreciated in their use by Calixto Noguera, whom Mariano Montilla described as "an unknown son of the fatherland" and a "seditious enemy of the whites." In 1822, Noguera had expressed his discontent with Cartagena's government by using the image of General Píar, the *pardo* Venezuelan general executed by Bolívar in 1817 for fomenting racial war. Noguera said that, even if Píar had died, there was no lack of other Píars in Cartagena.[33] It is notable that a Cartagenero was using the image of Píar five years after his death: *pardos* were clearly aware of important *pardo* figures and racial conflicts in other regions. This should not be surprising, considering the extent to which the revolutionary army moved *pardos* back and forth among Venezuela, Colombia, Peru, and Ecuador. In 1828, Noguera was again accused of wanting to finish off the whites when he sided with Padilla in support of the convention.[34]

Although in some cases, talk of race war came in response to concrete manifestations of racial hostility, such rumors seem to have often been merely the product of elite paranoia. One way to address this problem is to try to determine whether some *pardos* truly aspired to fomenting race war, but the evidence available makes such a determination impossible. It does, however, allow an analysis of these rumors as an expression of deep social and political tensions. Thus, a more useful approach to understanding the significance of the rumors is to analyze the events that favored their emergence. From this perspective, it is possible to understand the kinds of political tensions that led to rumors of race war and the effect that such rumors had on these tensions.

An analysis of the political circumstances surrounding these rumors and accusations reveals that they surfaced at foundational moments of the Revolution, when the extent and meaning of revolutionary change and its influence over the power relations between blacks and whites were at stake. In some cases, rumors coincided with the placing of local authority in the hands of Afro-Colombians. For example, in the cases of Justice Valentín Arcia, a *pardo* carpenter, and Colonel Remigio Márquez, who became commander general of the city of Mompox, race-war rumors arose when *pardo* public officers tried to exert their authority over the white elite.

Other racial rumors coincided with major political changes, such as the establishment of creole revolutionary juntas or the calling of constitutional conventions. These constituted veritable foundational moments of the revolutionary era, during which notions such as tyranny, anarchy, demagoguery, equality, and liberty—and their implications for social and racial relations—were passionately debated. For example, the accusations against master gunpowder maker Buenaventura Pérez coincided with the establishment of revolutionary juntas in 1811.[35] Similarly, rumors of race war emerged during the First Republic of Cartagena when Congress gathered to elect a governor in 1814. Conflicts between two local factions over who would be the new governor gave rise to rumors about a *pardo* conspiracy to place one of their own in office.[36] The accusation against General José Prudencio Padilla coincided with local debates over the convenience of adopting the Bolivian Constitution in Colombia, during the 1828 constitutional convention in Ocaña. Rumors of race war surfaced again in 1832 in Cartagena, Santa Marta, and Mompox, coinciding not only with the Christmas Rebellion in Jamaica but also with the defeat of the Bolivarian party, attempts by radical liberals to redefine Cartagena's power relations, and the meeting of yet another constitutional convention. In short, rumors of race war coincided with moments when national or local political changes promoted acute conflicts and negotiations over racial, social, and political relations. The rumors revealed both elites' anxieties at losing local control and *pardos'* rising political expectations. They also revealed the fact that, in the first decades of the nineteenth century, it was unclear which ways of addressing and managing contemporary inequality—if any—would be legitimate.

The Erasure of Racial Grievances

Behind most alleged racial conspiracies stood the pressure exerted by *pardos* to force the elite to fulfill their promises of racial equality. Although *pardos* agreed with the political elite on the virtues and desirability of racial harmony and equality, they had quite a different perspective on whether this republican ideal had been realized. Unlike the elite, they did not think that their political struggle for racial equality had ended. Again and again, *pardos* complained about persistent practices of racial discrimination. The language they used to express their grievances is exemplified in the following satirical denunciation of racial discrimination in a Cartagena café. A *pardo* artisan publicized the discrimination in a printed pamphlet that appeared in January 1832, a few months after the liberal triumph and during the meeting of the 1831–32 constitutional convention:

WARNING[:]
In the café of Mr. Cayetano Corrales in the street of Saint Augustine anybody's money is welcome; but only men of high status (those called *whites*) can take a seat, converse, and play cards, enter and leave at pleasure because they have money or blue blood. An honest and decent artisan who does not enjoy those eminent qualities and characteristics can leave his money, but then has to leave, himself, immediately, because it would be a sacrilegious impertinence to stay in the company of such distinguished men. Long live the aristocracy, long live the arrogance of the fatuous and the foolish like Mr. Corrales, and death to him who without being *white*, having blue blood, or epaulettes, shamefully goes in and lets himself be insulted and scorned for staying around.

AN HONEST PARDO[37]

AVISO[:]
En el café, bollería y garito del Señor Cayetano Corrales, situado en la calle de San Agustín, se admite el dinero de todo el que tenga la necesidad de ir allí a gastarlo; pero solamente tienen derecho a tomar asiento,

tertuliar, jugar los trucos y las barajas, entrar, salir endonde quiera y como gusten los señores de alta categoría; (pues, aquellos que llaman *blancos*) bien porque tienen dinero, o bien porque son procedentes de la sangre azul. Un artesano honrado, decente y hombre de bien si carece de aquellas eminentes cualidades y circunstancias, que largue los reales, bueno; pero debe también largarse luego, porque detenerse un punto en la asamblea de tan distinguidísimos señores, es un sacrílego atrevimiento. Viva la aristocracia, viva el envanecimiento de fatuos y mentecatos como el Sr. Corrales, y muera el que sin ser *blanco* [cursilla en el original] ni tener sangre azul, plata o charreteras tenga la poca vergüenza de ir a darle provecho, y a la vez motivo a que le desprecien y lo insulten si se detiene.

UN PARDO HONRADO

This pamphlet employs the language of racial grievances used by most *pardos* accused of racial enmity against whites. One salient characteristic of the pamphlet is its emphasis on the aristocratic nature of racial inequality—a recurrent theme of early republican racial language. Discrimination against honest *pardos* was a sign of arrogant aristocratic behavior. The pamphlet sets the "arrogance," "blue blood," and "high status" of those who discriminated against *pardos* against the "decency" of the victimized artisans, who embodied the republican values of work and honesty. The author was also willing to use racial terms and identification. He might have believed that the labels *pardo* and *white* should belong to the past, but because his experiences told him otherwise, he publicly used them to expose discrimination. He was unwilling to bury and silence race as long as it continued to be used to discriminate against *pardos*.

Pardos of all social backgrounds seem to have shared the elite association between republicanism and racial harmony and the notion that race war was undesirable. The *pardo* senator Remigio Márquez forcefully rejected any connection between his popularity among the lower classes of Mompox and his color. According to him, such an idea was an insult to the Mompox people and a sign of his opponents' criminal attempts to "sow detestable principles in our Republic."[38] At the other end of the social spectrum, the *pardo* sailors who entertained themselves by talking about the imminence of race war in Colombia did so with a distant and disapproving tone.[39] Still, although *pardos* agreed on the desirability of racial harmony and equality, they did not believe that their political struggle had ended and were therefore willing to openly talk about race to denounce discrimination.[40] The open exposure of racial discrimination in the "honest *pardo*" pamphlet was also accepted among a group of artisans who had gathered to celebrate a baptism. Discussing discrimination against *pardos* by local authorities, one stated, "When a white fights with a black, the black goes to jail, while the white keeps laughing."[41] Another told his fellow artisans that "their economic difficulties were not caused by the city's monetary problems but by the actions of eight or ten whites."[42] Arcia denounced the difficulties that *pardo* public officers had in securing the respect of the white elite, and Padilla condemned discrimination against *pardos* in military promotions.[43] If for the white elite racial language was something to be publicly silenced, and racial harmony a reality, for *pardos* racial harmony was only a desired future, and race an all-too-present category that should, but did not, belong to the past. The difference lay not in the values espoused but in the meaning, implications, and political use of these values.

Cartagena's judicial authorities declared the pamphlet signed by the "honest *pardo*" a "subversive printing"; its author, Agustín Martínez, was accused of sedition and banished for two years.[44] He learned the hard way that it was dangerous to seek public redress for racial discrimination, but his experience was not unique. Justice Arcia, in 1822, had faced a long trial for writing a dialogue that openly addressed the persistence of racial and social discrimination. Although he was eventually set free by the central authorities, he first suffered prison in Cartagena and Bogotá. The fifty artisans who discussed discrimination during the baptism were jailed for "trying to rob, murder, and maybe even destroy the government." When the government decided that the alleged conspiracy was merely an act of drunkenness, the artisans were set free.[45] Senator Márquez was forced to leave his town; although he was never jailed and Congress eventually declared him innocent, he had to endure the stress and humiliation of a publicized trial for sedition.[46] Others were less fortunate. General Padilla, who used his prestige and strong following among *pardos* to support the pro-Santander bloc, was executed. Two of the alleged leaders of racial conspiracies in Santa Marta and Mompox in 1832 suffered the same fate, while two of their accomplices were banished. Trial after trial conveyed the message that the public expression of racial grievances was dangerous and could lead to fatal personal and political consequences.

The criminal cases of *pardos* accused of sedition and racial enmity reveal the mechanisms through which local authorities inscribed the expression of racial grievances in a language of race war. Elite testimony reveals not only recalcitrance at accepting *pardo* authority—hardly surprising—but also difficulty in expressing antagonism. Elites could not openly accuse *pardos* of not knowing their place, of not respecting natural hierarchies, because such notions had been declared despotic and antipatriotic. Indeed, none of these *pardos* was accused or punished for denouncing racism. Instead, they were subjected to trial for fomenting race war. By thus inscribing *pardos'* defiance of elite authority in terms of racial enmity, the white elite managed to expunge *pardos'* actions from the sphere of legitimate politics.

Local elites referred to racial harmony as something that had already been achieved. It was a present reality, not something to be desired. They described their towns as places where racial peace and harmony already reigned. Justice Arcia's complex conflicts with the local white elite, for example, were summarized as follows: "He does not cease to cry out against the class of whites, with no consideration of the fact that we are all undifferentiated members of society. He has set himself on dividing the marriage in which this tranquil town has reposed, promoting a criminal aversion against whites."[47] Since harmony and equality were already present, Arcia's racial complaints could only be a manifestation of his aversion against whites. Similarly, the accusations against Senator Márquez argued that before his arrival, the city of Mompox had enjoyed "Octavian peace" and "fraternal union" among whites and *pardos*.[48]

Once they had been declared unnecessary, racial grievances became dangerous attempts to disrupt public order. *Pardos'* political denunciations, framed as righteous attempts to impose republican law on despotic elite cliques, were now described as factious attempts to promote race war. Thus, the white elite attributed any expression of racial conflict to the bad influence of disruptive figures who set themselves the task of breaking the union, peace, and tranquility of their towns. In the case of Senator Márquez, his enemies went so far as to accuse him of drawing attention to the presence of people of different colors in the city.[49] By associating racial grievances with race war, local authorities inscribed them within a general discourse of revolt and sedition. The authorities, for example, bypassed the complaints of the "honest *pardo*" altogether, presenting them as a pretext that concealed darker intentions. He was accused and convicted for his "alarming and threatening expressions against the government" and for "attempting to provoke a popular commotion with his pamphlet."[50] He was also accused of spreading "seditious ideas" against the government —ideas capable of "inciting rebellion or at least perturbing public order." His prosecutor claimed that since the publication of his pamphlet the city had been "in constant alarm, fearing an insurrection at any moment."[51]

In this way, the elite inverted notions of victimization. *Pardos* ceased to be victims of discrimination and became agents of racial hate, while the elite ceased to be upholders of racial hierarchies and became victims of racial hate. The notion of racial grievance had no place within an elite discourse that declared equality as something already achieved. By their association with race war and sedition, open debates about race and racial identification became marked as unpatriotic and antinational and were thus expunged from legitimate public discourse.

Also consolidating the association between racial grievance and race war was the use of race-war accusations against liberals. Significantly, in Cartagena, this tactic was used by both the Bolivarians and, following their defeat, the representatives of the new Santanderian government. In 1828, the Bolivarian governor of Cartagena, Mariano Montilla, effectively used this tactic to delegitimize Padilla's attempt to become a local champion of the self-proclaimed liberals of the pro-Santander coalition. This accusation also helped tarnish those liberals who defended Padilla at the Ocaña Convention, where liberal deputies were usually unafraid of accusing their opponents of racial discrimination. When the convention questioned the actions and position of Afro-Colombian men, the liberals tended to take the Afro-Colombian side. For example, when the convention debated whether Antonio Baena, an elected *pardo* deputy from Cartagena, met the property qualifications to be admitted into the assembly, liberals were unanimously in his favor. Francisco del Real, a close friend of Baena, was his most fervent defendant, speaking at length on Baena's behalf and "shedding tears" over the injustice being done. He attacked those "aristocrats who opposed his admission" only "because he belonged to a certain class."[52] Likewise, when the convention discussed the tumult in Cartagena, liberals supported Padilla. The liberal openness to discussing matters of race contrasted dramatically with the Bolivarian view that any public discussion of racial conflict or discrimination was imprudent.[53]

Liberals paid a high price for their support of Padilla: it displaced them from their position as righteous saviors of republican institutions to being seen as promoters of social chaos and disorder. Their link to Padilla put them on the defensive. On April 10, Bolívar sent a strong letter to the convention, accusing its members of "applauding a rebellion against order, military discipline, and public safety."[54] Bolívar's loyal secretary Daniel O'Leary noticed the panic and embarrassment that Bolívar's message caused among the "sans-culottes." According to him, their imprudence in supporting Padilla had given the pro-Bolívar bloc a precious opportunity to destroy the convention, since the twenty-six deputies who had voted for Padilla could be accused of rebellion.[55] Even Vice President Santander had to defend himself against accusations of complicity in the events in Cartagena. In a proclamation to the Colombians, he stated that he was guilty only of loving liberty and, since 1818, of being a friend of Padilla—who, he reminded the public, was a war hero (Benemérito de la Patria).[56]

Again in 1831–32, radical liberals faced charges of promoting race war. National and local circumstances had changed. The pro-Bolívar party had been defeated in Bogotá, and its representatives in Cartagena were ousted from government in April 1831, after a regional insurrection.[57] Empowered by these changes, a group of Cartagena's liberals organized as the Veteranos Defensores de la Libertad (Veteran Defenders of Liberty), a group that included among its members well-known *pardo* liberals such as Juan José Nieto, Calixto Noguera, and Juan Madiedo.[58] The activities of liberal Veteranos, particularly the group's *pardo* members, were soon considered threatening by the local government. As early as September 1831, Cartagena's new civilian authority, Manuel Romay, wrote that "the Veteranos society organized without the government's knowledge or approval. . . . Their leading members have taken it upon themselves to compose almost all of this town's newspapers, which reveals their intentions and aspirations. It is feared that the society will lead to the subversion of public order."[59] Yet Romay and the region's commander general initially decided to be prudent, since the society enjoyed support and protection in the city—support that likely derived from its members' long and active trajectory in support of the liberal cause.

While it is not exactly clear what the "intentions and aspirations" of the liberal Veteranos were, they did seek an active role in politics. They published several newspapers; they were not afraid of denouncing the shortcomings of the local government in fulfilling liberal aspirations; they were outspoken in denouncing their political opponents and urging the government to take a strong stand against the "despots and oligarchs" who had supported the previous government.[60] Two of the accusations the governor made against the Veteranos were provoked by their denunciations of his inability to fulfill the liberals' request for social and political change. In fact, the liberal government had been in power only two months when Governor Vicente García del Real jailed Veterano Francisco Correa for sedition. His incarceration and trial were based solely on the testimony of one witness, who had heard Correa commenting that "the apathy of the current governor Vicente García del Real endangered the patria, necessitating a popular commotion to place the provincial government in different hands."[61] Although Correa was freed for lack of proof, the governor continued to levy accusations against *pardo* Veteranos. He accused Juan Madiedo, director of the Veteranos, of questioning the legitimacy of his government. Indeed, not only had Madiedo denounced the unconstitutional imprisonment of Francisco Correa, but he had also stated that Governor García del Real only exercised a "tolerated authority" (*autoridad tolerada*) as a member of the previous administration. Madiedo would, he said, prove these claims and denounce the government in the press.[62] Madiedo's words reveal his belief that the government's authority rested solely on the citizens' willingness to accept it and that he had the right to use the press to denounce a government he found illegitimate. Veteranos' active use of the press was in fact their most bothersome tactic for Governor García del Real. According to him, Madiedo was always looking for a way to "slander the magistrates with his writings and inventions." Governor García del Real asked the vice president to take measures against the Veteranos because "they were men who threatened the peace of the province, which they would maintain in constant unrest and rebellion." In the governor's apocalyptic version, "there would be no commerce, distrust would put down roots, and honest citizens would always be insulted, mostly by the press."

The Veteranos also represented a tradition of expressing racial grievances and denouncing discrimination. They openly honored Padilla, who had denounced racial discrimination in 1824 and again in 1828. One of their leading members, Calixto Noguera, had been accused in 1822 of being a seditious enemy of the whites for allegedly exalting the memory of the *pardo* general Manuel Píar.[63] In 1828, the governor again accused Noguera of being an enemy of the whites for siding with Padilla.[64] After the liberal triumph, this tradition of denouncing racial discrimination continued with the January 1832 publication of the "honest *pardo*" pamphlet. Its author, Agustín Martínez, was the brother-in-law of Veterano Julián Figueroa, a fact that was used by the governor to support his characterization of Veteranos as dangerous subversives.[65]

The new government continued to make the association among radical liberalism, race war, and sedition utilized by the previous conservative government of Mariano Montilla. Like his predecessor, Governor García del Real sought to delegitimize the activities of his liberal *pardo* opponents by linking them with race war. According to him, Juan Madiedo, Julián Figueroa, Manuel Azanza, Pedro Laza, and Manuel Vives—all but the last members of the Veteranos—were "turbulent men who, under the mask of liberals, preach and promote rebellion." Governor García del Real predicted a "revolution of classes [races]" if such men were not contained.[66] To bolster his denunciations, the governor linked Veteranos to the printing of the "honest *pardo*" broadside and to the recent racial scares in Río Hacha, Santa Marta, and Mompox, which had resulted in the execution of three men. Thus, radical liberals, often *pardos*, were not true liberals but seditious advocates of race war and rebellion.[67] This linkage between radical liberalism and race war would affect the legitimacy of racial grievances, which could have become part of broader liberal antiaristocratic rhetoric, as at the 1828 Ocaña Convention. Instead, radical liberals learned that they would pay a high price for playing the race card in favor of their *pardo* supporters, as it linked them with race war and sedition and perhaps led them to eventually distance themselves altogether from explicit racial politics.

In many ways, these years continued a contest over the meaning of *pardo* politics, a struggle that had begun during the First Republic and would continue throughout the nineteenth century.[68] One side sought to vindicate *pardo* veterans as righteous defenders of republican values. Significantly, one of the first events sponsored by the Veteranos was a ceremony to restore the glory of General Padilla, vindicating his memory and celebrating him as a martyr for liberty, who after his heroic contribution to Colombia's freedom had fallen victim to Montilla's and Bolívar's tyrannical rule. The magnificent funeral held to memorialize Padilla, which took place in the city's cathedral, was presided over by the bishop. Although it is not clear whether the Veteranos initiated this event, they certainly played a crucial and visible role in its staging. They attended the funeral wearing black mourning clothes and a liberal red ribbon; they gave long speeches and sent representatives to present their condolences to Padilla's family. This commemoration of Padilla's glory had enormous symbolic meaning: Padilla represented *pardos*' political protagonism in building the fatherland, a role that the Veteranos sought to continue. He also symbolized the connection between racial equality and the antiaristocratic republican rhetoric of the Revolution. The construction of Padilla as a martyr against tyranny provided a useful cautionary tale filled with values dear to the Veteranos. It not only emphasized *pardos*' military role in the construction of the Republic but also depicted any repression of *pardo* liberals and war veterans as a sign of tyranny.

Conservative reading and writing presented a very different picture of *pardos*' activism. According to José Manuel Restrepo, a historian and former interior minister, in Cartagena "*pardos* were terrible."[69] Restrepo wrote in his diary that the "demagogic party" in Cartagena had tried to depose the government and nominate as governor Juan Madiedo (president of the Veteranos), a "crazy prattler." Restrepo concluded that this attempt showed that the "spirit of revolution" was still alive.[70] Restrepo's narrative transformed the Veteranos into demagogues and their leader into a "prattler" devoid of any legitimacy. At issue was whether *pardo* republicans should be immortalized as heroes who had fought for freedom or as demagogues" and "crazy prattlers" who aspired to destroy order and promote race war.

The nationalist discourse of racial harmony was further consolidated by the ways in which local actors—*pardos* and the elite—related to the central state. Neither local authorities nor *pardos* could take the support of the central state for granted. It was divided among various institutions, such as Congress, the Supreme Court, and the ministry of the interior, which responded to local racial conflicts in different and sometimes contradictory ways. Not all *pardos*, for example, were found guilty by the central authorities. In some cases, the central state not only declared *pardos* innocent but accused the local elite instead.[71] In others, they rejected the gravity of *pardos'* racial speech. In one instance, the interior minister not only dismissed allegedly severe *pardo* racial speech as an inconsequential act of drunkenness but also reminded Cartagena's government "that it is important as well as just" to ensure that a fair administration of justice would eliminate any residue of old racial resentments among various sectors of the population.[72] In the case of Padilla, on the other hand, the mostly liberal constitutional congress of Ocaña supported him at first, but the central government in Bogotá decreed his execution. In certain other cases, central authorities simply accepted local rulings.

Success in obtaining a favorable decision from the central authorities depended, among other things, on the actors' ability to frame their position according to legitimate republican principles. It was particularly important that they express their support for racial equality and public order. When *pardos* denounced racial inequality, local authorities had to convince the state of their success at promoting racial harmony and equality in their towns. The governor of Cartagena felt compelled to enumerate his efforts to lead people of all colors (*clases*) to "the most perfect union and harmonic society" before denouncing Calixto Noguera as an enemy of the whites. Local elites needed to clarify that whatever racial conflicts surfaced in their towns did not originate with their discriminatory behavior but, in the words of Cartagena's governor, with the "ignorant ambition" of "ungrateful men" who were not satisfied with the benefits the Republic had bestowed on them.[73] Thus, every time *pardos* raised the issue of racial discrimination, local elites, in addition to repressing and silencing them, had to reiterate a public commitment to racial equality. The central state thus played a crucial role in the transformation of racial grievances into a taboo subject— not by further repressing *pardos* but by upholding the notion of racial harmony. By the central state's forcing recalcitrant local elites to comply with a larger degree of racial equality than they may have been willing to accept, the fiction of harmony was maintained.

During the first decades of the nineteenth century, conflicts between *pardos* and the elite set the foundations for Colombian nationalist constructs of racial harmony. On the one hand, *pardos'* pressure forced the elite to deepen their official allegiance to racial harmony. On the other, elite repression—through executions, jail, and banishment, as well as through emphasis on the antinational nature of racial talk— forced upon *pardos* the realization that public denunciation of racial grievances was dangerous, if not unpatriotic. Arguably, elite repression eventually forced *pardos* to find alternative forms to express their political and social claims—forms that were not racially explicit. At the same time, conflicts between *pardos* and the elite forced overt racism out of the elite's official discourse, which needed to adapt its exclusionary practices to legal equality and to a political allegiance to racial harmony. Thus, these years laid the foundations for one of the most salient characteristics of Spanish American racial constructs: the absence of overt racism from state politics. No matter what the degree of their exclusionary desires and practices, Spanish American elites had to adapt them to nationalist ideologies of racial equality and harmony.

Conclusion

7

THE ENLIGHTENMENT ideals of liberty, equality, and citizenship faced perhaps their strongest challenges and reached their most dramatic consequences in the colonial settings of the Americas. Here these ideals most directly confronted their extreme opposites: slavery, colonialism, and racism. The power of these oppositions was only matched by the violence and length of the struggles to resolve them. Here democracy was for the first time linked to human equality regardless of color and geographical origin. And here anticolonial wars first faced a question that would become common in the anticolonial wars of the modern era: how can unifying national identities be constructed in societies beset by racism and racial and ethnic conflicts? The answer to this question, never easy or automatic, was not determined by white elites alone but also by indigenous peoples and people of African descent.

One fascinating aspect of this story is how various regions in the Americas constructed different national racial imaginaries out of similar pasts of slavery and colonialism. Although much more research needs to be done about the impact of the Age of Revolution on modern race relations, some common threads seem to have shaped it. In the late eighteenth century, white creoles across the Americas sought to reassert their European identity to confront a new imperial environment that increasingly questioned the equality between European- and American-born whites. European scientists like de Pauw, Buffon, and Abbé Raynal had popularized the notion of America's inferiority, arguing that its geography had degenerative effects on animals, plants, and men. This degeneration also influenced Americans of European descent, who allegedly suffered the enfeebling effects of the American environment. Colonial intellectuals like Thomas Jefferson and Antonio Clavigero responded by defending the Americas' nature and inhabitants. White colonials also confronted accusations of racial mixing that threw their equality with European-born whites into question.[1] Moreover, in the last quarter of the eighteenth century, white colonials saw their racial and social prominence challenged by demographic changes and new imperial policies. In Colombia, Venezuela, and Saint Domingue, white creoles responded with anger to colonial reforms that recognized the demographic and economic importance of free people of African descent and sought to encourage their loyalty and participation in militias.[2] Threatened by these changes, white colonials across the Americas asserted their European ascendancy and distinguished themselves from local blacks and mulattoes. In 1795, the Caracas town council wrote to the Crown about the need to "keep *pardos* in their present subordination, without any laws that confuse them with whites, who abhor and detest this union."[3] In the United States, James Otis similarly insisted that the northern colonies were "well settled, not as the common people of England foolishly imagine, with a compound of mongrel mixture of English, Indian and Negro, but with freeborn British white."[4] In Haiti, the white colonial intellectual Emilien Petit proposed strict racial segregation as a way to strengthen French identity and loyalty among white colonials.[5] But while it seemed, in the late eighteenth century, that white creoles across the Americas would construct a white-only national identity, only the United States followed this path.

By the 1820s, Colombians had developed a nationalist ideology that proclaimed the equality and harmony of its peoples of European, African, and indigenous descent. This ideological transformation echoed similar changes in the other Spanish American republics and foreshadowed the racial ideology of Cuban patriots in the late nineteenth century. In contrast, Haiti had constructed a nationalist identity that excluded whites. The United States alone had constructed its national identity as white, excluding nonwhites from the nation's imagined community. These divergent continental paths sprang from the anticolonial wars of the Age of Revolution, during which the new American nations developed new national identities, struggling over who would be included and who excluded from national polities.

These wars were instrumental for creating the collective identities that distinguished the new nations from their former European metropoles. In Colombia, insurgent nationalism was in large part constructed in opposition to Spain. As Linda Colley states so clearly, "Men and women decide who they are by reference to who and what they are not."[6] Colombia clearly was not Spain. Patriots distinguished themselves from Spain for the most part in political terms. Spain was old and despotic, while Colombia was new, free, and full of potential. Colombia was a land of beginning, where happiness and political virtue were possible.[7] Spain was all that hindered Colombia's future potential. Spanish colonialism held back Colombian economic development through excessive taxes, state monopolies, and laws against free trade. Spanish obscurantism kept creoles in ignorance, and Spanish tyranny prevented them from acquiring the necessary tools for self-government. Only free of Spanish rule could Colombia fulfill its natural potential. Patriot racial constructs fitted within these dichotomies. Spanish tyranny had caused Colombian racial differences. Cruel Spaniards had decimated indigenous populations and imported slaves to the Americas. Such racial antagonism as existed among Colombians was the product of a history of Spanish cruelty and indifference toward blacks and Indians. At Cádiz, Spaniards had denied people of African descent their rightful enjoyment of full citizenship. In contrast, Colombians loved their fellow citizens regardless of color. They opposed and despised racial discrimination and slavery as elements of an old despotic regime. Under the Republic, only enlightenment, harmony, and unity would reign.

If this period enshrined for the first time the principle of racial equality as a fundamental value for modern democracies, it also set limits on its full implementation. In Colombia, blacks had actively participated in the Wars of Independence and had been instrumental in the establishment and consolidation of the state's official commitment to racial equality and the elimination of any form of legal discrimination. Their participation, however, was not easily controlled. *Pardos* had joined the patriot movement as fellow citizens with equal rights; they had been told that they were the sovereign people. Yet the meaning of this was fluid and contested. *Pardos* pressed for notions of justice and equality that went beyond the elite's original intentions, profoundly challenging elite social and political control. Race-war rumors tended to surface when this pressure seemed most threatening. For contemporary Cartageneros, Haiti, more than Jacobin France, symbolized the revolutionary excesses of a world turned upside down. Thus, although some allegations of Jacobinism were made, they did not acquire the prominence of accusations of race war. Images of Haitian black revolutionaries resonated with local images of *pardo* patriots who challenged the political and social control of the creole elite. At times, rumors emerged when *pardos* rose to political positions that gave them power over the white elite. *Pardos* with political authority were symbolically charged figures; they embodied revolutionary change.

At other times, rumors arose at foundational political moments, such as the summoning of juntas or constitutional conventions. The armed insurrections that often accompanied these political conjunctures, and the passionate debates over the new republic's racial and social relations, provoked profound fear and uncertainty. Race-war rumors and threats may thus have reflected the creole fear—or the *pardo* hope—that elite inability to fulfill *pardos'* expectations might lead to violent conflict. They were both a reflection and an expression of the political fluidity of the independence period.

The concept of race war would have a profound effect on Colombian racial constructs. It was key to consolidating the nationalist discourse of racial harmony, yet at the same time it set boundaries on the legitimate ways in which racial equality could be addressed. Colombian policy makers used the threat of race war to convince recalcitrant elites that anything short of full legal equality and an official commitment to manumission could result in a full-scale racial conflict, as had happened in Haiti. Accusations of racial enmity also deprived *pardos'* grievances of political legitimacy. They challenged the ability of *pardo* authorities to exert power over the local elite, helping to stigmatize *pardo* attempts to punish the illegal activities of the creole elite as a sign of seditious enmity toward whites. *Pardos* who denounced racial discrimination faced similar charges, which often ended in banishment or execution. This sent a clear message: it was dangerous and unpatriotic to seek public redress for racial inequality. Still, each time creole elites accused *pardos* of racial enmity, they were forced to reiterate their commitment to racial harmony and equality. To legitimize their accusations of race war, local elites had to claim that racial harmony already reigned in their towns, that social disruption resulted only from the actions of individual seditious *pardos*. Such discourse thus set limits on elite expressions of racial fears and prejudices. No matter what their racial prejudices, they had to officially acknowledge their commitment to racial harmony and equality.

The differences and similarities among Colombia, Haiti, and the United States suggest that the revolutionary wars were crucial in shaping modern national racial identities. Unlike in Spanish America, racial equality did not become a source of conflict between French and Haitians. Racial equality for free men of African descent was first declared in Paris but opposed by the colonial white planter class. The violent military, political, and ideological conflicts of the Haitian Revolution were not between colonials and colonizers but between those in favor of the Republic and those against it. When the republicans triumphed, the white colonial planters, not the French, were excluded from the republican patriot imaginary. In the 1790s, Bastille Day and Emancipation Day were celebrated together, and both the French general Léger-Félicité Santhonax and the black general Touissant L'Overture were revered as founding fathers of Haitian republicanism. It was not until Napoleon sought to reinstate slavery in 1802 that a distinction between liberty-loving Haiti and a tyrannical France was established. By then, white colonials had been eliminated from the national imaginary. The national pantheon of founding fathers included only men of African descent like Vincent Ogé, Jean Baptiste Chavanne, and L'Overture. Those white men who were included in nationalist representations were European abolitionists, not white Haitians.[8] When national images and ceremonies proclaimed racial harmony, it was between blacks and mulattoes, not between whites and blacks. Haiti had become a black and mulatto nation.[9]

The revolutionary wars in the United States followed yet another path. Abolition and racial equality did not become a republican or patriot slogan in the United States. There was no clear-cut distinction between royalists and American patriots on racial issues. If anything, patriot propaganda tended to portray Britain as the champion of blacks' rights.[10] Unlike in Haiti and Spanish America, the ideology of racial equality in the United States did not become a source of national unity and pride in the fight against the Old Regime, instead remaining a contested and controversial position. This disconnection between nationalism and racial equality became apparent in the Fourth of July celebrations of the 1810s, 1820s, and 1830s, when free blacks were harassed and expelled from the celebrations by rowdy mobs claiming that Independence Day "belongs exclusively to the white population."[11] Even at a symbolic level, the American Revolution had failed to inaugurate a new era in race relations. The struggle for racial equality in the United States would become linked to bloody regional conflicts, not to a unified front against a common enemy.

These divergent associations between patriot nationalism and race developed during the wars would have an enormous influence on the construction of modern identities, determining whether racial equality would become a core element of the national ideology, as in Spanish America, or a precarious concept constantly subjected to challenge, as in the United States. In Colombia, the Revolution transformed racial equality into an unchallengeable nationalist principle. In spite of the numerous civil wars and constitutional changes that shifted Colombia back and forth from federalism to centralism, and from universal manhood suffrage to restricted suffrage, the principle of legal racial equality was never questioned. The power and endurance of this nationalist notion became apparent during the height of scientific racism in the late nineteenth century, when Latin American intellectuals refrained from wholeheartedly accepting European racist notions. They rejected the condemnation of miscegenation, hoping that their nations would progressively whiten through racial mixing between white immigrants and local blacks. Even these modified racist notions failed to affect the political discourse, which continued to emphasize racial unity and equality to attract black voters.[12] Modern struggles to end formal and informal racial inequality would have to confront the legacy of the Age of Revolution. In the United States, blacks would be excluded from the national imaginary and denied equal legal rights, yet they would form powerful and lasting political organizations to fight against formal and informal discrimination and prejudice. In Colombia, blacks would enjoy legal equality, yet they would face great difficulty in fighting prejudice and informal discrimination in a cultural environment that made the denunciation of racism taboo and black organizations a sign of unpatriotic divisiveness.

Paradoxically, the Colombian nationalist ideology of racial harmony and equality was further consolidated by discrimination against blacks in the United States. When the United States replaced Spain as the region's new imperial power, it also took Spain's place in the nationalist rhetoric that distinguished between Colombian racial tolerance and imperial discrimination. In the midst of U.S. expansionism in Central America and Panama, Colombian intellectuals started to highlight the differences between U.S. racism and the liberties that people of color enjoyed in Colombia.[13] Over time, Spain ceased to be seen as the source of slavery and racism. It instead began to be recognized as the cultural foundation of Colombian tolerance in a new nationalist rhetoric that distinguished between Anglo-Saxon racism and Hispanic tolerance. Already in 1869, Sergio Arboleda attributed to Spanish Catholicism a special degree of racial tolerance. According to him, under its influence, "the Spanish slave was not, like the English, a beast of labor, but . . . the labor partner of his master and almost a family member. Of all the slaves in the American colonies, the Spanish were the less miserable." Arboleda also foreshadowed future arguments that linked Iberian law with racial tolerance. Because of Spanish laws, he argued, "blacks multiplied and were incorporated in the new society, without the diversity of their color or origin being an obstacle: they were Christian, and baptism made them equal to the other members of the Church." "Of all the nations that colonized these countries," Arboleda declared, "Spain was the only one capable of creating this society of heterogeneous elements."[14] Racial equality had ceased to be a republican novelty, instead becoming part of an Iberian and Catholic cultural heritage that distinguished Latin America from the Anglo-Saxon United States.

Another important legacy of this period was the linkage established between racial equality and the egalitarian, antiaristocratic rhetoric of liberal politics. From the first years of the Revolution, blacks and mulattoes denounced racial discrimination as a sign of unrepublican aristocratic behavior. As Colombian republicans began to divide into two camps, the antiaristocratic card became particularly popular among self-proclaimed liberals, which on the Caribbean coast sometimes led to the identification of liberalism with *pardo* politics. This trend continued well into the nineteenth century, when liberals became the champions of abolition and numerous blacks and mulattoes joined their military ranks in the century's civil wars.[15] Liberalism and black politics continued to be linked during the 1930s and 1940s, as black and mulatto workers joined the Liberal Party in their struggles against oil and banana companies, while conservatives used racial stereotypes to tarnish their Liberal enemies.[16] Indeed, the foremost figure of twentieth-century Liberalism, José Eliecer Gaitán, was called "*el negro* Gaitán."

Now, as a new century begins and the two hundredth anniversary of the Wars of Independence fast approaches, what legacy of this period should we appropriate? Perhaps the *pardo* republicans should serve as our guide. They supported the ideal of racial equality and harmony without forgetting to denounce discrimination. They knew that fulfillment of this ideal required constant condemnation of the racist practices that to this day continue to plague Colombia and other American nations.

NOTES

1. The importance of this scene for understanding Afro-Colombians' patriot politics is highlighted in Múnera, *El fracaso*, 191–99.

2. See nn. 33, 34, this chapter.

3. I am borrowing the term *enlightened illusion* from Castro-Leiva, *La Gran Colombia*. I am also inspired by Rancière's critique of revisionist analysis, which declared the French Revolution an illusion; see *Names of History*, 22, 31–39.

4. Colmenares, *Las convenciones*, 78–89, 94–95.

5. José Manuel Restrepo, *Historia de la Revolución*, 1: 37.

6. José Manuel Restrepo, *Historia de la Revolución*, 1: 190.

7. José Manuel Restrepo, *Historia de la Revolución*, 1: 189.

8. For the importance of language and ideology for power structures, see Bourdieu, *Language and Symbolic Power*, 43–89; Lincoln, *Authority Construction and Corrosion*, 9–11, 47–54; Wolf, *Envisioning Power*, 56, 129.

9. José Manuel Restrepo, *Historia de la Revolución*, 1: 89–94.

10. See the following analyses of Bolívar's intellectual legacy: Carrera-Damas, *El culto a Bolívar*; Lynch, *Simón Bolívar*, 92–94, 119–22; Brading, *First America*, 603–20; Castro-Leiva, *La Gran Colombia*; Pagden, *Spanish Imperialism*, 133–53.

11. Bolívar, *Obras completas*, 1: 168.

12. This line of argumentation is strikingly similar to the French revisionist blame of intellectuals for the excesses of the French Revolution. See Rancière, *Names of History*, 40.

13. Bolívar, "Discurso Pronunciado por el Libertador ante el Congreso de Angostura el 15 de Febrero de 1819, día de su instalación," in *Obras completas*, 3: 681–82.

14. Carrera-Damas, *Venezuela*, 113–33.

15. Simon Bolívar to Francisco de Paula Santander, San Carlos, June 13, 1821, in *Obras completas*, 1: 565.

16. "Contestación de un Americano Meridional a un caballero de esta Isla," Kingston, Sept. 6, 1815, in Bolívar, *Obras completas*, 1: 172.

17. Simón Bolívar to José Antonio Páez, Mar. 6, 1826, in *Obras completas*, 2: 322–23.

18. Jaime E. Rodríguez, *Independence of Spanish America*, 220; Brading, *First America*, 613.

19. Uribe, "Enigma of Latin American Independence," analyzes the "limited impact" of social history in the historiography of the Wars of Independence. For a broader assessment of the difficulties of social history in providing a comprehensive analysis of political culture in Latin America, see Taylor, "Between Global Process."

20. Lynch's comprehensive *Spanish American Revolutions* provides an excellent summary of the monographs produced in the 1950s and 1960s. In the 1960s, several excellent historical monographs on the independence period emphasized the importance of lower-class participation. Yet these works tended to emphasize its apolitical nature. In his analysis of the Hidalgo revolt, e.g., Hamill summarizes lower-class participation as follows: "The vast majority of the Indians and castes in New Spain were content to remain aloof from the conflict except when it swept directly over them. They were the inert ingredients, the innocent sufferers, who had no knowledge of what the war was all about. . . . This is not

to say that the lower classes had no part in the revolt. Rather, it is to emphasize that they remained apart from the contest because of ignorance and the lack of opportunity to share in politics" (*Hidalgo Revolt*, 48).

21. One of the best-known academic representatives of this view is Burns, *Poverty of Progress*.

22. Lievano-Aguirre, *Los grandes conflictos sociales*, 4: 135.

23. James Sanders points to Colombia's pioneering role in the development of modern democratic politics. See Sanders, "'Citizens of a Free People.'"

24. Guerra, *Modernidad e independencias*, 41. For an analysis of the influence of the Haitian Revolution on Venezuela's slave population, see Arcaya, *Insurrección de los negros*; Brito Figueroa, *Las insurrecciones*, 41–88; Julius S. Scott, "Common Wind."

25. Guerra, *Modernidad e independencias*, 36.

26. For an analysis and critique of the weight that nineteenth-century narratives still carry for contemporary understanding of Indian politics in Colombia, see Saether, "Independence and the Redefinition"; Earle, "Creole Patriotism."

27. Qtd. in Pagden, *Spanish Imperialism*, 148.

28. Pagden, *Spanish Imperialism*, 152–53.

29. Annino, *Historia de las elecciones*, 7–9.

30. Adelman, *Republic of Capital*; Annino, *Historia de las elecciones*; Brading, *First America*; Chust, *La cuestión nacional americana*; Garrido, *Reclamos y representaciones*; Guerra, *Modernidad e independencias*; Pagden, *Spanish Imperialism*, 133–53; Posada-Carbó, *Elections*; Rieu-Millan, *Los diputados americanos*; Jaime E. Rodríguez, *Independence of Spanish America*; Uribe, *Honorable Lives*.

31. Here I am also inspired by Guha, "Prose of Counter-Insurgency"; Trouillot, "An Unthinkable History: The Haitian Revolution as a Non-Event," in *Silencing the Past*, 70–107.

32. Annino, "Introducción," in *Historia de las elecciones*, 7–13.

33. Early historical works addressing peasant politics in Latin America tended to focus on the second part of the nineteenth century and the early twentieth century. See, e.g., Mallon, *Peasant and Nation*; Alonso, *Thread of Blood*; Rappaport, *Politics of Memory*; Joseph and Nugent, *Everyday Forms*. More recent works have offered careful analyses of lower-class politics during the Wars of Independence. Guardino, e.g., examines the emergence of radical liberalism among the peasants of Guerrero. Thurner's analysis of Peruvian peasants' appropriation of terms such as *republic* and *republican* provides a new perspective on the history of political ideology during the postindependence period. See Guardino, *Peasants, Politics*; Thurner, *From Two Republics*. For analyses of the changing political ideology among the lower classes, see also Arrom, "Popular Politics"; Chambers, *From Subjects to Citizens*; Garrido, *Reclamos y representaciones*; Guedea, "De la infidelidad."

34. See Guardino, *Peasants, Politics*; Blanchard, "Language of Liberation"; Meisel, "From Slave to Citizen-Soldier"; Múnera, *El fracaso*; Andrews, *Afro-Argentines of Buenos Aires*, 42–113; Towsend, "'Half of My Body Free'"; Mallo, "La Libertad."

35. See Julius S. Scott, "Common Wind"; Gaspar and Geggus, *Turbulent Time*; Geggus, "Racial Equality"; Dubois, *Colony of Citizens*; Trouillot, *Silencing the Past*; Múnera, *El fracaso*. Zuluaga studies the black royalist guerrillas in the region of Patía in "Clientelismo y Guerrilla." Garrido examines the shifts in lower-class political language during the transition from colonial to republican rule, showing how peasant communities quickly learned to use the new republican rhetoric; see *Reclamos y representaciones*. For an analysis of pop-

ular support of royalist and republican guerillas in New Granada, see Hammett, "Popular Insurrection."

36. Van Young, *Other Rebellion*. Walker takes a similar approach in *Smoldering Ashes*.

37. Helg, *Liberty and Equality*, 122, 258.

38. See Lasso, "Haiti as an Image."

39. For elite use of the republican rhetoric of equality, see Lynch, *Spanish American Revolutions*; Wright, *Café con Leche*; Andrews, *Afro-Argentines of Buenos Aires*, 42–63.

40. Graham, *Idea of Race*.

41. Stoking, *Race, Culture and Evolution*; Young, *Colonial Desire*.

42. John Wood Sweet, *Bodies Politic*; Horsman, *Race and Manifest Destiny*; Blackburn, *Overthrow of Colonial Slavery*, 267–91.

43. I am inspired by recent works on the French Caribbean that set the debates over manumission and racial equality at the center of analysis of the Age of Revolution. See Dubois, *Colony of Citizens*; Trouillot, *Silencing the Past*; Geggus, "Racial Equality."

44. Freyre, *Masters and the Slaves*; Vasconcelos, *La raza cósmica*; Ortiz, *Contrapunteo cubano*; Siso, *La formación*; Tannenbaum, *Slave and Citizen*; Harris, *Patterns of Race*; Degler, *Neither Black nor White*.

45. Fernandes, *A integração do negro*; Viotti da Costa, "The Myth of Racial Democracy: A Legacy of the Empire, in *Brazilian Empire*, 234–46; Skidmore, *Black into White*; Andrews, *Blacks and Whites*; Wade, *Blackness and Race Mixture*; Wright, *Café con Leche*. For an excellent recent comparative analysis of race relations in Latin America, see Andrews, *Afro-Latin America*.

46. Appelbaum, Macpherson, and Rosemblatt, *Race and Nation*; Wade, *Blackness and Race Mixture*.

47. It is not clear when the myth of racial democracy was created in Brazil. Viotti da Costa explains how "the myth of racial democracy was created and destroyed" yet traces the origins of this myth to the 1930s. According to her, the myth emerged from the traditional planter elite, who felt besieged by new social forces—working-class, modern Pulista elites who mocked the past. Freyre sought to confront the new modernizing forces with a positive aspect of Brazilian tradition—racial democracy. See "Myth of Racial Democracy." Flory's analysis suggests instead that the myth's origins can be traced to the anti-Portuguese nationalism of the 1820s and 1830s; see "Race and Social Control." For an insightful analysis of the relationship between Freyre's personal life and his racial ideas, see Needell, "Identity, Race, Gender."

48. As Ferrer has shown, it was during the common struggle between black and white patriots against Spain that a nationalist construct associating Cubanness with racial harmony developed. See *Insurgent Cuba*, 112–37.

49. In 1970, Mörner pointed out the need for a "thorough study of the ethnic aspects of the struggle for emancipation." To his surprise, "not even Bolívar's somewhat contradictory views on race have ever been submitted to a systematic and objective analysis." See *Race and Class*, 200–205. After thirty years, his statement remains largely valid.

50. A few recent comparative works are Andrews, "Brazilian Racial Democracy"; Marx, *Making Race and Nation*; Cooper, Holt, and Scott, *Beyond Slavery*; Skidmore, "Racial Mixture"; Darién Davis, *Slavery and Beyond*; Landers, *Against the Odds*; Torres and Whitten, *Blackness in Latin America*.

51. De la Fuente, *Race, Inequality, and Politics*; Ferrer, *Insurgent Cuba*; Helg, *Our Rightful Share*; Schmidt-Nowara, *Empire and Antislavery*.

52. Similarly, John Wood Sweet argues that modern segregation patterns were first established in the North during the revolutionary era; see *Bodies Politic.*

53. For example, in her excellent comparison of postabolition Louisiana and Cuba, Rebecca J. Scott is able to use the Cuban patriot ideology of racial equality as one of the factors explaining differences in race and labor relations, but she is unable to explain how this factor itself emerged. See "Fault Lines, Color Lines, and Party Lines: Race, Labor, and Collective Action in Louisiana and Cuba, 1862–1912," in Cooper, Holt, and Scott, *Beyond Slavery,* 61–106, and *Degrees of Freedom,* 129–53, 189–252.

54. See Anderson, *Imagined Communities;* Colley, *Britons.*

55. For the pervasiveness of racial fears among the elite, see Lynch, *Spanish American Revolutions;* Safford, "Race, Integration, and Progress"; Wright, *Café con Leche,* 30–42.

56. For race-war threats in Panama, see Castillero-Calvo, "El movimiento de 1830"; Lasso, "La crisis política"; Espinar, "Resumen Histórico." For Guayaquil, see Lasso, "Threatening Pardos," 125–27.

57. Lynch defines *pardo* as "mulatto, of mixed white and Black descent, free coloureds"; see *Spanish American Revolutions,* xxviii.

58. The Constitution of Cartagena established that members of the Senate were required to have enough property to live comfortably but did not specify an exact amount. See "Constitución del Estado de Cartagena de Indias sancionada por la Convención General en 14 de junio de 1812 2° de la Independencia," in Guerra and Pombo, *Constituciones de Colombia,* 2: 132, 153.

59. The 1821 Constitution entitled to vote all Colombians who had one hundred pesos' worth of real estate or a useful trade, profession, or commerce with an open house or shop—thus including many black artisans. Dependents were excluded. Members of the electoral college, however, were required to be literate; to be at least twenty-five years old; and to own five hundred pesos' worth of real estate, to have employment or rent worth three hundred pesos annually, or to have a scientific degree. See Uribe Vargas, *Las constituciones de Colombia,* 2: 710–13.

60. Sabato, *La política en las calles,* 15.

Chapter 2

1. Grahn, "Contraband, Commerce, and Society"; Múnera, *El fracaso,* 131–32.

2. This figure is from the 1780 census. See Tovar Pinzón, *Convocatoria al poder;* MacFarlane, *Colombia before Independence,* 114, 117.

3. MacFarlane, *Colombia before Independence,* 116–25, 178–81; Múnera, *El fracaso,* 76–91.

4. Múnera, *El fracaso,* 104–39.

5. Múnera, *El fracaso,* 92.

6. Múnera, *El fracaso,* 94–95.

7. Kuethe, "Status of the Free *Pardo*"; Sanchez, "African Freedman." For a recent work on pardo militias in Mexico, see Vinson III, *Bearing Arms.*

8. Colmenares, "El tránsito"; MacFarlane, *Colombia before Independence,* 143; Meisel-Roca, "Esclavitud, mestizaje y haciendas"; Tovar Pinzón, *Grandes empresas agrícolas,* 41–130.

9. Tovar Pinzón, *Convocatoria al poder,* 483.

10. Mörner, *Race Mixture,* 60–70.

11. King, "Case of Jose Ponciano de Ayarza"; Ots-Capadequi, "Sobre las confirmaciones reales."

12. See "R.C. declarando la forma en que se ha de guardar y cumplir en las Indias la pragmática sanción de 23 de marzo de 1776 sobre contraer matrimonios," in Konetzke, *Colección de documentos*, 3: 438–42. For an analysis of the impact of the Real Pragmática on race relations, see Stolcke, *Marriage, Class, and Colour*. For changing eighteenth-century notions about *resguardos*, see Safford, "Race, Integration, and Progress."

13. King, "Case of Jose Ponciano de Ayarza," 644.

14. See "Informe que el Ayuntamiento de Caracas hace al Rey de España referente a la Real Cédula de 10 febrero de 1795, 28 de noviembre de 1796," in Blanco, *Documentos para la historia*, 292.

15. Gerbi, *Dispute of the New World*; Brading, *First America*, 428–32; Lynch, *Spanish American Revolutions*, 1–37; Phelan, *People and the King*.

16. For an analysis of the conflicts between Spanish authorities and the *cabildos* of Cartagena, Guayaquil, and Panama, see Kuethe, "Status of the Free *Pardo*," 110–11.

17. Archivo General de Simancas (AGS hereafter), Secretaría de Guerra, 7069, exp. 36-1, fol. 5. See also Kuethe, *Military Reform*, 176–79.

18. The literature on the Comunero rebellion is large. For a classic account in English, see Phelan, *People and the King*. An excellent account that incorporates recent literature on the subject is MacFarlane, *Colombia before Independence*, 248–71.

19. For an analysis of Spanish tactical use of coastal *pardo* militias to control Andean disaffection, see Kuethe, *Military Reform*, 165–83.

20. For tensions and conflicts between creoles and Spaniards in Bogotá in the 1790s, see MacFarlane, *Colombia before Independence*, 272–93.

21. Archivo General de Indias, Sevilla (AGI hereafter), Santa Fé, 997.

22. Múnera, *El fracaso*, 96–97.

23. AGS, Secretaría de Guerra, 7069, exp. 36, fols. 1–6.

24. "[La gente de color] es la verdadera clase de pueblo de util servicio, robusta, agil, y apta para todo género de fatiga" (AGS, Secretaría de Guerra, 7069, exp. 36, fols. 1–2). For the scant military inclination of white creoles, see AGI, Cuba, 717. Antonio Francisco Merleno wrote in 1796 that Americans, in particular whites, were little inclined to military service or to any kind of physical effort.

25. Corráles, *Documentos para la historia*, 1: 20–21.

26. Lynch, *Spanish American Revolutions*, 21–24.

27. "Actas del Ayuntamiento de Caracas," in Blanco, *Documentos para la historia*; "Informe que el Ayuntamiento de Caracas," 284–98.

28. "Informe que el Ayuntamiento de Caracas," 296.

29. "Informe que el Ayuntamiento de Caracas," 293.

30. "Informe que el Ayuntamiento de Caracas," 296.

31. AGS, Secretaría de Guerra, 7069, exp. 36-1, fols. 1–6. For similar petitions in Brazil, see Roossell-Wood, "Colonial Brazil."

32. AGS, Secretaría de Guerra, 7069, exp. 36-1, fol. 2.

33. AGS, Secretaría de Guerra, 7069, exp. 36-1, fol. 4.

34. AGS, Secretaría de Guerra, 7069, exp. 36-1, fol. 6.

35. Tate Lanning, "Documents"; King, "Case of Jose Ponciano de Ayarza." On Pedro Romero, see Múnera, *Fronteras imaginadas*, 153–74.

36. Tate Lanning, "Documents," 441.

37. Tate Lanning, "Documents," 448.

38. Tate Lanning, "Documents," 442.

39. The last time a mulatto had sought royal approval to obtain a university degree

was thirty years earlier. In 1765, Cristóbal Polo sought and obtained the king's approval of his university degrees, again with the caveat that his case must not be used as a precedent. See Tate Lanning, "Documents," 435–36.

40. Tate Lanning, "Documents," 441.

41. Helg, "Fragmented Majority," 57.

42. Brito Figueroa, *Las insurrecciones*, 72–76.

43. Pombo, *Comercio y contrabando*, 57–58. See also MacFarlane, *Colombia before Independence*, 311–14.

44. Nariño translated the 1789 version of the "Declaration of the Rights of Man," which had seventeen articles. This new translation followed instead the more radical version that preceded the Constitution of 1793, which had thirty-five articles. See Grases, "Estudio histórico-crítico," 127.

45. "Ordenanzas de la Conspiración de Gual y España," in Grases, *La con-spiración*, 175–76. The original reads as follows: "La igualdad natural entre todos los habitantes de las Provincias y distritos y se encarga que entre blancos, indios, *pardos*, y morenos, reine la mayor armonía, mirándose como hermanos en Jesucristo iguales por Dios, procurando aventajarse sólo unos y otros en méritos y virtud que son las dos únicas distinciones reales y verdaderas que hay de hombre a hombre y habrá en lo sucesivo entre todos los individuos de nuestra República."

46. Grases, *La conspiración*, 171.

47. Grases, *La conspiración*, 177–78.

48. Blanco and Aizpurua, *Documentos para la vida pública*, 332, 340.

49. Blanco and Aizpurua, *Documentos para la vida pública*, 340–41.

50. García-Chuecos, "Estudio histórico critico," in *Documentos relativos*, 13–15, 21–23.

51. Blanco and Aizpurua, *Documentos para la vida pública*, 332.

52. Blanco and Aizpurua, *Documentos para la vida pública*, 332–44; Julius S. Scott, "Common Wind," 248–61.

53. Brito Figueroa, *Las insurrecciones*, 59–81; Arcaya, *Insurrección de los negros*.

54. Pedro Medinueta to President and Captain General of Caracas, Santa Fé, Aug. 29, 1797, in García-Chuecos, *Documentos relativos*, 139–40.

55. "Instrucciones que deberán observarse en las elecciones parroquiales, en las de partido y en las capitulares, para el nombramiento de diputados en la Suprema Junta de la provincia de Cartagena," Dec. 11, 1810, in Corráles, *Efemérides y anales*, 2: 48.

56. See *Derechos del hombre*.

57. See chap. 3.

58. AGS, Secretaría de Guerra, 7064, exp. 33, fol. 1.

59. Archivo Histórico Nacional de Colombia (AHNC hereafter), Colonia, Milicias y Marina, 113, fols. 76–87.

60. AGI, Estado, 53, no. 77, fols.1–2; Kuethe, *Military Reform and Society*, 141–43.

61. Brito Figueroa, *Las insurrecciones*, 79.

62. Helg, "Fragmented Majority," 157–61.

Chapter 3

1. Vann Woodward, *Strange Career*; Marx, *Making Race and Nation*, 120–44.

2. James, *Black Jacobins*; Geggus, *Slavery, War and Revolution*.

3. The complex political and ideological changes of these years have been studied in detail elsewhere. See Guerra, *Modernidad e independencias;* Jaime Rodríguez, *Independence of Spanish America,* 36–106.

4. Chust, *La cuestión nacional americana.*

5. Chust, *La cuestión nacional americana,* 52.

6. The best analysis of the Cádiz debates over *pardo* representation remains King, "Colored Castas." See also Rieu-Millan, *Los diputados americanos,* 152–73; Chust, *La cuestión nacional americana,* 53–73, 150–73. In her recent analysis of early modern Spain and Spanish America, Herzog highlights *castas'* exclusion from citizenship in the Cádiz Constitution but does not notice the fervent debate over this issue, the fact that patriots united against it, or that all the republican constitutions in Spanish America granted legal equality to all citizens regardless of color. See Herzog, *Defining Nations.* As Jordana Dym points out, however, some regions bypassed Cádiz's regulations and included peoples of African descent in their electoral lists. Dym, "Our Pueblos," 454–57.

7. King, "Colored Castas," 43–44.

8. Manuel Alfredo Rodríguez, "Los pardos libres," 50.

9. Guerra, *Modernidad e independencias,* 327–33.

10. Chust, *La cuestión nacional americana,* 128–29.

11. See, e.g., Arguelles's arguments on Jan. 23, 1811, in *Diario de sesiones,* vol. 3.

12. Sessions of Jan. 23–25, 1811, *Diario de sesiones,* vol. 3; *El amigo de los hombres* (Philadelphia: 1812; Cartagena: Imprenta del Gobierno, 1813). When the example of Haiti was used to persuade creoles from Cartagena against declaring a junta, Antonio de Villavicencio, a royal emissary, responded: "It is completely absurd to fear an outcome similar to that of Saint Domingue, because of differences in circumstances and precedents. We recognize our king Ferdinand VII and we have not proclaimed liberty and equality or abolished the slavery of blacks, whose number was as excessive in Saint Domingue as it is scarce here. To all of those who share these fears with me I tell them to hide them." (Era el absurdo mayor temer un resultado igual al de la Isla de Santo Domingo por la diferencia de circunstancias, de antecedentes y de datos mucho mas cuando tenemos a Fernando VI por Rey reconocido y el nuevo gobierno no habiendo proclamado la libertad, e igualdad, ni abolido la esclavitud de los negro cuyo número era tan excesivo en Santo Domingo como aquí escaso. A cuantos me manifiestan estos temores, les predico que los oculten y que solo el presumirlos es un desvarío de una imaginación pusilánime e ignorante.) See Antonio de Villavicencio to Virrey Amar, May 30, 1810, AGI, Santa Fé, 747, doc. 34.

13. Chust, *La cuestión nacional americana,* 149–51.

14. Sept. 10, 1811, *Diario de sesiones,* 3: 1808.

15. Sept. 7, 1811, *Diario de sesiones,* 3: 1796.

16. Chust, *La cuestión nacional americana,* 160.

17. Sept. 7, 1811, *Diario de sesiones,* 3: 1797; Rousseau, *Social Contract and Discourses,* 26–28. For an analysis of Spanish American ideas about factionalism during the revolutionary era, see Dealy, "Prolegomena."

18. Sept. 7, 1811, *Diario de sesiones,* 3: 1795–97.

19. Riue-Millan, *Los diputados americanos,* 154.

20. "Las distintas jerarquías que hay en el cielo nos convencen de que las hay en la tierra" (Sept. 6, 1811, *Diario de sesiones,* 3: 1788).

21. For an analysis of characteristics of citizenship in Spain and America during these years, see Guerra, "El soberano."

22. Sept. 7, 1811, *Diario de sesiones,* 3: 1798.

23. Sept. 10, 1811, *Diario de sesiones*, 3: 1809.

24. Sept. 6, 1811, *Diario de sesiones*, 3: 1789–90.

25. Sept. 5, 1811, *Diario de sesiones*, 3: 1781.

26. Sept. 7, 1811, *Diario de sesiones*, 3: 1799; Chust, *La cuestión nacional americana*, 153–57. For the reevaluation of mechanical arts during the Enlightenment, see Sewell, *Work and Revolution*, 64–72, 77–86.

27. "Carta 6a de Juan Sintierra sobre un artículo de la Nueva Constitución de España," *El Español*, Oct. 30, 1811.

28. Sept. 1811, *Diario de sesiones*, 3: 1781.

29. Sept. 7, 1811, *Diario de sesiones*, 3: 1799.

30. Corráles, *Documentos para la historia*, 1: 198.

31. Antonio Nariño asked the following of Cartagena's junta: "In the sudden state of revolution it is said that the people assume sovereignty; but in fact, how do they exercise it? By their representatives, is the reply. And who names the representatives? The people. And who convokes this people? When? Where? Under what formula?" (qtd. in Jaramillo-Uribe, *El pensamiento colombiano*, 152). Although Nariño's questions were intended to satirize Cartagena's fondness for liberal notions of representation, he pointed out the crucial question of how, in fact, the people were to exercise sovereignty.

32. Múnera was the first historian to note the crucial role that *pardos* played in Cartagena's achievement of independence. See "Failing to Construct," 237–40.

33. Múnera, *El fracaso*, 157–59, 175–76.

34. Corráles, *Documentos para la historia*, 1: 127. For Pedro Romero, see Múnera, *Fronteras imaginadas*, 153–74.

35. Corráles, *Documentos para la historia*, 1: 127–28.

36. "Informe del Comandante de Ingenieros, Don Vicente Talledo, al Virrey Amar, sobre conatos de revolución en Cartagena y Mompox," in Corráles, *Documentos para la historia*, 1: 53–54.

37. "Testimonio de lo que resulta de la Causa Principal contra Don José Manuel de la Paz, Administrador General de Tabacos de la Villa de Mompox: Indiciado de haber entrado en la conspiración tramada en Mompox contra las armas del Rey," AGI, Cuba, 719 A. Similarly, the list of patriot conspirators in 1819 Ocaña includes men and women, whites and blacks, free and slaves. See "Relación de las personas que resultaron cómplices en la sorpresa y asesinato verificado en esta ciudad de Ocaña el 10 de Noviembre de 1819," AGI, Cuba, 719 A.

38. "Instrucciones que deberán observarse en las elecciones parroquiales, en las de partido y en las capitulares, para el nombramiento de diputados en la Suprema Junta de la provincia de Cartagena," Dec. 11, 1810, in Corráles, *Efemérides y anales*, 2: 48.

39. Corráles, *Documentos para la historia*, 1: 129.

40. Corráles, *Documentos para la historia*, 1: 127.

41. Cartagena, Feb. 7, 1811, AGI, Santa Fé, 747, doc. 43.

42. This point is made by Múnera, "Failing to Construct," 238. See Corráles, *Documentos para la historia*, 1: 368.

43. Pombo and Guerra, *Constituciones de Colombia*, 170.

44. Carrera-Damas, *Boves*. For a summary of *pardos'* military role in the Llanos, see, e.g., Blackburn, *Overthrow of Colonial Slavery*, 340–60; Lynch, *Spanish American Revolutions*, 190–227; Masur, *Simon Bolívar*.

45. This account of *pardos'* political activities in Caracas is based on Manuel Alfredo Rodríguez, "Los pardos libres," 51.

46. The analysis of Venezuela's debates is based on Session of July 31, 1811, Sánchez, *Libro de actas*, 254–62; Manuel Alfredo Rodríguez, "Los pardos libres," 52.

47. Parra Pérez, *La Constitución federal*, 205.

48. This rhetorical tactic was shared by other contemporary nationalist ideologies. See Hobsbawm, *Nations and Nationalism*, 91; Colley, *Britons*, 6–7, 368.

49. *Derechos del hombre* (1813). For the 1797 version, see Grases, "Estudio histórico-crítico."

50. Anderson emphasizes the sense of newness shared by Spanish American patriots yet restricts it to the elite; see *Imagined Communities*, 193. Hunt's conception of the French Revolution as a "liminal period . . . in which the nation appeared to hover on the margins between what had been declared old and what was hoped for as new" is also appropriate for the Wars of Independence; see Hunt, *Politics, Culture, and Class*, 180; Furet, *Interpreting the French Revolution*. The irremediable differences between Spain and America would be a constant element of patriot rhetoric throughout the independence period. See, e.g., "Cuartel General del Libertador en Turbaco to Sr. Brigadier and Jefe Supremo de la Plaza de Cartagena," Aug. 28, 1820, AGI, Santa Fé, 1017.

51. *Derechos del hombre* (1813), 21.

52. *Derechos del hombre* (1813), 16, 16 n. 6.

53. *El Español*, July 30, 1810, 282.

54. *El Español*, July 30, 1810, 282–83.

55. Brading, *First America*, 573–77. In 1811 Cartagena, the newspaper *El Argos Americano* reproduced fragments of *El Español* coverage of the Cádiz debates.

56. "Sobre las facultades intelectuales de los negros," *El Español*, Oct. 30, 1811, 3–25.

57. "Carta 6a de Juan Sintierra sobre un artículo de la Nueva Constitución de España," *El Español*, Oct. 30, 1811, 65–79.

58. "Carta 6a de Juan Sintierra."

59. "Reflexiones políticas y morales de un descendiente de Africa a su nación en que manifiesta sus amorosas quejas a los americanos sus hermanos," Imprenta de los huérfanos por D. Bernardino Ruiz, AGI, Signatura IA-27/9, Registro 15497.

60. King, "Colored Castas and American Representation," 34; King, "Royalist View," 533.

61. "Declaración de los capitanes Don Juán Jaldon y Don Andrés María Alvarez sobre lo ocurrido en su enviada a San Juan de Pyra para tratar con el Jefe disidente Paez," Aug. 5, 1820, AGI, Indiferente, 1568.

62. "Proclama de José Francisco Bermúdez," Cartagena, Aug. 8, 1815, AHNC, Restrepo, rollo 5, fol. 179.

63. *Observaciones de G.T. sobre la ley de Manumisión del Soberano Congreso de Colombia* (Bogota: Por José Manuel Galarza, 1822), Colección de Libros Raros y Manuscritos, Biblioteca Luis Angel Arango; "Los Hacendados y Vecinos de la Provincia de Cartagena de Colombia al Congreso," Nov. 30, 1822, Archivo Legislativo del Congreso de Colombia (ALCC hereafter), Camara, Peticiones, 33, fols. 24–31.

64. This is not to deny that some parties were more strongly associated with blacks' demands than others. The early federalist faction and later the Liberal Party tended to enjoy a larger degree of *pardo* support than the Conservative Party. For an examination of the relationship between abolitionism and the Liberal Party in the 1840s and early 1850s, see Sanders, *Contentious Republicans*.

65. Freyre's historical analysis of race relations in colonial Brazil has been instrumental in the popularity of this notion of racial tolerance. As far as I can tell, in Colombia,

the idea of Spanish racial tolerance was developed in the 1860s by conservative intellectuals who wanted to rescue the positive legacy of Spanish rule, in particular the role of the church. See Soroa, *La República*, 34–35.

66. Bolívar, "A los pueblos de Venezuela," Guyana, Aug. 5, 1817, in *Obras completas*, 647.

67. This speech, which took place in Mompox during the December 1823 Independence Day celebrations, was printed in *Gaceta de Cartagena de Colombia*, Jan. 17, 1824.

68. Mariano Montilla to Sr. Secretario de Guerra y Marina, Cartagena, May 10, 1822, AHNC, República, Secretaría de Guerra y Marina, t. 14, fol. 317.

69. Chust, *La cuestión nacional americana*, 102.

70. "Los Hacendados y Vecinos de la Provincia de Cartagena de Colombia al Congreso," Nov. 30, 1822, ALCC, Cámara, Peticiones, 33, fols. 24–31; *Observaciones de G.T.*; Jaramillo-Uribe, "La controversia jurídica," 76–80.

71. Restrepo-Piedrahita, *Actas del Congreso*, 1: 97.

72. Restrepo-Piedrahita, *Actas del Congreso*, 219–20.

73. Bierck, "Struggle for Abolition," 373–78; González, "El proceso de manumisión," 196.

74. *Gaceta de Cartagena de Colombia*, Jan. 29, 1825.

75. Art. 12, Ley de manumisión de esclavos, Cúcuta, July 19, 1821, in Restrepo-Piedrahita, *Actas del Congreso*, 2: 52.

76. *Gaceta de Cartagena de Colombia*, Jan 1, 1825.

77. *Gaceta de Cartagena de Colombia*, Jan. 17, 1824.

78. *Gaceta de Cartagena de Colombia*, Jan. 1, 1825.

79. Session of May 16, 1823, in *Santander y el Congreso de 1823*, 3: 67.

80. Castro-Leiva, *La Gran Colombia*, 110, 125.

81. "Discurso pronunciado por el Libertador ante el Congreso de Angostura el 15 de febrero de 1819," in Bolívar, *Proclamas y discursos*, 228; *Selected Writings of Bolívar*, 1: 191.

82. For the relevance of this notion for Colombian political ideology, see Castro-Leiva, *La Gran Colombia*, 110–15; Castro-Leiva, "Ironies"; Sabato, "On Political Citizenship," 1301.

83. Rousseau, *Social Contract and Discourses*, 26–28.

84. Castro-Leiva, *La Gran Colombia*, 110, 125.

85. Jan. 12, 1825, in Cortazar and Cuervo, *Congreso de 1825*, 85: 77.

86. Castro-Leiva, "Ironies," 59.

87. "Los peligros que con el tiempo pudiera experimentar la República por la diferencia de castas," Senate to Francisco de Paula Santander, June 7, 1823, in *Santander y el Congreso de 1823*, 1: 309.

88. *Selected Writings of Bolívar*, 2: 191–92.

89. "Independencia," *Gaceta de Cartagena de Colombia*, 2. The *Gaceta de Cartagena* published this history of independence in various segments.

90. *Observaciones de G.T.*, 37–38.

91. AHNC, República, Secretaría de Interior y Relaciones Exteriores, 153, fol. 624.

92. See del Río, "Meditaciones Colombianas," 308; Múnera, *Fronteras imaginadas*, 148. In the excellent essay "En busca del mestizaje" (*Fronteras imaginadas*, 129–52), Múnera highlights the importance of the idea of *mestizaje* among nineteenth-century Colombian intellectuals.

93. Del Río, "Meditaciones Colombianas," 307.

94. Del Río, "Meditaciones Colombianas," 309.

95. Del Río, "Meditaciones Colombianas," 308.

96. This was hardly a problem faced exclusively by Colombians or Spanish Americans. As Bell shows, French revolutionaries, while invoking the nation, confronted the problem of how to create the Frenchman who did not yet exist. See "Unbearable Lightness." See also Hunt, *Politics, Culture, and Class*, 72–86.

97. Since the United States left the legal status of people of African descent to individual states, legislation varied. Some states abolished slavery and granted full citizenship right to blacks; others promoted slavery and disenfranchisement of free blacks. For a summary of the various states' legislation, see Blackburn, *Overthrow of Colonial Slavery*, 111–27, 267–91.

98. This quote from the Haitian Constitution comes from Sheller, *Democracy after Slavery*, 73. Nicholls acknowledges the ideological and political dimension of this notion of "black," which included the hundreds of Polish soldiers who fought with Dessalines. Yet he links it to twentieth-century notions of black liberation rather than to contemporary notions of race, nation, and citizenship. See *From Dessalines to Duvalier*, 35–36. Geggus points out the use of a shared black identity in contemporary attempts to unify nations divided by class and color. Yet he also points out that the first constitution represented only a very short-lived attempt to stress blackness. See "Naming of Haiti," 45–46.

99. José Manuel Restrepo, "Memoria que le secretario de estado y del despacho del interior presentó al Congreso de Colombia sobre los negocios de su departamento. Año de 1823–13," Biblioteca Nacional de Colombia, Miscelánea no 1.160.

100. José Manuel Restrepo, "Memoria que le secretario de estado," 14.

101. Bushnell, *Santander Regime*, 173.

102. José Manuel Restrepo, "Memoria que le secretario de estado," 14–15. This theme recurred in Bolívar's speeches in favor of abolition. His address to the Congress of Angostura, along with his constitutional project for Bolivia, expressed his belief in the incompatibility between republicanism and slavery. See Bolívar, *Proclamas y discursos*, 232, 332.

103. The 1821 Constitution declared all free men born in Colombia's territory to be Colombians. It did not distinguish between Colombians and citizens, which were thought to be the same. The difference was instead established between those who were entitled to vote and those who were not.

104. *Gaceta de Cartagena de Colombia*, Jan. 29, 1825.

105. José Félix Restrepo, *Sobre la manumisión de los esclavos, pronunciado en el soberano congreso de Colombia reunido en la villa de Rosario de Cúcuta* (1822), in José Félix Restrepo, *Obras completas*, 337–39.

106. Art 6, Ley de manumisión de esclavos, Cúcuta, July 19, 1821, in Restrepo-Piedrahita, *Actas del Congreso*, 2: 51.

107. AHNC, República, Gobernación de Cartagena, 42, fols. 10–16; ALCC, Cámara, Informe de Comisiones, 48, fols. 223–52.

108. AHNC, República, Gobernación de Cartagena, 42, fol. 15.

109. AHNC, República, Gobernación de Cartagena, fol. 14.

110. AHNC, República, Gobernación de Cartagena, fols. 10–16.

111. Bushnell, *Santander Regime*, 183–93.

112. Decree establishing elementary schools in the cities of Honda, Mariquita, Ibagué, Ambalema, and Espinal, *Boletín de Historia y Antigüedades* 10 (May 1915): 109, 78.

113. Session of May 16, 1823, in *Santander y el Congreso de 1823*, 3: 67–68.

114. *Gaceta de Cartagena de Colombia*, June 7, 1823.

Chapter 4

1. "La Junta de Cartagena a Su Majestad y el Consejo de Regencia," Nov. 20, 1810, AGI, Santa Fé, 747, doc. 46; Pombo and Guerra, *Constituciones de Colombia*, 75–83; "Suplemento al 'Argos Americano' del lúnes 18 de Noviembre de 1811," in Corráles, *Documentos para la historia*, 1: 351.

2. For an analysis of the First Republic, see De la Vega, *Cartagena de Indias;* Guzzo, "Independence Movement." For an examination of the Spanish role in this period, see Earle, *Spain and the Independence.*

3. On creoles' fears of crowd mobilization in Colombia, see, e.g., Lievano-Aguirre, *Los grandes conflictos sociales*, 277–97. This, of course, was not unique to Colombia or Spanish America. In 1959, Rudé described how the French bourgeoisie confronted a similar predicament. See *Crowd in the French Revolution.*

4. For the rhetorical use of the sovereign people as an actor, see Guerra, *Modernidad e independencias*, 351.

5. "Instrucciones que deberá observarse en las elecciones parroquiales, en las de partido y en las capitulares, para el nombramiento de diputados en la Suprema Junta de la provincia de Cartagena," Dec. 11, 1810, in Corráles, *Efemérides y anales*, 2: 48.

6. "Defensa hecha por el señor José María García de Toledo de su conducta pública y privada, contra las calumnias de los autores de la conmoción del 11 y 12 del presente mes," in Corráles, *Documentos para la historia*, 1: 373.

7. Corráles, *Documentos para la historia*, 1: 373.

8. My analysis of Cartagena's crowd builds on the theoretical insights of Lucas, "Crowd and Politics"; Natalie Z. Davis, *Society and Culture;* Rudé, *Crowd in the French Revolution;* Thompson, *Customs in Common.*

9. Manuel Trinidad Noriega to Don Francisco Bustamante, Feb. 10, 1811, in Corráles, *Efemérides y anales*, 2: 64–70.

10. Corráles, *Efemérides y anales*, 2: 67–68.

11. Corráles, *Efemérides y anales*, 2: 66.

12. Corráles, *Efemérides y anales*, 2: 67.

13. While *zambo* is usually applied to people of mixed Indian and African descent, here it seems to denominate dark people of mixed descent.

14. Corráles, *Efemérides y anales*, 2: 68.

15. AGI, Santa Fé, 747, doc. 43.

16. Jiménez Molinares, *Linajes cartageneros*, 3–9.

17. Lemaitre, *Historia general de Cartagena*, 3: 28–31.

18. Jiménez Molinares, *Los mártires de Cartagena*, 1: 302.

19. Jiménez Molinares, *Los mártires de Cartagena*, 1: 242–44.

20. Jiménez Molinares, *Los mártires de Cartagena*, 1: 246.

21. Múnera, *El fracaso*, 193–94.

22. King, "Royalist View," 533.

23. Manuel Marcelino Núñez, "Exposición de los acontecimientos memorables relacionados con mi vida política, que tuvieron lugar en este país desde 1810 en adelante," Feb. 22, 1864; "Diligencias actuadas que tienen relación con la trans-formación política de Cartagena de Indias, que se toman de una documentación del Coronel Bonifacio Rodríguez," both in Corráles, *Documentos para la historia*, 1: 412–13.

24. "Una especie de revolución del pueblo, tramada por unos cuantos, con gratificationes a algunos pocos de la gente de color" (AGI, Santa Fé, 747, doc. 100).

25. AGI, Santa Fé, 747, doc. 94.

26. "Defensa hecha por el señor," 1: 380, 390. For a description of the Nov. 12 events, see Jiménez Molinares, Los mártires de Cartagena, 1: 258.

27. Jiménez Molinares, Los mártires de Cartagena, 1: 281.

28. Jiménez Molinares, Los mártires de Cartagena, 1: 260. See also "Ley del estado de Cartagena de Indias, da honores a los ciudadanos Pedro Gual, Manuel del Castillo, y José María García de Toledo," Feb. 13, 1815, in Corráles, Efemérides y anales, 2: 180.

29. Jiménez Molinares, Los mártires de Cartagena, 1: 288.

30. "Noticias sobre el estado de la Plaza de Cartagena," AHNC, Anexo, Historia, fols. 445–53.

31. See, e.g., Edicto del Presidente Manuel Rodriguez Torices, AHNC, Restrepo, 5, fol. 51.

32. AHNC, Anexo, Historia, 27, fols. 197–98.

33. Jiménez Molinares, Los mártires de Cartagena, 1: 275.

34. Tisnes, La independencia, 243–55; Lemaitre, Historia general de Cartagena, 3: 36.

35. For the active participation of pardos in the Republic of Cartagena, see Múnera, El fracaso, chap. 6.

36. Jiménez Molinares, Los mártires de Cartagena, 1: 280–81.

37. "Respecto a que el Obispo es Fernandino, que salga Jacobino"; "Noticias sobre el estado de la Plaza de Cartagena," Oct. 15, 1812, AHNC, Anexo, Historia, fols. 445–53.

38. "Defensa hecha por el señor," 1: 369.

39. Verna, Petión y Bolívar, 337, 316.

40. "Allí mandaba yo cincuenta haitianos corsaristas que se pusieron a mis ordenes," one Cartagenero wrote in his account of the siege. See Corráles, Documentos para la historia, 1: 183.

41. Verna, Petión y Bolívar, 312.

42. Jiménez Molinares, Los mártires de Cartagena, 1: 288.

43. Jiménez Molinares, Los mártires de Cartagena, 1: 287.

44. Jiménez Molinares, Los mártires de Cartagena, 2: 3–4.

45. "Manuel del Castillo, general en jefe de los ejércitos de la República, to the oficiales y soldados del ejército del Magdalena," Oct. 30, 1814, AHNC, Restrepo, rollo 5.

46. Jiménez Molinares, Los mártires de Cartagena, 2: 6.

47. Jiménez Molinares, Los mártires de Cartagena, 2: 7–9.

48. Pedro Gual, "Primer oficio del gobernador de la provincia de al secretario del Estado y Relaciones Exteriores del Gobierno de la Unión," Jan. 30, 1815, AHNC, Restrepo, rollo 5, fols. 113–17; "Extracto de las sesiones del Colegio Electoral y Revisor de la Constitución del Estado de Cartagena de Indias," in Corráles, Efemérides y anales, 2: 162–65.

49. Gual, "Primer oficio del gobernador," fol. 114.

50. José Salvador de Narváez, "Operaciones del Ejército de Cartagena situado en la línea occidental del río Magdalena, desde el 22 de diciembre de 1814 hasta el 18 de enero de 1815, con motivo de lo ocurrido en el Colegio electoral y Revisor el 17 de Diciembre citado," Jan. 30, 1815, in Corráles, Efemérides y anales, 2: 172–73.

51. Salvador de Narváez, "Operaciones del Ejército de Cartagena," 177; Gual, "Primer oficio del gobernador," fol. 115.

52. Salvador de Narváez, "Operaciones del Ejército de Cartagena," 175, 178–79.

53. Gual, "Primer oficio del gobernador," 114.

54. "El honor vindicado y brevísima exposición de los motivos que han obligado al pueblo de Cartagena a rechazar el nombramiento de Gobernador en el señor García de Toledo," AHNC, Restrepo, rollo 5, fols. 281–83.

55. "El honor vindicado y brevísima exposición," fol. 281.

56. "El honor vindicado y brevísima exposición," fol. 281.

57. Salvador de Narváez, "Operaciones del Ejército de Cartagena," 175–76; Gual, "Primer oficio del gobernador," fols. 115–16.

58. Salvador de Narváez, "Operaciones del Ejército de Cartagena," 176–77. For a list of the exiled men, see Jiménez Molinares, Los mártires de Cartagena, 2: 196–97.

59. "Ley del Estado de Cartagena de Indias de honores a los ciudadanos Pedro Gual, Manuel del Castillo y José María García de Toledo," Feb. 13, 1815, in Corráles, Efemérides y anales, 2: 181–83.

60. "Ley del Estado de Cartagena," 2: 181–83.

61. "Ley del Estado de Cartagena," 2: 181–83.

62. Qtd. in Jiménez Molinares, Los mártires de Cartagena, 1: 287.

63. Jiménez Molinares, Los mártires de Cartagena, 2: 191–92.

64. Jiménez Molinares, Los mártires de Cartagena, 2: 193.

65. Jiménez Molinares, Los mártires de Cartagena, 2: 194–95.

66. Jiménez Molinares, Los mártires de Cartagena, 2: 197.

67. Jiménez Molinares, Los mártires de Cartagena, 2: 199–200.

68. "Proclama de José Francisco Bermúdez," Cartagena, Aug. 8, 1815, AHNC, Restrepo, rollo 5, fol. 179. See chap. 4 for an analysis of this speech.

69. Earle, Spain and the Independence, 81.

70. This summary is based on Earle, Spain and the Independence.

71. Lemaitre, Historia general de Cartagena, 3: 151–64.

72. Jiménez Molinares, Los mártires de Cartagena, 2: 350.

Chapter 5

1. AHNC, Anexo, Guerra y Marina, 106, fol. 448.

2. AHNC, Anexo, Guerra y Marina, 106, fol. 448.

3. José Manuel Restrepo, Historia de la Revolución, 1: 164.

4. AHNC, Anexo, Guerra y Marina, 106, fols. 445–46.

5. AHNC, Anexo, Guerra y Marina, 106, fols. 455–56.

6. AHNC, Anexo, Guerra y Marina, 106, fol. 459.

7. "Inmediatamente lo convido para que se uniese con una juntica que tenia hecha contra los blancos, con la expreson que si no lo hacian asi estos se cagaban" (AHNC, Anexo, Guerra y Marina, 106, fol. 446).

8. There is a large literature on this aspect of popular support for the legitimacy of the Spanish colonial state. For Colombia, see Phelan, People and the King. For a social-history approach to the ways in which the lower classes related to the colonial state, see Nash and Sweet, Struggle and Survival.

9. AHNC, Anexo, Guerra y Marina, 106, fol. 447.

10. "Que a nadie le ha dicho de que no hay justicia en esta villa, pero que él si lo dice, pues es verdad que no la hay, pues el que quiere le pega y se queda con su trabajo" (AHNC, Anexo, Guerra y Marina, 106, fol. 447).

11. "Buenaventura Pérez, Patrimonial y Vecino de esta villa, maestro polvorista o cohetero; . . . parezco y digo, Que en el anterior gobierno compuesto de opresores de la libertad de este pueblo, se me denunció por un satélite de los déspotas del cabildo de chapetones que había en él; y fui conducido a prisión a pedimento del empecinado Don Nicolás Pérez, del egoísta Don Tomas Gartero, del Orgulloso Don Ignacio Camacho, apoyos de la ambición y el despotismo del bárbaro intrigante presidente de la extinguida Junta" (AHNC, Anexo, Guerra y Marina, 106, fol. 460).

12. AHNC, Anexo, Guerra y Marina, 106, fol. 460.

13. See AHNC, Anexo, Guerra y Marina, 106, fol. 450.

14. AHNC, Anexo, Guerra y Marina, 106, fol. 462.

15. AHNC, Anexo, Guerra y Marina, 106, fol. 470.

16. AHNC, Anexo, Guerra y Marina, 106, fol. 467.

17. AHNC, Anexo, Guerra y Marina, 106, fol. 477.

18. "Viva la patria ya muchachos descansaran sus espaldas de los planazos de Juan Gutiérrez" ("Testimonio de la causa criminal contra Juan José Mexias," AGI, Cuba, 890 B, fol. 4). Camarones is a small town near the city of Rio Hacha on the Caribbean coast.

19. "Ya tendremos alivio ya no seremos oprimidos como lo estabamos con el gobierno anterior" (AGI, Cuba, 890 B, fol. 7).

20. AGI, Cuba, 890 B, fol. 13.

21. The following discussion is based on "Cornelio Ortiz contra el Juez Letrado de Hacienda de la Provincia de Mariquita," AHNC, República, Asuntos Criminales, 38, fols. 755–63.

22. AHNC, República, Asuntos Criminales, 38, fol. 755.

23. AHNC, República, Asuntos Criminales, 38, 761.

24. AHNC, República, Asuntos Criminales, 38, 762.

25. Blackburn, *Overthrow of Colonial Slavery*, 333–75.

26. ALCC, Cámara, Informe de Comisiones, 48, fols. 223–52.

27. ALCC, Cámara, Informe de Comisiones, 48, fol. 233.

28. Zuluaga, "Clientelismo y Guerrilla," 111–36.

29. MacFarlane, "Cimarrones and Palenques," 146–48.

30. ALCC, Cámara, Informe de Comisiones, 48, fol. 232.

31. ALCC, Cámara, Informe de Comisiones, 48, fols. 243–44.

32. AHNC, República, Asuntos Criminales, 66, fols. 745–46.

33. Jaramillo-Uribe, "La controversia jurídica y filosófica."

34. ALCC, Cámara, Informe de Comisiones, 48, fols. 231–35.

35. ALCC, Cámara, Informe de Comisiones, 48, fols. 223–24.

36. ALCC, Cámara, Informe de Comisiones, 48, fols. 250–51.

37. The discussion of Arcia is based on "Causa criminal contra Valentin Arcia, alcalde ordinario de segunda nominación de Majagual por hablar mal contra los blancos y contra el gobierno," AHNC, República, Asuntos Criminales, 61, fols. 1143–1209; AHNC, República, Asuntos Criminales, 96, fols. 244–322.

38. Guarico was the Spanish name for Cap-Français, where the Haitian Revolution had begun.

39. AHNC, República, Asuntos Criminales, 61, fols. 1143–1209.

40. "Si en todos los lugares de Colombia se trataba a los de su calidad con el mismo desprecio, no quisiere Dios que se suscitase otra guerra de aquellos contra los blancos" (AHNC, República, Asuntos Criminales, 61, fols. 1143–1209).

41. For an interesting analysis of shifting notions of honor from colonial times to the early republican era, see Chambers, *From Subject to Citizens*, 161–87. For *pardos'* place in Colombia's late colonial social order, see Garrido, "'Free Men of All Colors.'"

42. "Despertad Majagualeños a las puertas del sentido os toco y vuelvo a decir / Despertad Majagualeños con vos grande y enronquecida repito / Despertad Majagualeños; no estén aletargados / mirad que quien tiene enemigos no duerme. . . . / En todo Colombia el despotismo no tiene lugar; / los Americanos a las Bayonetas lo han de desterrar / El yugo tirano no se vea en Majagual / pues de lo contrario habéis de esperar / la muerte propicia a nuestro umbral" (AHNC, República, Asuntos Criminales, 61, fols. 1143–1209).

43. AHNC, República, Asuntos Criminales, 96, fols. 244–322.

44. AHNC, República, Asuntos Criminales, 96, fols. 244–322.

45. AHNC, República, Guerra y Marina, 29, fols. 144–45.

46. AHNC, República, Congreso, 25, fol. 552.

47. AHNC, República, Congreso, 25, fol. 568.

48. José Manuel Restrepo, *Historia de la Revolución*, 1: 152.

49. Cochrane, *Viajes por Colombia*, 53. Throughout his travels on the Magdalena River, Cochrane continued to complain about the boatmen's bad work habits and "unruliness" (59–70).

50. José Manuel Restrepo, *Memoria que el secretario*, 24.

51. Cortazar and Cuervo, *Congreso de 1825*, 85: 444; José Manuel Restrepo, *Esposición*.

52. AHNC, República, Ministerio del Interior, 13, fols. 459–61.

53. AHNC, República, Congreso, 25, fols. 551–56.

54. AHNC, República, Congreso, 25, fols. 561–66.

55. For an analysis of smuggling in colonial New Granada, see Grahn, *Political Economy of Smuggling*.

56. AHNC, República, Secretaría de Guerra y Marina, 30, fols. 324–50.

57. AHNC, República, Historia, 1, fols. 168–69.

58. AHNC, República, Secretaría de Guerra y Marina, 30, fols. 324–50.

59. AHNC, República, Secretaría de Guerra y Marina, 30, fols. 616–21.

60. AHNC, República, Congreso, 25, fol. 704.

61. Session of Apr. 20, 1824, in *Santander y el Congreso de 1824*, 1: 103; AHNC, República, Congreso, 25, fol. 703.

62. AHNC, República, Congreso, 25, fols. 573–74.

63. AHNC, República, Congreso, 25, fols. 573–74.

64. AHNC, República, Congreso, 25, fols. 573–74.

65. AHNC, República, Asuntos Criminales, 66, fols. 804–11.

66. AHNC, República, Asuntos Criminales, 66, fols. 804–11. The quote comes from a copy that a local official sent to his superiors in Cartagena.

67. Remigio Marquez to los Señores del Senado Conservador, June 22, 1823, AHNC, República, Congreso, 25, fol. 567.

68. Manuel Romay to Domingo Caycedo, Cartagena, Sept. 2, 1831, in Caycedo, *Archivo epistolar*, 3: 161.

69. For the details of Padilla's life, see Otero-D'Acosta, *Vida del Almirante José Padilla;* Uribe White, *Padilla.*

70. Bushnell, *Santander Regime,* 319.

71. This portrayal is based on two contemporary descriptions, one from 1817 and one from 1828, which are quoted at length in Uribe White, *Padilla, xv.*

72. Martín-Maillefer, *Los novios de Caracas,* 91.

73. "Boletín de Ejército Defensor de Cartagena," Aug. 27, 1815, in Montilla, *General de División,* 1: 566–67.

74. Verna, *Petión y Bolívar,* 167–254.

75. Mariano Montilla to Simón Bolívar, in Montilla, *General de División,* 1: 565.

76. Mariano Montilla to F. de P. Santander, Apr. 10, 1822, Apr. 30, 1822, in Montilla, *General de División,* 2: 923, 927.

77. For marriage and race in colonial Spanish America, see Stolcke, *Marriage, Class, and Colour;* Lavrin, *Sexuality and Marriage.*

78. Mariano Montilla to F. de P. Santander, Feb. 20, 1823, in Montilla, *General de División,* 2: 969.

79. General José Padilla, "Al respetable público de Cartagena," Nov. 15, 1824, AHNC, Restrepo, fondo 11, caja 88, 170, fols. 125–26; trans. in Helg, *Liberty and Equality,* 197.

80. Padilla, "Al respetable público de Cartagena," trans. in Helg, *Liberty and Equality,* 195.

81. Bushnell, *Santander Regime,* 338–59.

82. José Padilla to Francisco de Paula Santander, Cartagena, Aug. 18, 1827, in Caicedo, Trujillo de Epps, and Anzola de Pineda, *La convención de Ocaña,* 3: 125–26.

83. General Montilla to Secretario del Libertador, Turbaco, Mar. 7, 1828, and Comandante General del Magdalena [José Montes] to Secretario General del Libertador, both in Corráles, *Efemérides y anales,* 2: 357–59.

84. This description is based on Vicente Ucros to Señor Secretario de Estado, General Montilla to Secretario del Libertador, Turbaco, Mar. 7, 1828, Comandante General del Magdalena to Secretario General del Libertador, and General Padilla to the Comisión de la Gran Convención, Mompox, Mar. 12, 1828, all in Corráles, *Efemérides y anales,* 2: 354–63, 369–73.

85. Vicente Ucros to Señor Secretario de Estado, General Montilla to Secretario del Libertador, Turbaco, Mar. 7, 1828, Oficio del Comandante General del Magdalena to Secretario General del Libertador, and General Padilla to la Comisión de la Gran Convención, Mompox, Mar. 12, 1828, all in Corráles, *Efemérides y anales,* 2: 354–63, 369–73.

86. A copy of the town council act of Mar. 12, 1828, summarizing the events appears in Magdalena Padilla, *A la impostura y la intriga, la justicia y la verdad* (Cartagena: Impreso por Manuel M. Guerrero, 1828), AHNC, República, Negocios Judiciales, 2, fol. 451.

87. According to Montilla, an Englishman told him that Padilla had armed the people of Getsemaní and the slaves. See Mariano Montilla to Señor Secretario de Estado y General de S. E. el Libertador, Turbaco, Mar. 7, 1828, in O'Leary, *Memorias,* 26: 63.

88. "Que esta era una buena noche para acabar con los blancos" (AHNC, República, Asuntos Criminales, 44, fols. 86–118).

89. AHNC, República, Asuntos Criminales, 44, fols. 86–118.

90. AHNC, República, Asuntos Criminales, 44, fols. 86–118.

91. AHNC, República, Asuntos Criminales, 44, fols. 86–118.

92. Bushnell, *Santander Regime*, 334.

93. See Uribe Vargas, *Las constituciones de Colombia*, 2: 710–12, 748–49, 790–92.

94. José Manuel Restrepo, *Historia de la Revolución*, 6: 86–92; Daniel F. O'Leary to Simón Bolívar, Ocaña, Mar. 22, 1828, and Daniel O'Leary to Simón Bolívar, Ocaña, May 22, 1828, May 27, 1828, all in O'Leary, *Memorias*, 29: 179–80, 306–9.

95. Uribe provides an excellent analysis of the social differences between aristocrats and liberals, or *provinciales*. See Uribe, *Honorable Lives*, 71–102.

96. Maingot, "Social Structure."

97. *El Calamar*, Cartagena, Mar. 28, 1828 (Imprenta de Eduardo Hernandez), and Magdalena Padilla, *A la impostura*, both AHNC, República, Negocios Judiciales, 2, fols. 451–53; Mariano Montilla to Simón Bolívar, Cartagena, Feb. 9, 1828, in Montilla, *General de División*, 1: 587.

98. Mariano Montilla to Canónigo Juan Marimon, June 27, 1815, in Montilla, *General de División*, 2: 649–51.

99. Mariano Montilla to Simón Bolívar, Apr. 3, 1828, in Montilla, *General de División*, 1: 590.

100. Daniel O'Leary to Simón Bolívar, Mar. 22, 1828, Apr. 25, 1828, both in O'Leary, *Memorias*, 29: 180, 248.

101. López, *José Padilla*, 19.

102. Simón Bolívar to José Antonio Páez, Magdalena, Mar. 6, 1826, in Bolívar, *Obras completas*, 2: 322–23.

103. José Manuel Restrepo, *Diario político y militar*, 1: 377; Daniel O'Leary to Simón Bolívar, Mar. 20, 1828, in O'Leary, *Memorias*, 29: 166–67.

104. Mariano Montilla to Simón Bolívar, Mar. 18, 1828, Apr. 3, 1828, both in Montilla, *General de División*, 1: 588–92.

105. Mariano Montilla to Simón Bolívar, in O'Leary, *Memorias*, 29: 243.

106. José Padilla to Francisco de Paula Santander, Cartagena, Feb. 9, 1828, in Caicedo, Trujillo de Epps, and Anzola de Pineda, *La convención de Ocaña*, 3: 183.

107. The account of Padilla's speech and of racial rumors during the tumults in Cartagena is based on the testimony of fifteen *pardo* and white witnesses interrogated in summary proceedings. See "Cartagena, Sumaria averiguación para aclarar asuntos relacionados con la seguridad pública y con la subordinación y disciplina en las clases del ejército," AHNC, República, Asuntos Criminales, 44, fols. 86–118.

108. "Cartagena, Sumaria averiguación."

109. Padilla's sister printed and distributed an account of the town council proceedings of Mar. 12, 1828. See Magdalena Padilla, *A la impostura*, AHNC, República, Negocios Judiciales, 2, fol. 451.

110. AHNC, República, Historia, 2, fols. 375–411.

111. "El desenlace de tales sucesos no puede haber sido más feliz, y nos ha evitado que Padilla se pusiera al frente de los *pardos* porque él es un negro" (José Manuel Restrepo, *Diario político y militar*, 1: 375); Simón Bolívar to General Pedro Briceño Méndez, Sativá, Mar. 24, 1828, in O'Leary, *Memorias*, 29: 189.

112. Simón Bolívar to Daniel O'Leary, Bucaramanga, Mar. 31, 1828, Simón Bolívar to Daniel O'Leary, Bucaramanga, Apr. 9, 1828, and Simón Bolívar to Briceño Méndez, Apr. 15, 1828, all in O'Leary, *Memorias*, 29: 197, 206, 212.

113. Mariano Montilla to Colonel Daniel O'Leary, Cartagena, Mar. 18, 1828, in

Montilla, *General de División*, 2: 656. Contemporary documents alternatively used the terms *guerra de clases* and *guerra de colores* to refer to race war. When O'Leary wrote about Píar, e.g., he said, "No pudiendo conseguirlo desacreditando la administración de éste, intentó hacerlo, provocando los odios y la guerra entre las clases de blancos y *pardos*" (O'Leary, *Memorias*, 27: 399).

114. Mariano Montilla to Señor Secretario de Estado y General de S. E. el Libertador, Turbaco, Mar. 7, 1828, in O'Leary, *Memorias*, 26: 63.

115. *El Calamar*, Cartagena, Mar. 28, 1828 (Imprenta de Eduardo Hernández), AHNC, República, Negocios Judiciales, 2, fols. 452–53.

116. López, *José Padilla*, 170.

117. Otero-D'Acosta, *Vida del Almirante*, 150–51.

Chapter 6

1. "Es muy probable, y el Libertador siempre lo pronostica, que concluida la guerra con los españoles tengamos otra con los negros" (José Manuel Restrepo, Mar. 23, 1823, in *Diario político y militar*, 1: 211).

2. Senate to Francisco de Paula Santander, June 7, 1823, in *Santander y el Congreso de 1823*, 1: 309.

3. Francisco de Paula Santander to the Minister of the Interior, Sept. 7, 1824, ALCC, Senado, Consultas, 58, fols. 43–44.

4. AHNC, República, Ministerio de Interior, 1, fols. 154, 163.

5. AHNC, República, Ministerio de Interior, 1, fols. 5–32

6. AHNC, República, Gobernación de Cartagena, 42, fols. 2–8; AHNC, República, Ministerio de Interior, 1, fols. 99–105.

7. AHNC, República, Ministerio de Interior, 1, fol. 351–53.

8. Helg, "Simón Bolívar."

9. For an analysis of the relationship between rumors and existing social conflicts, see Lincoln, *Authority Construction and Corrosion*, 45–50; Knopf, *Rumors, Race and Riots*, 20; Guha, *Elementary Aspects*, 251–77; Lefebvre, *Great Fear of 1789*.

10. Bourdieu, *Language and Symbolic Power*, 43–89; Wolf, *Envisioning Power*, 56.

11. For a recent study that makes this claim for Colombia, see Helg, *Liberty and Equality*, 216.

12. "Santo Domingo es un funesto ejemplo, y de allí deben partir las centellas del incendio" (José Manuel Restrepo, Mar. 23, 1823, *Diario político y militar*, 1: 211).

13. For the Christmas Rebellion, see Hart, *Slaves Who Abolished Slavery*, 244–73; Craton, *Testing the Chains*, 291–321.

14. AHNC, República, Gobernación de Cartagena, 42, fols. 2, 8.

15. Francisco de Paula Santander to the Minister of the Interior, Sept. 7, 1824, ALCC, Senado, Consultas, 58, fols. 43–44.

16. See the 1780 and 1825 censuses for the province of Cartagena, in Tovar Pinzón, *Convocatoria al poder del número*.

17. On public order and abandoned hacienda slaves, see Bell-Lemus, "Deser-ciones, fugas, cimarronajes, rochelas," in *Cartagena de Indias*, 75–103; AGI, Cuba, 717, Cartagena, Mar. 1816. For a congressional dossier on the freedom of slave-soldiers, see, e.g., ALCC, Senado, Consultas, 58, fols. 28, 45–47.

18. AHNC, Anexo, Tierras de Bolívar, t. único, no, 2883, fols. 78–80.

19. AHNC, Anexo, Tierras de Bolívar, t. único, no, 2883, fol. 83.

20. AHNC, Anexo, Tierras de Bolívar, t. único, no. 2883, fol. 84.

21. AHNC, Anexo, Esclavos, 2, fol. 458.

22. See chap. 4.

23. Simón Bolívar to Francisco de Paula Santander, Apr. 7, 1825, in Bolívar, *Obras completas*, 2: 114.

24. AHNC, República, Secretaría de Guerra y Marina, 14, fols.115–16.

25. See chap. 3 for the importance of Haitian sailors in the First Republic of Cartagena. See chap. 4's account of the trials of Valentín Arcia and Remigio Márquez for uses of Haitian images in local conflicts. For the influence of the Haitian Revolution in the Spanish Caribbean, see Julius S. Scott, "Common Wind"; Childs, "Black French General Arrived."

26. AHNC, República, Ministerio de Interior, 1, fol. 155. This account is particularly reliable because the author did not seek to accuse anybody but only made the government aware of the thoughts of local blacks. Neither coercion nor personal antagonism was involved in this account.

27. AHNC, República, Ministerio de Interior, 1, fol. 155.

28. AHNC, República, Ministerio de Interior, 1, fol. 155.

29. AHNC, República, Ministerio de Interior, 1, fol. 155.

30. AHNC, República, Asuntos Criminales, 61, fols. 1143–1209.

31. See chap. 4.

32. In 1816, the Venezuelan general Píar was accused of fomenting race war and was executed by Bolívar. In 1831, José Domingo Espinar, a black general from Panama, would be the target of similar accusations. For Píar's trial, see Lynch, *Spanish American Revolutions*, 210–12; Lynch, "Bolívar and the Caudillos"; "Proceso de Píar," in O'Leary, *Memorias*, 15: 351–423. For an analysis of Jose Domingo Espinar, see Castillero-Calvo, "El movimiento de 1830."

33. AHNC, República, Guerra y Marina, 14, fols. 115–16.

34. Mariano Montilla to Simón Bolívar, in O'Leary, *Memorias*, 29: 243.

35. See chap. 4.

36. José Salvador de Narváez, "Operaciones del Ejército de Cartagena situado en la línea occidental del río Magdalena, desde el 22 de diciembre de 1814 hasta el 18 de enero de 1815, con motivo de lo ocurrido en el Colegio electoral y Revisor el 17 de Diciembre citado," Jan. 30, 1815, in Corráles, *Efemérides y anales*, 2: 172–76; Pedro Gual, "Primer oficio del gobernador de la provincia de al secretario del Estado y Relaciones Exteriores del Gobierno de la Unión," Jan. 30 1815, AHNC, Restrepo, 5, fols. 115–16.

37. AHNC, República, Gobernación de Cartagena, 42, fol. 5.

38. Remigio Márquez to Señores del Senado Conservador, June 22, 1823, AHNC, República, Congreso, 25, fol. 567.

39. AHNC, República, Ministerio de Interior, 1, fol. 155.

40. Alejandro De la Fuente has noticed similar conflicts between the elite and Afro-Cubans over the meaning and implications of the nationalist myth of racial democracy in postindependence Cuba. See De la Fuente, *Nation for All*, 28–30.

41. AHNC, República, Ministerio de Interior, 1, fol. 353.

42. AHNC, República, Ministerio de Interior, 1, fol. 353.

43. See the stories of Arcia and Padilla in chap. 4.

44. AHNC, República, Ministerio de Interior, 1, fol. 102.

45. AHNC, República, Ministerio de Interior, 1, fols. 351–53.

46. See chap. 4.

47. AHNC, República, Asuntos Criminales, 61, fols. 1143–1209.

48. AHNC, República, Historia, 1, fols. 168–69.

49. AHNC, República, Historia, 1, fols. 168–69.

50. AHNC, República, Ministerio de Interior, 1, fol. 102.

51. AHNC, República, Ministerio de Interior, 1, fol. 102.

52. Daniel O'Leary to Simón Bolívar, Apr. 9, 1828, in O'Leary, *Memorias*, 29: 199.

53. Daniel O'Leary to Simón Bolívar, Apr. 9, 1828, Mar, 20, 1828, both in O'Leary, *Memorias*, 29: 170, 199.

54. "Mensaje del Libertador sobre los asuntos de Cartagena," Bucaramanga, Apr. 10, 1828, in O'Leary, *Memorias*, 29: 249.

55. Daniel O'Leary to Simón Bolívar, Ocaña, Apr. 26, 1828, Apr. 25, 1828, both in O'Leary, *Memorias*, 29: 248, 252–53.

56. "Proclama a los colombianos," Ocaña, Apr. 28, 1828, in Caicedo, Trujillo de Epps, and Anzola de Pineda, *La convención de Ocaña*, 3: 250.

57. Lemaitre, *Historia general*, 4: 63–75.

58. "Sociedad de Veteranos Defensores de la Libertad," in Corráles, *Efemérides y anales*, 3: 104–5.

59. Manuel Romay to Vice-President Domingo Caycedo, Cartagena, Sept. 2, 1831, in Caycedo, *Archivo epistolar*, 3: 160–61.

60. AHNC, República, Ministerio de Interior, 1, fols. 121–24. For Veteranos' active publishing in Cartagena, see Helg, *Liberty and Equality*, 231.

61. AHNC, República, Ministerio de Interior, 1, fols. 157–58.

62. AHNC, República, Ministerio de Interior, 1, fol. 110.

63. AHNC, República, Secretaría de Guerra y Marina, 14, fol. 115.

64. Mariano Montilla to Simón Bolívar, in O'Leary, *Memorias*, 29: 243.

65. AHNC, República, Gobernación de Cartagena, 42, fol. 4.

66. AHNC, República, Gobernación de Cartagena, 42, fol. 4; AHNC, República, Ministerio de Interior, 1, fols. 158–60, 124; AHNC, República, Gobernación de Cartagena, 42, fol. 4. For the names of the Veteranos, see "Sociedad de Veteranos Defensores de la Libertad," in Corráles, *Efemérides y anales*, 3: 104–5.

67. In her analysis of the Veteranos and the 1831 liberal revolt, Helg argues that this revolt continued traditional patterns of hierarchical citizenship in which the lower classes did not enjoy political autonomy. She bases her argument on the leading elite role in the surrender of Cartagena to the liberal troops, on the fact that the liberal press did not contain any explicit mention of racial issues, and on the assumption that Restrepo's 1831 mention of a racial conspiracy only derived from his continuing fears of pardocracy. See Helg, *Liberty and Equality*, 232–34. Yet the records of the minister of the interior show that even though the official press did not contain any explicit mention of race, broadsides such as the "honest *pardo*" pamphlet did. Moreover, racial conspiracies were real enough that several men were executed or banished because of them. Finally, *pardos'* active political participation in itself embodied—perceptibly—an active challenge to the traditional power of the white elite.

68. Conservatives continued to use accusations of race war to tarnish liberals at least until the 1870s. See Sanders, *Contentious Republicans*, 164.

69. José Manuel Restrepo, *Diario político y militar*, 2: 294; AHNC, República, Ministerio de Interior, 1, fol. 353; AHNC, República, Gobernación de Cartagena, 42, fol. 5.

70. José Manuel Restrepo, *Diario político y militar*, 2: 220.

71. See the cases of Pérez and Márquez in chap. 4.

72. AHNC, República, Ministerio de Interior, 1, fol. 351.

73. AHNC, República, Secretaría de Guerra y Marina, 14, fol. 115.

Chapter 7

1. Gerbi, *Dispute of the New World*, 3–79, 195–208, 252–68.

2. For Saint Domingue, see Garrigus, *Before Haiti*, 123.

3. "Informe que el Ayuntamiento de Caracas," 293.

4. Otis, *Rights of the British Colonies*, 36.

5. Garrigus, *Before Haiti*, 111–14. For other examples of this intellectual trend, see chaps. 4 and 5.

6. Colley, *Britons*, 6.

7. For patriots' views of America, see Guerra, *Modernidad e independencias*, 348.

8. Célius, "Neoclassicism."

9. Nicholls, *From Dessalines to Duvalier*, 55–57, 71–73.

10. I am summarizing Holton, *Forced Founders*, 133–63; John Wood Sweet, *Bodies Politic*, 189, 191.

11. Leonard I. Sweet, "Fourth of July"; White, "'It Was a Proud Day'"; Nash, *Forgotten Fifth*, 121–68.

12. For Latin American ideas about race, see Graham, *Idea of Race*. For a careful analysis of the relationship between racial discourse and Afro-Cuban political participation, see De La Fuente, *Nation for All*.

13. I am building on McGuiness, "Searching for 'Latin America,'" 97.

14. Soroa, *La República*, 34.

15. Sanders, *Contentious Republicans*; Pacheco, *La Fiesta Liberal*; Appelbaum, *Muddied Waters*, 98–99.

16. Roldán, *Blood and Fire*, 38–40.

BIBLIOGRAPHY

Archives and Manuscript Collections

COLOMBIA

Archivo Histórico Nacional de Colombia (AHNC)

Sección Colonia

Milicias y Marina

Sección República

Asuntos Criminales
Congreso
Gobernación de Cartagena
Historia
Ministerio de Interior
Negocios Judiciales
Secretaría de Guerra y Marina
Secretaría de Interior y Relaciones Exteriores

Archivo Restrepo

Sección Anexo

Esclavos
Guerra y Marina
Historia
Tierras de Bolívar

Archivo Legislativo del Congreso de Colombia (ALCC)

Cámara
Informe de Comisiones
Peticiones
Senado

Biblioteca Luis Angel Arango

Biblioteca Nacional de Colombia

SPAIN

Archivo General de Indias, Sevilla (AGI)

Fondo Cuba
Fondo Estado
Fondo Indiferente
Fondo Santa Fé

Archivo General de Simancas (AGS)

Secretaría de Guerra

Newspapers

Argos Americano
El Calamar
El Español
Gaceta de Cartagena de Colombia

Published Documents

Blanco, José Félix, ed. *Documentos para la historia de la vida pública del Libertador*. Caracas: 1878.

Blanco, José Félix, and Ramón Aizpurua, eds. *Documentos para la vida pública del Libertador*. Caracas: Ediciones de la Presidencia de la República, 1977.

Bolívar, Simón. *Obras completas de Bolívar*. Ed. Vicente Lecuna. 3 vols. Habana: Editorial Lex, 1950.

———. *Proclamas y discursos: Discursos del Libertador*. Caracas: Lit. y Tip. del Comercio, 1939.

———. *Selected Writings of Bolívar*. Ed. Harold A. Bierck Jr. Trans. Lewis Bertrand. 2 vols. New York: Colonial Press, 1951.

Bolívar, Simón, and Francisco de Paula Santander. *A los colombianos: Proclamas y discursos, 1812–1840*. Ed. Luis Horacio Lopez D. Bogotá: Fundación para la Conmemoración del Bicentenario del Natalicio y el Sesquicent, 1988.

Caicedo, Luis Javier, Alicia Trujillo de Epps, and María Victoria Anzola de Pineda, comps. *La convención de Ocaña 1828*. 3 vols. Bogotá: Biblioteca Presidencia de la República, 1993.

Caycedo, Domingo. *Archivo epistolar del General Domingo Caycedo*. Bogotá: Editorial ABC, 1943.

Cochrane, Charles Stuart. *Viajes por Colombia 1823 y 1824: Diario de mi residencia en Colombia*. Bogotá: Banco de la República, 1994.

Corráles, Manuel Ezequiel, comp. *Documentos para la historia de la provincia de Cartagena de Indias, hoy Estado Soberano de Bolívar en la Unión Colombiana*. Bogotá: Imprenta Medardo Rivas, 1883.

———. *Efemérides y anales del Estado de Bolívar*. 3 vols. Bogotá: Casa Editorial de J. J. Pérez, 1889.

Cortazar, Roberto, and Luis Augusto Cuervo, eds. *Congreso de 1825: Senado, actas*. Bogotá: Imprenta Nacional, 1952.

del Río, Juan García. "Meditaciones Colombianas." In *Ensayos costeños de la colonia a la República: 1770–1890*, ed. Alfonso Múnera. Bogotá: Colcultura, 1994.

Derechos del hombre y del ciudadano con varias máximas republicanas y un discurso preliminar dirigido a los americanos. Santa Fé de Bogotá: Imprenta del Estado por el C. José Maria Ríos, 1813.

Diario de sesiones de las Cortes Generales y Extraordinarias. 9 vols. Madrid: 1870.

Espinar, José Domingo. "Resumen histórico que hace el General José Domingo Espinar de los acontecimientos políticos ocurridos en Panamá en el año de 1830, apellidados ahora Revolución de Castas por el Gobernador José de Obaldía." *Lotería* (1976).

García-Chuecos, Hector, ed. *Documentos relativos a la Revolución de Gual y España.* Caracas: Instituto Panamericano de Geografía e Historia, 1949.

Grases, Pedro. *La conspiración de Gual y España y el ideario de la independencia.* Caracas: Academia Nacional de la Historia, 1996.

————. "Estudio histórico-crítico sobre los derechos del hombre y del ciudadano." In *Derechos del hombre y del ciudadano,* ed. Pedro Grases and Pablo Ruggeri Parra, 103–246. Caracas: Academia Nacional de la Historia, 1959.

Grases, Pedro, and Pablo Ruggeri Parra, eds. *Derechos del hombre y del ciudadano.* Caracas: Academia Nacional de la Historia, 1959.

Konetzke, Richard. *Colección de documentos para la historia de la formación social de Hispanoamérica, 1493–1810.* 2 vols. Madrid: Consejos Superior de Investigaciones Científicas, 1962.

Montilla, Mariano. *General de División Mariano Montilla: Homenaje al bicentenario de su nacimiento 1782–1982.* Caracas: Ediciones Presidencia de la República, 1982.

O'Leary, Daniel. *Memorias del General O'Leary.* Vols. 18–29. Caracas: Imprenta el Monitor, 1884.

Otís, James. *The Rights of the British Colonies Asserted and Proved.* Boston: Reprinted for J. Almon, London, 1764.

Parra Pérez, C., ed. *La Constitución federal de Venezuela de 1811 y documentos afines.* Caracas: Academia Nacional de la Historia, 1959.

Restrepo, José Félix. *Obras completas.* Comp. Rafael Montoya y Montoya. Medellín: Editorial Bedout, 1961.

Restrepo, José Manuel. *Diario político y militar: Memorias sobre los sucesos importantes de la época para servir a la historia de la Revolución de Colombia y de la Nueva Granada, desde 1819 para adelante.* Bogotá: Imprenta Nacional, 1954.

————. *Esposición que el secretario de estado del despacho de interior del gobierno de la República de Colombia hace al Congreso de 1827 sobre los negocios de su departamento.* Bogotá: Imprenta de Pedro Cubides, 1827.

————. *Historia de la Revolución de la República de Colombia.* 6 vols. 1858. Reprint, Medellín: Editorial Bedout, 1974.

————. *Memoria que el secretario de estado y del despacho del interior presentó al Congreso de Colombia sobre los negocios de su departamento.* Biblioteca Nacional de Colombia, Miscelánea, no 1.160. Bogotá: Espínosa, 1823.

Restrepo-Piedrahita, Carlos, ed. *Actas del Congreso de Cucutá, 1821.* 3 vols. Bogotá: Fundación para la Conmemoración del Bicentenario del Natalicio y el Sesquicentenario de la muerte del General Francisco de Paula Santander, 1989.

Sánchez, Ramón Díaz, ed. *Libro de actas del Supremo Congreso de Venezuela, 1811–1812.* Caracas: Academia Nacional de la Historia, 1959.

Santander y el Congreso de 1823: Actas correspondencia, senado. 2 vols. Bogotá: Biblioteca de la Presidencia de la Republica, 1989.

Santander y el Congreso de 1824: Actas y correspondencia, senado. Bogotá: Biblioteca de la Presidencia de la República, 1989.

Soroa, G. de [Sergio Arboleda]. *La República en la América Española.* Bogotá: Imprenta a cargo de Foción Mantilla, 1869.

Tate Lanning, John. "Documents: The Case of José Ponseano de Ayarza: A Document on the Negro in Higher Education." *Hispanic American Historical Review* 24, no. 3 (1944): 432–51.

Torres, Gerónimo. *Observaciones de G.T. sobre la ley de manumisión del soberano Congreso de Colombia.* Bogotá: José Manuel Galarza, 1822.

Secondary Sources

Adelman, Jeremy, *Republic of Capital: Buenos Aires and the Legal Transformation of the Atlantic World.* Stanford: Stanford University Press, 1999.

Alonso, Ana María. *Thread of Blood: Colonialism, Revolution, and Gender on Mexico's Northern Frontier.* Tucson: University of Arizona Press, 1995.

Anderson, Benedict. *Imagined Communities: Reflections on the Origin and Spread of Nationalism.* London and New York: Verso, 1991.

Andrews, George Reid. *The Afro-Argentines of Buenos Aires, 1800–1900.* Madison: University of Wisconsin Press, 1980.

———. *Afro-Latin America, 1800–2000.* Oxford: Oxford University Press, 2004.

———. *Blacks and Whites in Sao Paulo, Brazil, 1888–1988.* Madison: University of Wisconsin Press, 1991.

———. "Brazilian Racial Democracy, 1900–1990: An American Counterpoint." *Journal of Contemporary History* 31, no. 3 (1996): 483–507.

———. "Spanish American Independence: A Structural Analysis." *Latin American Perspectives* 12, no. 1 (1985): 105–32.

Annino, Antonio, ed. *Historia de las elecciones en Iberoamérica, siglo XIX.* Mexico: Fondo de Cultura Económica, 1995.

Annino, Antonio, Luis Castro-Leiva, and Francois-Xavier Guerra, eds. *De los imperios a las naciones: Iberoamérica.* Zaragoza: Obra Cultural, 1994.

Appelbaum, Nancy P. *Muddied Waters: Race, Region, and Local History in Colombia, 1846–1948.* Durham: Duke University Press, 2003.

Appelbaum, Nancy P., Anne S. Macpherson, and Karin Alejandra Rosemblatt, eds. *Race and Nation in Modern Latin America.* Chapel Hill: University of North Carolina Press, 2003.

Arcaya, Pedro M. *Insurrección de los negros de la Serranía de Coro.* Caracas: Instituto Panamericano de Geografía e Historia, 1949.

Arrom, Sylvia M. "Popular Politics in Mexico City: The Parian Revolt, 1828." In *Riots in the Cities: Popular Politics and the Urban Poor in Latin America, 1765–1910,* ed. Silvia M. Arrom and Servando Ortoll, 71–96. Wilmington: Scholarly Resources, 1996.

Beezley, William H., Cheryl E. Martin, and W. E. French, eds. *Rituals of Rule, Rituals of Resistance: Public Celebrations and Popular Culture in Mexico.* Wilmington: Scholarly Resources, 1994.

Bell, David A. "The Unbearable Lightness of Being French: Law, Republicanism and National Identity at the End of the Old Regime." *American Historical Review* 106, no. 4 (2001): 1215–35.

Bell-Lemus, Gustavo. *Cartagena de Indias de la colonia a la república.* Bogotá: Fundación Simón y Lola Guberek, 1991.

Berlin, Ira, and Ronald Hoffman, eds. *Slavery and Freedom in the Age of the American Revolution.* Charlottesville: University Press of Virginia, 1983.

Bierck, Harold A., Jr. "The Struggle for Abolition in Gran Colombia." *Hispanic American Historical Review* 33, no. 3 (1953): 365–86.

Blackburn, Robin. *The Overthrow of Colonial Slavery, 1776–1848.* London: Verso, 1988.

Blanchard, Peter. "The Language of Liberation: Slave Voices in the Wars of Independence." *Hispanic American Historical Review* 82, no. 3 (2002): 499–523.

Borrego, María del C. *Palenques de negros en Cartagena de Indias a fines del siglo diecisiete.* Sevilla: Escuela de Estudios Hispanoamericanos, 1973.

Bourdieu, Pierre. *Language and Symbolic Power.* Cambridge: Polity Press, 1991.

Brading, David A. *The First America: The Spanish Monarchy, Creole Patriots, and the Liberal State, 1492–1867.* Cambridge: Cambridge University Press, 1991.

Brito Figueroa, Federico. *Las insurrecciones de los esclavos negros en la sociedad colonial venezolana.* Caracas: Editorial Cantaclaro, 1961.

Burns, Bradford E. *The Poverty of Progress: Latin America in the Nineteenth Century.* Berkeley: University of California Press, 1983.

Bushnell, David. *The Making of Modern Colombia: A Nation in Spite of Itself.* Berkeley: University of California Press, 1993.

———. *The Santander Regime in Gran Colombia.* Newark: University of Delaware Press, 1954.

Carrera-Damas, Germán. *Boves: Aspectos socioeconómicos de la guerra de independencia.* 3rd ed. Caracas: Ediciones de la Biblioteca, Universidad Central de Venezuela, 1972.

———. *El culto a Bolívar.* Caracas: Instituto de Antropología e Historia, 1969.

———. *Venezuela: Proyecto nacional y poder social.* Barcelona: Grijalbo, 1986.

Castillero-Calvo, Alfredo. "El movimiento de 1830." *Tareas* 5 (1961): 12–56.

Castro-Leiva, Luis. *De la patria boba a la teología bolivariana: Ensayos de historia intelectual.* Caracas: Monte Avila Editores, 1991.

———. *La Gran Colombia, una ilusión ilustrada.* Caracas: Monte Avila Editores, 1985.

———. "The Ironies of the Spanish American Revolutions." *International Social Science Journal* 41, no. 1 (1989): 53–68.

Célius, Carlo. "Neoclassicism and the Haitian Revolution." Paper presented at conference Haitian Revolution after Two Hundred Years. Providence, June 2004.

Chambers, Sarah C. *From Subjects to Citizens: Honor, Gender, and Politics in Arequipa, Peru 1780–1854.* University Park: Pennsylvania State University Press, 1999.

Chartier, Roger. *Cultural History: Between Practices and Representations.* Ithaca: Cornell University Press, 1988.

———. *The Cultural Origins of the French Revolution.* Durham: Duke University Press, 1991.

Childs, Matt D. "'A Black French General Arrived to Conquer the Island': Images of the Haitian Revolution in Cuba's 1812 Aponte Rebellion." In Geggus, *Impact of the Haitian Revolution,* 135–56.

Chust, Manuel. *La cuestión nacional americana en las Cortes de Cádiz (1810–1814).* Valencia: Fundación Instituto de Historia Social, 1999.

Clark, Meri L. "Education for a Moral Republic: Schools, Reform, and Conflict in Colombia, 1780–1845." Ph.D. diss., Princeton University, 2003.

Cobb, Richard. *The Police and the People: French Popular Protest, 1789–1820.* Oxford: Clarendon Press, 1970.

Cohen, David W., and Jack P. Greene, eds. *Neither Slave nor Free*. Baltimore: John Hopkins University Press, 1972.

Colley, Linda. *Britons: Forging the Nation, 1707–1837*. New Haven: Yale University Press, 1992.

Colmenares, Germán. *Las convenciones contra la cultura*. Bogotá: Tercer Mundo editores, 1987.

———, ed. *La Independencia: Ensayos de historia social*. Bogotá: Instituto Colombiano de Cultura, 1986.

———. "El tránsito a sociedades campesinas de dos sociedades esclavistas en la Nueva Granada, Cartagena y Popayán, 1780–1850." *Huellas* 29 (1990): 8–24.

Cooper, Frederick, Thomas C Holt, and Rebecca J. Scott. *Beyond Slavery: Explorations of Race, Labor, and Citizenship in Postemancipation Societies*. Chapel Hill: University of North Carolina Press, 2000.

Coronil, Fernando. "Beyond Occidentalism: Toward Nonimperial Geohistorical Categories." *Cultural Anthropology* 11, no. 1 (1996): 51–88.

———. *The Magical State: Nature, Money, and Modernity in Venezuela*. Chicago: University of Chicago Press, 1997.

Craton, Michael. *Testing the Chains: Resistance to Slavery in the British West Indies*. Ithaca: Cornell University Press, 1982.

Davis, Darién. *Slavery and Beyond: The African Impact on Latin America and the Caribbean*. Wilmington: Scholarly Resources, 1995.

Davis, David B. *The Problem of Slavery in the Age of Revolution, 1770–1823*. Ithaca: Cornell University Press, 1975.

Davis, Natalie Z. *Society and Culture in Early Modern Europe*. Stanford: Stanford University Press, 1975.

Dealy, Glen. "Prolegomena on the Spanish American Political Tradition." *Hispanic American Historical Review* 48, no. 1 (1968): 37–58.

Deas, Malcom. "La presencia de la política nacional en la vida provinciana, pueblerina y rural de Colombia en el primer siglo de la República." In *La unidad nacional en América Latina*, ed. Marco Palacios,149–73. México, D.F.: Colegio de México, 1983.

Degler, Carl. *Neither Black nor White: Slavery and Race Relations in Brazil and the United States*. New York: Macmillan, 1971.

De la Fuente, Alejandro. *A Nation for All: Race, Inequality, and Politics in Twentieth-Century Cuba*. Chapel Hill: University of North Carolina Press, 2001.

———. *Race, Inequality, and Politics in Twentieth-Century Cuba*. Chapel Hill: University of North Carolina Press, 2001.

De la Vega de, Alejandra Sourdis. *Cartagena de Indias durante la Primera República, 1810–1815*. Bogotá: Banco de la República, 1988.

Dirks, Robert. *Black Saturnalia: Conflict and Its Ritual Expression on British West Indian Slave Plantations*. Gainesville: University Press of Florida, 1987.

Dominguez, Jorge. *Insurrection or Loyalty: The Breakdown of the Spanish American Empires*. Cambridge: Harvard University Press, 1980.

Dubois, Laurent. *A Colony of Citizens: Revolution and Slave Emancipation in the French Caribbean, 1787–1804*. Chapel Hill: University of North Carolina Press, 2004.

Dym, Jordana. "'Our Pueblos, Fractions with No Central Unity': Municipal Sovereignty in Central America, 1808–1821." *Hispanic American Historical Review* 86, no. 3 (2006): 431–66.

Earle, Rebecca A. "Creole Patriotism and the Myth of the 'Loyal Indian.'" *Past and Present* 172 (2001): 125–45.

———. *Spain and the Independence of Colombia, 1810–1825*. Exeter: University of Exeter Press, 2000.

Edwards, Paul, and James Walvin. *Black Personalities in the Era of the Slave Trade*. London: Macmillan, 1983.

Engerman, Stanley L., and Eugene D. Genovese, eds. *Race and Slavery in the Western Hemisphere: Quantitative Studies*. Princeton: Princeton University Press, 1975.

Farge, Arlette. *Fragile Lives: Violence, Power and Solidarity in Eighteenth-Century Paris*. Cambridge: Harvard University Press, 1993.

Favre, Henry. "Bolívar y los Indios." *Histórica* 10, no. 1 (1986): 1–18.

Fernandes, Florestan. *A integracao do negro na sociedade de classes*. São Paulo: Dominus Editôra, 1965.

Ferrer, Ada. *Insurgent Cuba: Race, Nation, and Revolution, 1868–1898*. Chapel Hill: University of North Carolina Press, 1999.

Flory, Thomas. "Race and Social Control in Independent Brazil." *Journal of Latin American Studies* 9, no. 2 (1977): 199–224.

Frey, Sylvia R. *Water from the Rock: Black Resistance in a Revolutionary Age*. Princeton: Princeton University Press, 1991.

Freyre, Gilberto. *The Masters and the Slaves: A Study in the Development of Brazilian Civilization*. New York: Knopf, 1956.

Friedemann, Nina S. de. "Estudios negros en la antropología en Colombia." In *Un siglo de investigación social*, ed. Jaime Arrocha and Nina S. de Friedemann, 507–72. Bogotá: Etno, 1984.

Furet, François. *Interpreting the French Revolution*. Cambridge: Cambridge University Press, 1981.

Garrido, Margarita. "'Free Men of All Colors' in New Granada: Identity and Obedience before Independence." In *Political Culture in the Andes, 1750–1950*, ed. Nils Jacobsen and Cristóbal Aljovín de Losada, 165–83. Durham: Duke University Press, 2005.

———. *Reclamos y representaciones: Variaciones sobre la política en el Nuevo Reino de Granada, 1770–1815*. Bogotá: Banco de la República, 1993.

Garrigus, John D. *Before Haiti: Race and Citizenship in French Saint-Domingue*. New York: Palgrave Macmillan, 2006.

Gaspar, D. B., and D. P. Geggus, eds. *A Turbulent Time: The French Revolution and the Greater Caribbean*. Bloomington: Indiana University Press, 1997.

Geertz, Clifford. *Deep Play: Notes on the Balinese Cockfight*. Indianapolis: Bobbs-Merrill, 1972.

Geggus, David P., ed. *The Impact of the Haitian Revolution in the Atlantic World*. Columbia: University of South Carolina Press, 2001.

———. "The Naming of Haiti." *New West Indian Guide* 71 (1997): 43–68.

———. "Racial Equality, Slavery, and Colonial Secession during the Constituent Assembly." *American Historical Review* 94, no. 5 (1989): 1290–1308.

———. *Slavery, War, and Revolution: The British Occupation of Saint Domingue, 1793–1798*. Oxford: Clarendon Press, 1982.

Genovese, Eugene D. *From Rebellion to Revolution: Afro-American Slave Revolts in the Making of the Modern World*. Baton Rouge: Louisiana State University Press, 1979.

Gerbi, Antonello. *The Dispute of the New World: The History of a Polemic, 1750–1900.* Pittsburgh: University of Pittsburgh Press, 1973.

Gilroy, Paul. *The Black Atlantic: Modernity and Double Consciousness.* Cambridge: Harvard University Press, 1993.

Ginzburg, Carlo. *Clues, Myths, and the Historical Method.* Baltimore: Johns Hopkins University Press, 1989.

González, Margarita. "El proceso de manumisión en Colombia." *Cuadernos Colombianos* 2 (1974): 150–240.

Graham, Richard, ed. *The Idea of Race in Latin America, 1870–1940.* Austin: University of Texas Press, 1990.

———. *Independence in Latin America: A Comparative Approach.* 2nd ed. New York: McGraw-Hill, 1994.

Grahn, Lance Raymond. "Contraband, Commerce, and Society in New Granada, 1713–1763." Ph.D. diss., Duke University, 1985.

———. *The Political Economy of Smuggling: Regional Informal Economies in Early Bourbon New Granada.* Boulder: Westview Press, 1997.

Guardino, Peter. *Peasants, Politics, and the Formation of Mexico's National State.* Stanford: Stanford University Press, 1996.

Guedea, Virginia. "De la infidelidad a la infidencia." In *Patterns of Contention in Mexican History,* ed. Jaime E. Rodríguez, 95–123. Wilmington: Scholarly Resources, 1992.

Guerra, Francois-Xavier. *Modernidad e independencias: Ensayos sobre las revoluciones hispánicas.* Madrid: Mapre, 1992.

———. "El soberano y su reino: Reflexiones sobre la génesis del ciudadano en América Latina." In *Ciudadanía política y formación de naciones: Perspectivas históricas de América Latina,* ed. Hilda Sabato, 33–61. Mexico: Fondo de Cultura Económica, 1999.

Guerra, José Joaquín, and Manuel Antonio Pombo, comps. *Constituciones de Colombia.* 4 vols. Bogotá: Biblioteca Popular de la Cultura Colombiana, 1951.

Guha, Ranahit. *Elementary Aspects of Peasant Insurgency in Colonial India.* Delhi: Oxford University Press, 1983.

———. "The Prose of Counter-Insurgency." In *Selected Subaltern Studies,* ed. Ranajit Guha and Gayatri Chakravorty Spivak, 45–88. New York: Oxford University Press, 1988.

Guzzo, Peter. "The Independence Movement and the Failure of the First Republic of Cartagena." Ph.D. diss., Catholic University of America, 1972.

Hale, Charles. *Mexican Liberalism in the Age of Mora, 1821–1853.* New Haven: Yale University Press, 1968.

Halperín-Donghi, Tulio. *The Contemporary History of Latin America.* Durham: Duke University Press, 1993.

Hamill, Hugh, Jr. *The Hidalgo Revolt: Prelude to Mexican Independence.* Gainesville: University Press of Florida, 1966.

Hammett, Brian R. "Popular Insurrection and Royalist Reaction: Colombian Region, 1810–1823." In *Reform and Insurrection in Bourbon New Granada and Peru,* ed. J. R. Fisher, A. J. Kuethe, and A. McFarlane, 291–326. Baton Rouge: Louisiana State University Press, 1990.

Harris, Marvin. *Patterns of Race in the Americas.* New York: Walker, 1964.

Hart, Richard. *Slaves Who Abolished Slavery.* Mona: Institute of Social and Economic Research, 1980.

Haslip-Viera, Gabriel. "The Underclass." In *Cities and Society in Colonial Latin America,* ed. L. S. Hoberman and S. M. Socolow, 258–312. Albuquerque: University of New Mexico Press, 1986.

Hay, Douglas, ed. *Albion's Fatal Tree: Crime and Society in Eighteenth-Century England*. New York: Pantheon Books, 1975.

Helg, Aline. "Esclavos y libres de color: Negros y mulatos en la investigación y la historia de Colombia." *Revista Iberoamericana* 65 (1999): 697–712.

———. "A Fragmented Majority: Free 'Of All Colors,' Indians, and Slaves in Caribbean Colombia during the Haitian Revolution." In Geggus, *Impact of the Haitian Revolution*, 157–75.

———. *Liberty and Equality in Caribbean Colombia, 1770–1835*. Chapel Hill: University of North Carolina Press, 2004.

———. "The Limits of Equality: Free People of Colour and Slaves during the First Republic of Cartagena, Colombia, 1810–1815." *Slavery and Abolition* 20, no. 2 (1999): 1–30.

———. *Our Rightful Share: The Afro-Cuban Struggle for Equality, 1886–1912*. Chapel Hill: University of North Carolina Press, 1995.

———. "Simón Bolívar and the Spectre of *Pardocracia:* José Padilla in Post-Independence Cartagena." *Journal of Latin American Studies* 35, no. 3 (2003): 447–71.

Herzog, Tamar. *Defining Nations: Immigrants and Citizens in Early Modern Spain and Spanish America*. New Haven: Yale University Press, 2003.

Hobsbawm, Eric J. *The Age of Revolution, 1789–1848*. London: Weidenfield and Nicolson, 1962.

———. *Nations and Nationalism since 1780: Programme, Myth, Reality*. Cambridge: Cambridge University Press, 1990.

Hobsbawm, Eric, and Terence Ranger, eds. *The Invention of Tradition*. Cambridge: Cambridge University Press, 1983.

Holton, Woody. *Forced Founders: Indians, Debtors, Slaves, and the Making of the American Revolution in Virginia*. Chapel Hill: University of North Carolina Press, 1999.

Horsman, Reginald. *Race and Manifest Destiny: The Origins of American Racial Anglo-Saxonism*. Cambridge: Harvard University Press, 1981.

Hunt, Lynn. *Politics, Culture, and Class in the French Revolution*. Berkeley: University of California Press, 1984.

James, C. L. R. *The Black Jacobins: Toussaint L'Ouverture and the San Domingo Revolution*. New York: Vintage Books, 1989.

Jaramillo-Uribe, Jaime. "La controversia jurídica y filosófica librada en la Nueva Granada en torno a la liberación de los esclavos y la importancia económica-social de la esclavitud en el siglo XIX." *Anuario Colombiano de Historia Social y de la Cultura* 4 (1969): 63–86.

———. "Esclavos y señores en la sociedad colombiana del siglo XVIII." *Anuario Colombiano de Historia Social y de la Cultura* 1 (1963): 3–55.

———. *El pensamiento colombiano en el siglo XIX*. Bogotá: Planeta, 1996.

Jiménez Molinares, Gabriel. *Linajes cartageneros*. Cartagena: Imprenta Departamental, 1950.

———. *Los mártires de Cartagena de 1816 ante el consejo de guerra y ante la historia*. 2 vols. Bolívar: Imprenta Departamental, 1950.

Joseph, Gilbert M., and Daniel Nugent, eds. *Everyday Forms of State Formation: Revolution and the Negotiation of Rule in Modern Mexico*. Durham: Duke University Press, 1994.

King, James. "The Case of Jose Ponciano de Ayarza: A Document of Gracias al Sacar." *Hispanic American Historical Review* 31, no. 4 (1951): 640–47.

————. "The Colored Castas and American Representation in the Cortes of Cádiz." *Hispanic American Historical Review* 33, no. 1 (1953): 33–64.

————. "A Royalist View of the Colored Castes in the Venezuelan Wars of Independence." *Hispanic American Historical Review* 33, no. 4 (1953): 527–37.

Knopf, Terry Ann. *Rumors, Race and Riots.* New Brunswick: Transaction Books, 1975.

König, Hans-Joachim. *En el camino hacia la nación: Nacionalismo en el proceso de formación del estado y de la nación en la Nueva Granada, 1750–1856.* Bogotá: Banco de la República, 1994.

Kraay, Hendrik. "As Terrifying as Unexpected: The Bahian Sabinada, 1837–1838." *Hispanic American Historical Review* 72, no. 4 (1992): 501–27.

Kuethe, Allan. *Military Reform and Society in New Granada.* Gainesville: University Press of Florida, 1978.

————. "The Status of the Free *Pardo* in the Disciplined Militia of New Granada." *Journal of Negro History* 56 (1971): 105–17.

Landers, Jane, ed. *Against the Odds: Free Blacks in the Slave Societies of the Americas.* Portland: Frank Cass, 1996.

Lasso, Marixa. "La crisis política post-independentista: 1821–1841." In *Historia general de Panamá,* ed. Alfredo Castillero-Calvo, 2: 66–72. Panamá City: Comité Nocional del Centenario de la República de Panama, 2004.

————. "Haiti as an Image of Popular Republicanism in Caribbean Colombia." In Geggus, *Impact of the Haitian Revolution,* 176–90.

————. "Threatening Pardos: Pardo Republicanism in Colombia, 1811–1830." In *Transatlantic Rebels: Agrarian Radicalism in Comparative Context,* ed. Thomas Summerhill and James C. Scott, 117–35. East Lansing: Michigan State University Press, 2004.

Lavrin, Asunción, ed. *Sexuality and Marriage in Colonial Latin America.* Lincoln: University of Nebraska Press, 1989.

Lefebvre, Georges. *The Great Fear of 1789: Rural Panic in Revolutionary France.* New York: Pantheon Books, 1975.

Lemaitre, Eduardo. *Historia general de Cartagena.* 4 vols. Bogotá: Banco de la República, 1983.

Lievano-Aguirre, Indalecio. *Los grandes conflictos sociales y económicos de nuestra historia.* 4 vols. Bogotá: Ediciones Nueva Prensa, n.d.

Lincoln, Bruce. *Authority Construction and Corrosion.* Chicago: University of Chicago Press, 1994.

————. *Discourse and the Construction of Society: Comparative Studies of Myth, Ritual, and Classification.* New York: Oxford University Press, 1989.

Linebaugh, Peter. "All the Atlantic Mountains Shook." *Labour/Le Travailler* 10 (1982): 87–121.

Linebaugh, Peter, and Marcus Rediker. "The Many Headed Hydra." *Journal of Historical Sociology* 3 (1990): 225–53.

Liss, Peggy K. *Atlantic Empires: The Network of Trade and Revolution, 1713–1826.* Baltimore: Johns Hopkins University Press, 1983.

Lombardi, John. *The Decline and Abolition of Negro Slavery in Venezuela, 1820–1854.* Westport: Greenwood Publishing, 1971.

López, Víctor Manuel. *José Padilla: Almirante de Colombia.* Manizales: Editorial Renacimiento, 1960.

Lucas, Colin. "The Crowd and Politics between 'Ancien Regime' and Revolution in France." *Journal of Modern History* 60, no. 3 (1988): 421–57.

Lynch, John. "Bolívar and the Caudillos." *Hispanic American Historical Review* 63, no. 1 (1983): 3–35.

———, ed. *Latin American Revolutions, 1808–1826: Old and New World Origins.* Norman: University of Oklahoma Press, 1994.

———. *Simón Bolívar: A Life.* New Haven: Yale University Press, 2006.

———. *The Spanish American Revolutions, 1808–1826.* 2nd ed. New York: Norton, 1986.

MacFarlane, Anthony. "Building Political Order: The 'First Republic' in New Granada, 1810–1815." In *In Search of New Order: Essays on the Politics and Society of Nineteenth-Century Latin America,* ed. Eduardo Posada-Carbó, 8–33. New York: Cambridge University Press, 1993.

———. "Cimarrones and Palenques: Runaways and Resistance in Colonial Colombia." In *Out of the House of Bondage: Runaways, Resistance and Marronage in Africa and the New World,* ed. Gad Heuman, 131–51. London: Cass, 1986.

———. *Colombia before Independence: Economy, Society and Politics under Bourbon Rule.* Cambridge: Cambridge University Press, 1993.

Maingot, Anthony P. "Social Structure, Social Status, and Civil-Military Conflict in Urban Colombia, 1810–1858." In *Nineteenth-Century Cities: Essays in the New Urban History,* ed. Stepha Thernstrom and Richard Sennett, 297–355. New Haven: Yale University Press, 1969.

Mallo, Silvia C. "La libertad en el discurso del estado, de amos y esclavos, 1780–1830." *Revista Historia de América* 112 (1991): 121–46.

Mallon, Florencia. *Peasant and Nation: The Making of Postcolonial Mexico and Peru.* Berkeley: University of California Press, 1995.

Martín-Maillefer, P. D. *Los novios de Caracas, poema eclectico en dos cantos, seguidos de notas o consideraciones politicas y morales sobre algunos estados del Nuevo Mundo.* Caracas: Talleres de linotipo de El Universal, 1917.

Marx, Anthony W. *Making Race and Nation: A Comparison of South Africa, the United States, and Brazil.* Cambridge: Cambridge University Press, 1998.

Masur, Gerhard. *Simon Bolívar.* Caracas: Grijalbo, 1987.

McGuiness, Aims. "Searching for 'Latin America': Race and Sovereignty in the Americas in the 1850s." In *Race and Nation in Modern Latin America,* ed. Nancy P. Appelbaum, Anne S. Macpherson, and Karin Alejandra Rosemblatt, 87–107. Chapel Hill: University of North Carolina Press, 2003.

Meisel, Seth. "From Slave to Citizen-Soldier in Early Independence Argentina." *Historical Reflections* 29, no. 1 (2003): 65–82.

Meisel-Roca, Adolfo. "Esclavitud, mestizaje y haciendas en la provincia de Cartagena, 1531–1851." *Desarrollo y Sociedad* 4 (1980): 242–77.

Méndez, Cecilia. *The Plebeian Republic: The Huanta Rebellion and the Making of the Peruvian State, 1820–1850.* Durham: Duke University Press, 2005.

Mintz, Sidney W. "The Caribbean Region." In *Slavery, Colonialism and Racism,* ed. Sidney Mintz, 45–71. New York: Norton, 1974.

———. *Caribbean Transformations.* Chicago: Aldine, 1974.

Mintz, Sidney W., and Richard Price. *The Birth of African-American Culture: An Anthropological Perspective.* Boston: Beacon Press, 1992.

Mörner, Magnus, ed., *Race and Class in Latin America*. New York: Columbia University Press, 1970.

———. *Race Mixture in the History of Latin America*. Boston: Little Brown, 1967.

Múnera, Alfonso, ed. *Ensayos costeños, de la colonia a la República: 1770–1889*. Bogotá: Colcultura, 1994.

———. "Failing to Construct the Colombian Nation: Race and Class in the Andean Caribbean Conflict, 1717–1816." Ph.D. diss., University of Connecticut, 1995.

———. *El fracaso de la nación: Región, clase y raza en el Caribe colombiano (1717–1821)*. Bogotá: Ancora Editores, 1998.

———. *Fronteras imaginadas: La construcción de las razas y la geografía en el siglo XIX colombiano*. Bogotá: Planeta, 2005.

Nash, Gary. *The Forgotten Fifth: African Americans in the Age of Revolution*. Cambridge: Harvard University Press, 2006.

Nash, Gary B., and David G. Sweet, eds. *Struggle and Survival in Colonial America*. Berkeley: University of California Press, 1981.

Needell, Jeffrey D. "Identity, Race, Gender, and Modernity in the Origins of Gilberto Freyre's Oeuvre." *American Historical Review* 100, no. 1 (1995): 51–77.

Nicholls, David. *From Dessalines to Duvalier: Race, Colour and National Independence in Haiti*. 1979. Reprint, New Brunswick: Rutgers University Press, 1996.

Ortiz, Fernando. *Contrapunteo cubano del tabaco y el azúcar: Advertencia de sus contrastes agrarios, económicos, históricos y sociales, su etnografía y su transculturación*. Havana: J. Montero, 1940.

Otero-D'Acosta, Enrique. *Vida del Almirante José Padilla (1778–1828)*. Bogotá: Imprenta y Lit. de las fuerzas militares, 1973.

Ots-Capadequi, José María. "Sobre las confirmaciones reales y las 'gracias al sacar' en la historia del derecho indiano." *Estudios de Historia Novobispana* 2 (1968): 35–47.

Pacheco, Margarita. *La Fiesta Liberal en Cali*. Cali: Ediciones Univ. del Valle, 1992.

Pagden, Anthony. *Spanish Imperialism and the Political Imagination, 1513–1830*. New Haven: Yale University Press, 1990.

Phelan, John Leddy. *The People and the King: The Comunero Revolution in Colombia, 1781*. Madison: University of Wisconsin Press, 1978.

Pombo, José Ignacio de. *Comercio y contrabando en Cartagena de Indias*. Bogotá: Nueva Biblioteca Colombiana de Cultura, 1986.

Posada-Carbó, Eduardo, ed. *Elections before Democracy: The History of Elections in Europe and Latin America*. London: Macmillan Press, 1996.

Ramos-Pérez, Demetrio. *Bolívar en las Antillas: Una etapa decisiva para su línea política*. Madrid: Real Academia de la Historia-Gráficas 66, 1986.

Rancière, Jacques. *The Names of History: On the Poetics of Knowledge*. Minneapolis: University of Minnesota Press, 1994.

Rappaport, Joanne. *The Politics of Memory: Native Historical Interpretation in the Colombian Andes*. Cambridge: Cambridge University Press, 1990.

Reis, Joao Jose. "The Revolution of the Ganhadores: Urban Labour, Ethnicity and the African Strike of 1857 in Bahia, Brazil." *Journal of Latin American Studies* 29, no. 2 (1997): 355–93.

Rieu-Millan, Marie Laure. *Los diputados americanos en las cortes de Cádiz*. Madrid: Consejo Superior de Investigaciones Científicas, 1990.

Rodríguez, Jaime E. *The Independence of Spanish America*. Cambridge: Cambridge University Press, 1998.

Rodríguez, Manuel Alfredo. "Los pardos libres en la colonia y la independencia." *Boletín de la Academia Nacional de la Historia* 75, no. 299 (1992): 33–63.

Roldán, Mary. *Blood and Fire: La Violencia in Antioquia, Colombia, 1946–1953*. Durham: Duke University Press, 2002.

Roossell-Wood, A. J. R. "Colonial Brazil." In *Neither Slave nor Free*, ed. David W. Cohen and Jack P. Greene, 120–23. Baltimore: John Hopkins University Press, 1972.

Roseberry, William. *Anthropologies and Histories: Essays in Culture, History, and Political Economy*. New Brunswick: Rutgers University Press, 1989.

Rousseau, Jean-Jacques. *The Social Contract and Discourses*. New York: E. P Dutton and Company, 1950.

Rudé, George. *The Crowd in the French Revolution*. London: Oxford University Press, 1959.

Sabato, Hilda. *La política en las calles: Entre el voto y la movilización, Buenos Aires, 1862–1880*. Buenos Aires: Editorial Sudamericana, 1998.

———. "On Political Citizenship in Nineteenth-Century Latin America." *American Historical Review* 106, no. 4 (2001): 1290–326.

Saether, Steinar A. "Independence and the Redefinition of Indianness around Santa Marta, Colombia, 1750–1850." *Journal of Latin American Studies* 37 (2005): 5–80.

Safford, Frank. "Race, Integration, and Progress: Elite Attitudes and the Indian in Colombia, 1750–1870." *Hispanic American Historical Review* 71, no. 1 (1991): 1–33.

Sanchez, Joseph. "African Freedman and the Fuero Militar: A Historical Overview of Pardo and Moreno Militiamen in the Late Spanish Empire." *Colonial Latin American Historical Review* 3, no. 2 (1994): 165–84.

Sanders, James. "'Citizens of a Free People': Popular Liberalism and Race in Nineteenth-Century Southwestern Colombia." *Hispanic American Historical Review* 84, no. 2 (2004): 233–312.

———. *Contentious Republicans: Popular Politics, Race, and Class in Nineteenth-Century Southwestern Colombia*. Durham: Duke University Press, 2004.

Schmidt-Nowara, Christopher. *Empire and Antislavery: Spain, Cuba and Puerto Rico, 1833–1874*. Pittsburgh: University of Pittsburgh Press, 1999.

Schwarz, Roberto. *Misplaced Ideas: Essays on Brazilian Culture*. London: Verso, 1992.

Scott, James. *Domination and the Arts of Resistance: Hidden Transcripts*. New Haven: Yale University Press, 1990.

Scott, Julius S. "The Common Wind: Currents of Afro-American Communication in the Era of the Haitian Revolution." Ph.D. diss., Duke University, 1986.

Scott, Rebecca. *Degrees of Freedom: Louisiana and Cuba after Slavery*. Cambridge: Harvard University Press, 2005.

———. *Slave Emancipation in Cuba: The Transition to Free Labor, 1860–1899*. Princeton: Princeton University Press, 1985.

Sewell, William H., Jr. *Work and Revolution in France: The Language of Labor from the Old Regime to 1848*. Cambridge: Cambridge University Press, 1980.

Sheller, Mimi. *Democracy after Slavery: Black Publics and Peasant Radicalism in Haiti and Jamaica*. Gainesville: University Press of Florida, 2000.

Siso, Carlos. *La formación del pueblo Venezolano: Estudios sociológicos*. New York: Horizon House, 1941.

Skidmore, Thomas. *Black into White: Race and Nationality in Brazilian Thought.* Oxford: Oxford University Press, 1974.

———. "Racial Mixture and Affirmative Action: The Cases of Brazil and the United States." *American Historical Review* 108, no. 5 (2003): 1391–96.

Stoking, George. *Race, Culture and Evolution: Essays in the History of Anthropology.* Chicago: University of Chicago Press, 1982.

Stolcke, Verena. *Marriage, Class, and Colour in Nineteenth-Century Cuba: A Study of Racial Attitudes and Sexual Values in a Slave Society.* 1974. Reprint, Ann Arbor: University of Michigan Press, 1989.

Sweet, John Wood. *Bodies Politic: Negotiating Race in the American North, 1730–1830.* Baltimore: Johns Hopkins University Press, 2003.

Sweet, Leonard I. "The Fourth of July and Black Americans in the Nineteenth Century: Northern Leadership Opinion within the Context of Black Experience." *Journal of Negro History* 61, no. 3 (1976): 258–59.

Tannenbaum, Frank. *Slave and Citizen, the Negro in the Americas.* New York: Vintage Books, 1946.

Taylor, William. "Between Global Process and Local Knowledge: An Inquiry into Early Latin American Social History, 1500–1900." In *Reliving the Past: The Worlds of Social History,* ed. Oliver Zunz, 115–90. Chapel Hill: University of North Carolina Press, 1985.

Thompson, E. P. *Customs in Common.* London: Merlin Press, 1991.

Thurner, Mark. *From Two Republics to One Divided: Contradictions of Postcolonial Nation-making in Andean Peru.* Durham: Duke University Press, 1997.

Tisnes, Roberto M. *La independencia de la costa Atlántica.* Bogotá: Editorial Kelly, 1976.

Torres, Arlene, and Norman E. Whitten Jr., eds. *Blackness in Latin America and the Caribbean.* Bloomington: Indiana University Press, 1998.

Tovar Pinzón, Hermes. *Convocatoria al poder del número: Censos y estadísticas de la Nueva Granada 1750–1830.* Bogotá: Archivo General de la Nación, 1994.

———. *Grandes empresas agrícolas y ganaderas: Su desarrollo en el siglo XVIII.* Bogotá: CIEC, 1980.

———. "Guerras de opinión y represión en Colombia durante la Independencia." *Anuario Colombiano de Historia Social y de la Cultura* 2 (1983): 187–233.

Towsend, Camilla. "'Half of My Body Free, the Other Half Enslaved': The Politics of the Slaves of Guayas at the End of the Colonial Era." *Colonial Latin American Review* 7, no. 1 (1998): 105–28.

Trouillot, Michel-Rolph. "The Caribbean Region: An Open Frontier in Anthropological Theory." *Annual Review of Anthropology* 21 (1992): 19–42.

———. *Silencing the Past: Power and the Production of History.* Boston: Beacon Press, 1996.

Tutino, John. *From Insurrection to Revolution in Mexico: Social Bases of Agrarian Violence, 1750–1940.* Princeton: Princeton University Press, 1986.

Uribe, Victor M. "The Enigma of Latin American Independence." *Latin American Research Review* 32, no. 1 (1997): 236–55.

———. *Honorable Lives: Lawyers, Family, and Politics in Colombia, 1780–1850.* Pittsburgh: Pittsburgh University Press, 2000.

Uribe Vargas, Diego, comp. *Las constituciones de Colombia: Historia crítica y textos.* 2 vols. Madrid: Ediciones Cultura Hispánica, 1977.

Uribe White, Enrique. *Padilla: Homenaje de la Armada Colombiana al héroe de Maracaibo.* Colombia: Imprenta de las Fuerzas Militares, 1973.

Vann Woodward, C. *The Strange Career of Jim Crow.* New York: Oxford University Press, 1957.

Van Young, Eric. "Conclusion—Was There an Age of Revolution in Spanish America?" In *State and Society in Spanish America during the Age of Revolution,* ed. Victor M. Uribe-Uran, 219–46. Wilmington: Scholarly Resources, 2001.

———. *The Other Rebellion: Popular Violence, Ideology, and the Mexican Struggle for Independence, 1810–1821.* Stanford: Stanford University Press, 2001.

———. "Quetzalcóatl, King Ferdinand, and Ignacio Allende Go to the Seashore; or, Messianism and Mystical Kingship in Mexico, 1800–1821." In *The Independence of Mexico and the Creation of the Nation,* ed. Jaime Rodríguez, 109–27. Los Angeles: Latin American Center Publications, 1989.

Vasconcelos, José. *La raza cósmica misión de la raza iberoamericana.* Paris: Agencia Mundial de Librerias, 1920(?).

Verna, Paul. *Petión y Bolívar: Cincuenta años (1790–1830) de relaciones haitiano-venezolanas y su aporte a la emancipación de Hispanoamérica.* Caracas: 1969.

Vinson III, Ben. *Bearing Arms for His Majesty: The Free Colored Militia in Colonial Mexico.* Stanford: Stanford University Press, 2001.

Viotti da Costa, Emilia. *The Brazilian Empire: Myths and Histories.* Chicago: University of Chicago Press, 2000.

Wade, Peter. *Blackness and Race Mixture: The Dynamics of Racial Identity in Colombia.* Baltimore: Johns Hopkins University Press, 1993.

Walker, Charles. *Smoldering Ashes: Cuzco and the Creation of Republican Peru, 1780–1840.* Durham: Duke University Press, 1999.

White, Shane. "'It Was a Proud Day': African Americans, Festivals, and Parades in the North, 1741–1834." *Journal of American History* 81 (1994): 38–41.

Williams, Eric. *Capitalism and Slavery.* 1944. Reprint, New York: Capricorn Books, 1966.

Wolf, Eric R. *Envisioning Power: Ideologies of Dominance and Crisis.* Berkeley: University of California Press, 1999.

Wright, Winthrop. *Café con Leche: Race, Class, and National Image in Venezuela.* Austin: University of Texas Press, 1990.

Young, Robert. *Colonial Desire: Hybridity in Theory, Culture, and Race.* London: Routledge, 1995.

Zuluaga, "Clientelismo y Guerrilla en el Valle del Patía, 1536–1811." In *La Independencia: Ensayos de historia social,* ed. Germán Colmenares, 111–36. Bogotá: Instituto Colombiana de Cultura, 1986.

INDEX

O'Leary, Daniel, 127, 144
Ortiz, Cornelio, 97–99
Ortiz, Fernando, 10
Ortiz, José Diego, 33
Otis, James, 152

Padilla, José Prudencio, 115–28, 136–38, 141, 142, 144–49
Paez, José Antonio, 3, 55, 124
Pagden, Anthony, 5–6, 7
Panama, 11, 13–14
pardos: as artisans, 18, 73–75, 102, 110; Bourbon policies on, 20–21; in Cartagena, 44–47; citizenship of, 38–43, 45–47, 52–56; in country-side, 19; definition of, 14; in First Republic, 68–90; loyalty of, 22, 24–26; in military, 18–19, 21–26; and patriotism, 49–57, 69; and politics, 10, 21, 134–35, 147–48, 154–55; and race war, 135–36; racial grievances of, 139–50; social status of, 105, 117–18; in Venezuela, 47–49; and Wars of Independence, 1–9. *See also* blacks; race
patriotism. *See* nationalism
patron-client relations, 130
peasant studies, 7
peasants, 103
Pérez, Buenaventura, 92–96, 138
Pérez, Nicolás, 95
Pétion, Alexandre, 116
Petit, Emilien, 153
Pey, Joseph Miguel, 27
Píar, Manuel, 137, 147, 180n32
Picornell, Juan Bautista Mariano, 30–32, 49–50
Piñeres brothers. *See* Gutiérrez de Piñeras, Gabriel; Gutiérrez de Piñeras, Germán
Piñeres, Vicente, 125
Piñeristas, 68, 73–88
"Political and Moral Reflections," 52–54
politics: class and, 1–6, 69, 71–73, 86–87; of First Republic, 77–79; *pardos* and, 10, 21, 134–35, 147–48, 154–55; race and, 8–9, 15, 21; Spanish American, 7
Polo, Cristóbal, 23

Pombo, José Ignacio de, 17, 28–29
Ponce, Dr. (judge), 97–99
Ponseano, José, 27
popular sovereignty, 36, 44, 69–72, 83
prisoners, Spanish, 81, 87–88
Public Health Committee, 85, 87, 88

race: Bourbon policies on, 20–25; citizen-ship and, 36–43; discrimination based on, 9, 11, 52, 103, 139–41, 158; and equality, 9–13, 28–30, 34–43, 48–49, 57, 74, 89, 118–28, 131, 139, 150, 154–59; and factions, 61; geog-raphy and, 14; and intelligence, 51; military and, 25–27; and politics, 15; republicanism and, 61–65; social sta-tus and, 19–20, 24–27; tensions concerning, 19–33; and Wars of Independence, 1–9. *See also* blacks; *pardos*
race relations, 10–12, 152–53
race war, 129–50; concept of, 10, 12–13, 155, 179n113; *pardos* and, 135–36; political circumstances for rumors of, 137–38; racial grievances and, 139–50; rhetorical significance of, 102–5, 114–15, 121, 127, 130–33, 137–38, 155; rumors of, 121–22, 130, 133–38; threats of, 85, 111, 129–30
racial democracy. *See* myth of racial democ-racy
racial differences, 61–65
racial equality, 9–13, 28–30, 34–43, 48–49, 57, 74, 89, 118–28, 131, 139, 150, 154–59
racial grievances, 132–33, 139–50
racial harmony: creole elite and, 142, 149–50, 155; myth of, 10, 14; nationalism and, 9–13, 57–67, 89, 131–33, 149–50, 155, 158; *pardos* and, 139–42, 149–50, 155, 158; republicanism and, 50, 56
racial mixing, 62–64, 152. *See also* misce-genation
racism, 10, 21, 51, 63, 157
Raynal, Abbé, 152
Real, Francisco del, 144
representation, political, 37–43, 69–70
republicanism: race and, 61–65; racial